The History of British Society
Britain in the Nineteen Thirties

The History of British Society
Edited by E. J. Hobsbawm, Professor of History
Birkbeck College, University of London

Britain in the Nineteen Thirties

Noreen Branson and
Margot Heinemann

Weidenfeld and Nicolson
5 Winsley Street London W1

SBN 297 00277 5 Case Bound
SBN 297 00280 5 Paperback

Printed in Great Britain by Cox & Wyman Ltd
London, Fakenham and Reading

Contents

General
Editor's Preface

Social history is a comparatively new *genre*, though the name itself has long been familiar. It has been widely used as part of the combination 'social and economic history', as a label for the history of labour and popular movements and other topics of interest to scholars of the left, for miscellaneous studies of customs, social behaviour and everyday life, or even, as with the late G. M. Trevelyan, as a residual category of traditional history: 'history with the politics left out'. Its aim today is the ambitious one of writing the history of society. Ideally, it ought therefore to embrace and coordinate the numerous historical specialisms, since all are relevant to its task. In practice, social historians are, at least for the present, likely to concentrate on a number of topics which have tended to be neglected, or to be treated only peripherally, by the general and specialist historians, with some honourable exceptions.

Class and social structure is the most obvious of these, but the historical demographers have also opened up the study of the pattern of birth, marriage, death, household and kinship, 'urban studies' has explored the cities, while the pattern of culture (in the anthropologists' sense of the word) and ideas has attracted what the French call the historians of 'mentalities'. More generally, all aspects of the life and activities of the common people, that is to say, those who have left little documentation behind as individuals, have been studied with increasing intensity. A great deal of work in social history has concentrated in these areas since 1950, when the subject began to be systematically developed. However, these studies have been unsystematic, both because the topics themselves have been treated patchily, and because other and

viii Britain in the Nineteen Thirties

equally relevant ones have been neglected, Though of course a good deal of important material has been accumulated by historians of one kind or another in other contexts.

The present series attempts to bring together, for the period from the industrial revolution on, what we know (and don't yet know) about the structure and changes in British society. Since social history is itself in the process of development, the individual authors have been left free to define their field, though they have all agreed to treat certain common questions and subjects. Though they are all experts, they have not written for a specialist public, but for students – of history, of sociology, or indeed of any subject which requires some understanding of British society since 1780 – and for the general reader, who, contrary to a widespread opinion, is not a myth. Not everyone who wants to know about the past and the present also wants to pass an examination. However, it may be hoped that the attempt to draw together the threads of our present knowledge, and at least some of those of historical discussion, may help to advance the work of the numerous and active force of social historians, if only by stimulating them to do better than the authors of this series.

E. J. Hobsbawm

Preface

We are here concerned primarily with the everyday lives and attitudes of the British people during the thirties – with living standards, work, homes, schooling; what happened to the ordinary person who got ill or had a baby; what it was like to be old, to be young, to be unemployed. And since the majority of the British people, then as now, were wage-earners or small salary-earners, our study concerns itself mostly with them, though not to the exclusion of the well-to-do and the ruling elite.

As we wished to present in some depth the quality of life for the majority in 1931–39 and in particular to show how and why it changed, we have had regretfully to exclude much material, fascinating in itself, which concerned the doings of royalty and high society, or which made fugitive headlines in the press. A brilliant surface mosaic of the thirties scene was already available in *The Long Weekend* by Robert Graves and Alan Hodge, which concentrated, as the authors said, on the West End rather than Wigan. We have tended to tilt the balance the other way. For the full flavour of upper-class life – including the political lobbies and the constitutional crisis around the abdication of Edward VIII – the reader should turn to the letters and diaries of Harold Nicolson, the Channon diaries, or the memoirs of Winston Churchill and Harold Macmillan.

For reasons of space we have been highly selective in our treatment of culture and the arts, tracing one or two crucial movements rather than attempting to cover the whole field. We have also limited our use of statistics to those necessary to establish an argument or a point of analysis, and have not attempted a full record of figures readily available in other sources.

We are not setting out to add one more to the many valuable books on the economic, political, constitutional and diplomatic history of the thirties. The reader who seeks a general outline history of the period is well provided for in C. L. Mowat's *Britain Between the Wars*, and the economic history is documented in S. Pollard's *The Development of the British Economy, 1914–1950*.

We would like to thank the many people who have helped us in the writing of the book, giving generously of their time to provide us with material and advice. In particular we are grateful to J. D. Bernal, Isabel Brown, the late J. R. Campbell, F. Le Gros Clark, Tony and Susan Cox, Nan Green, Charles Hoyle, Frank Jackson, J. W. Jones, James Klugmann, Sheila Lynd, E. Melling, Max and Margaret Morris, W. S. Sedley. We would like to thank the staffs of the National Federation of Old Age Pensions Associations, the Cyclists' Touring Club, and the Royal Automobile Club for the trouble taken to answer our questions.

To the Labour Research Department and its staff we owe a very special debt. Its unique library of material on the labour movement, and the close contact with working-class organisations through our years of work there, have been the basis without which we could never have attempted to write this book.

Neither the LRD nor the friends we have mentioned are responsible for anything in the book, and the views we have expressed in it are entirely our own.

N. Branson
M. Heinemann

London, 1970

Economic and Political Setting

After the First World War, British economy and society never regained the relative stability and confidence of the pre-war years. During the nineteen twenties it was, indeed, widely believed that depression in the basic exporting industries and acute labour unrest, culminating in the General Strike of 1926, were merely the aftermath of the post-war dislocation of the European economy, a turbulence which would die away as production and trade resumed their normal peace-time rhythm. In the later twenties this seemed to be happening. The prosperity of the United States, moreover, was a shining example of what capitalist enterprise could achieve when joined to modern mass-production technology. There post-war problems had been easily overcome, production was soaring, and a high-wage economy seemed to secure the interests of business and labour alike. This was the new way forward to which capitalists and labour leaders confidently pointed in the later twenties. Henry Ford, it was said, had refuted Karl Marx.

This prospect was shattered by the devastating economic crisis which, beginning with the New York stock market crash in 1929, engulfed the United States and spread rapidly throughout the world. It was immeasurably the worst slump ever known. Except for the Soviet Union (and that was still economically a backward country), no nation escaped. Industrial countries and colonial areas both suffered its devastating impact, and the crisis was proportionately most severe of all in the United States, where production fell in three years to less than half the 1929 boom level. In Britain unemployment reached an all-time record figure of just under three million by the beginning of 1933, or 23 per cent of all insured workers. Moreover, the process of recovery in the years from 1934 to 1937 was exceptionally slow and uneven. Even when output once again began to rise it was more slowly than before, and was dependent largely on armaments expenditure. By 1938 there were already signs of a new recession. The feeling became widespread that this was no longer a mere local or incidental maladjustment, but a mortal disease that called in question the continued existence of the capitalist system itself.

Compared with pre-war depressions, this one had certain new features. Maintenance of prices and restriction of production, rather than reduction of costs, became the main objectives of industry and of governments. Fear of over-production led to the introduction of tariffs, cartels and price-rings, restriction schemes and production quotas. Farmers were subsidized in the US and elsewhere to burn wheat and coffee, and not to raise hogs. In Britain potatoes were ploughed back into the ground, cotton-mills, coalmines and shipyards closed, whole industrial areas left derelict. At the same time advertising and selling-schemes proliferated as businessmen struggled for a share of the dwindling and impoverished markets. 'Poverty in the midst of plenty' was an overwhelming reality.

The world crisis and the catastrophic slump in export markets made it obvious that the foundations of British economic power, depending as it so largely did on international financial and trading connections, had been seriously weakened. The very position of the City of London as a world banking and financial centre was challenged by the run on the pound in the summer of 1931. There was a kind of 'moment of truth'. Faced with a threat to the world standing of British capitalism itself, the Labour Prime Minister, Ramsay MacDonald, and some other Labour leaders crossed over to join forces with the Conservatives, the traditional party of big business – an action whose aftermath of shock and demoralization weakened the labour movement and established what were in effect Conservative-led governments for the rest of the decade.

Britain, however, was still the centre of the greatest Empire the world had seen, though it was an Empire in which strains and cracks were beginning to show. It embraced five hundred million people, roughly a quarter of the population of the world, of which four hundred and thirty million were subject colonial peoples, including three hundred and sixty million in India. Moreover the colonies contained some of the world's richest sources of raw materials – oil in the East and West Indies and in Burma, copper and gold in Africa, tin and rubber in Malaya.

Britain's relationship with the Empire enabled her to import food and raw materials cheaply; and during the slump the rapid fall in the price of imported food, which traditionally formed an exceptionally large part of the British working-class diet, was one of the factors which helped ruling circles to avoid a decisive conflict with the working people at home. In addition, the Imperial Preference system allowed Britain to give tariff protection to her own industry in home and Empire markets. True, the shrinkage in world trade as a result of currency restrictions and tariff barriers in the long run reduced opportunities for British exports, and so tended to unbalance the British economy still further. But for the time being the income from overseas investments, shipping and financial services ('invisible exports'), the inheritance from the days when Britain was still economically the most powerful nation, was more than large enough to offset the adverse balance of visible trade which continued year by year throughout the decade.

However, this privileged position was also a source of weakness. The tendency of British investors to export capital to the colonies, rather than invest it in modernizing production at home, had contributed to the technical backwardness of the older basic industries in Britain, which by their very age included a great deal of obsolete plant, and were already losing ground in world markets to Japan, Germany and the US. It was these industries which were hit hardest by the slump. And as production recovered after 1934, unemployment still remained relatively high in these older industries. In 1938 there was still one man in eight out of work in the country as a whole. Moreover the unemployed now included not merely those in less-skilled and casual work, but great numbers of highly-skilled men in what had previously been considered steady jobs, who now found themselves out of work not merely for weeks but for years at a time.

Despite the heavy unemployment, and continued attempts by employers to reduce wages, there was a relatively small fall in money wage rates in Britain. For those fully employed, real wages were roughly maintained during the acute crisis, and began to rise immediately afterwards. This reflected the defensive strength of the trade union movement despite its depleted numbers; the employers were unable in most industries to make wage-cuts commensurate with the fall in prices. Real wages were indirectly supported also by the resistance of the unemployed to cuts in benefit, which kept the dole for a family man at a level not far below the lowest wage.

The fall in the cost of living meant that the middle class and salaried workers, and the better-paid workers in relatively sheltered occupations, began to have some extra purchasing power. This contributed to the expansion from 1934 onwards of consumption industries such as private housebuilding, furniture, motor cars and entertainment. The gradually-rising standard of those in steady employment also helps to explain to some extent the relative passivity of the trade union movement, at a time when the unemployed were engaged in bitter and massive conflict with the state authorities.

During the years of blackest depression profits were remarkably well maintained by comparison with earlier depressions.* Meanwhile the concentration of industrial and economic power continued apace throughout the decade. Although many small firms still survived, the tendency was towards the buying up of independent businesses by holding companies, often with the support of the banks and insurance companies, and the formation of increasingly powerful price-rings and trade associations. Industry both needed and accepted increasing government intervention, and this led to a degree of integration between industry and the machinery of the state, symbolized in the Tory company-director MP, the main support of the two National governments of 1931

---

*According to Lord Stamp's profit-index, dividends on preference and ordinary shares maintained an average figure of more than 6 per cent even in the bad years of 1931–3 (against 10·5 per cent in 1929) and in no year fell much below 6 per cent. (See M. Dobb, *Studies in the Development of Capitalism*, p. 329.)

and 1935. Almost all the main trusts had directors in Parliament, among them the successive Prime Ministers Baldwin (from Baldwin's steel trust) and Chamberlain (whose family munitions firm had recently been taken over by Imperial Chemical Industries). Government intervention was not designed even in form (like the US anti-trust legislation) to save the community from monopoly, but rather to save business by underwriting monopoly. Privileged and protected markets secured by tariffs and import quotas, as well as direct government contracts, especially for armaments, assumed increasing importance in the industrialists' calculations.

All these changes brought about a decline in the numbers and influence of the independent small producers and farmers. Industry was increasingly dominated by the owners of large blocks of shares, who appointed full-time professional managers, and through them controlled vast masses of capital held in smaller units. The so called 'rise of the middle class' was more strictly a rise in the number of clerical, technical and administrative workers, whose incomes were in many cases comparable with those of skilled industrial workers, and who, like them, were affected by unemployment. Meanwhile the glaring contrast between the way of life of the rich and that of millions of the poor forced itself even on the casual observer and the most cursory reader of the popular press.

The early thirties thus faced large sections of the British people with a virtual breakdown of the whole economic system under which they lived. One of the richest countries in the world was patently unable to provide great numbers of its people with any way of making a living. Not only the working-class movement, but a growing number of middle class and professional people suffered from a sense of insecurity. The idea of a planned economy had a powerful appeal in this situation, and there was keen interest in the experience both of the Roosevelt New Deal and of the Five Year Plans in the Soviet Union, which, although still poor and backward, was manifestly building up a modern industry at full speed at a time when so much of industry was lying idle in the capitalist world. Especially did the new radical trends in the middle class affect the younger scientists, who, aware of new breakthrough discoveries in physics and biology, were conscious also that their potential growth and usefulness for mankind was not being, and perhaps never could be, developed within the existing economic order.

It was not only the left who began to believe that Britain could not continue as it was – that the crisis and the social gulf it opened was so deep that even in England revolution was a serious possibility within the next few years. Young Conservatives and Liberals, as well as Labour, produced blueprints for a planned economy, which they hoped might forestall more violent upheavals. Harold Macmillan, then a Conservative backbench MP, has written of the thirties mood:

> Up to 1931 there was no reason to suppose that (changes) would not, or could not, follow the same evolutionary pattern which had resulted from the increased creation and distribution of wealth throughout the nineteenth century ... Now, after 1931, many of us felt that the disease was more deep-rooted. It had become evident that the structure of capitalist society in its old form had broken down, not only in Britain but all over Europe and even in the United States. The whole system had to be reassessed. Perhaps it could not survive at all; it certainly could not survive without radical change. ... Something like a revolutionary situation had developed, not only at home but overseas.[1]

Much of the conflicting attitudes and policy in ruling circles can be traced back to this basic sense of insecurity and threat. In spite of the 'diehards' (who believed in the strong hand with strikers at home and with Indian nationalists or foreign encroachers abroad) and the conscience-stricken group of northern Tory MPs (who wanted to see bolder schemes of public works and welfare), the main body of Conservatives supported business-as-usual leaders – first Baldwin, then Chamberlain – who gave confidence and reassurance by appearing to believe that no radical changes were called for, that the old principles of thrift and sound finance would see the country through, and that all reasonable men could agree to solutions on these lines.

The Tory leadership of the period, indeed, was notably aged, backward-looking and inert. Baldwin, the ironmaster, habitually spoke oratorically of England in terms of the rural landscape of squire and parson. Chamberlain behaved as if Birmingham business ethics and municipal accounting would deal with the crisis and with Hitler. 'One of the major reasons why he (Chamberlain) was defective on defence', wrote his former Air Minister Lord Swinton, 'was his determination that industry should not be deflected from business as usual.'[2] Chamberlain, moreover, was convinced that a profitable business deal could be done between his own industrial backers and Hitler's, which would enable German industry to find outlets in Eastern Europe while Britain continued in her old way. The main weight of ruling circles and of governments was indeed exerted to prevent any kind of far-reaching change – in the circumstances a hopeless undertaking.

The dominant leadership of the trade union and labour movement, though naturally more closely concerned with the suffering brought about by poverty and unemployment, offered little in the way of fundamental challenge to these attitudes. After the experience of 1926 they shared the fear that uncontrolled rioting and revolutionary movements might break out. During the thirties, after the defeat of 1931, the prospect of another Labour government seemed distant indeed; and meanwhile there were continual unofficial contacts and private consultations between Conservative ministers and trade union leaders on key policies, the assumption being that the over-riding interests of both sides was in stability and order.[3] The major movements of protest and opposition – by the unemployed, the industrial workers, the tenants, the East End anti-fascists – in the main began outside the national official machinery of the labour movement, usually from local and sometimes from wholly unofficial and banned organizations. And in the 'black spots' of non-unionism in the Midlands and the South-East, it was in general the shop stewards and trades councils, rather than the TUC and the national officials, who against heavy odds got a foothold for the unions in the engineering and arms industries and laid the foundation for the great advances in organization in the forties and fifties.

To some extent, as we have said, the imperial heritage of British

B

capitalism gave the governing class during the thirties the flexibility and ability to compromise under popular pressure which their German or Austrian counterparts did not possess. This privileged position, however, was being strongly challenged; firstly by the rapid advance of rival capitalist powers – Germany, Italy, Japan and above all the United States – which had more modern industries and were determined, especially after Hitler came to power in 1933, to carve out preferential markets and spheres of influence of their own; and secondly by the growing national revolt in the colonial territories themselves, in China, in the Middle East, and above all in India, with large-scale strikes and civil disobedience. Throughout the decade British rulers manoeuvred amid these conflicting pressures, but were unable to achieve more than a partial and precarious economic recovery. But any hope that the immediate rival, Germany, might embroil itself directly with what was seen as the main long-term danger, the Soviet Union, proved to be an illusion. The day of reckoning came in 1939 – and the Second World War left the fundamental dilemma of the British economy and social system still unsolved.

1931: The Political Watershed

It was on 24 August 1931 that the announcement came: the Labour government had resigned, but Labour's Prime Minister, Ramsay MacDonald, was forming a new government with the cooperation of Conservative and Liberal leaders. This was no mere reshuffle at the top with politicians changing places in a political game – one of those things that *they* do while *we* watch. It had an impact in countless working-class homes. Years later ageing Labour supporters were still saying, 'I remember the time when Ramsay MacDonald went over', as though nothing that had ever happened since had made an equal impression.

For them indeed it was the culminating point of months of disillusionment. The Labour government had entirely failed to cope with the ever-increasing unemployment. 'New thinking' – from J. M. Keynes among others – had been proposing government investment and big public works programmes to break the vicious circle and restore industrial activity. But since the beginning of the year there had been one ominous sign after another that 'orthodox' thinking, urging retrenchment and wage cuts, was gaining ground.

By the spring of 1931 engineers, agricultural workers, dyers and potters were all facing demands for wage reductions, and railwaymen's wages had already been cut. Meanwhile the National Confederation of Employers' Associations was demanding that all state and municipal wages should be reduced, and in its evidence to the Royal Commission on Unemployment Insurance argued that unemployment pay was 'insidiously sapping the whole social and financial stability of the country' since it was preventing 'unemployment from acting as a corrective factor in the adjustment of wage levels'. As if to confirm this standpoint, the Royal Commission in its Interim Report which appeared in June advocated heavy reductions in unemployment benefit.

At the end of May the editor of *The Economist* stated that 'we must make preparations to bring about as smoothly and as harmoniously as possible a general fall in wages'. The Macmillan Report[1] published in July called for an increase in wholesale prices by cartelization and international agreement; it recognized that this would involve a reduction in real wages. An addendum, signed among others by Sir T. Allen of the Co-operative Movement and Ernest Bevin of the TGWU and TUC, stated:

> A readiness to accept the fact that the value of incomes is something which must be accommodated to changing circumstances is, indeed, an essential of the sound working of the economic system.

Almost immediately after came the Report of the May Committee[2] urging cuts of £96 million in government expenditure, including wage and salary reductions for civil servants, teachers, police, workers in government factories and dockyards, and severe cuts in unemployment pay.

And then in August an acute financial emergency had blown up. On top of the trade depression there was a crisis of confidence in the pound and a drain on gold. At last came the final letdown – the Labour government had resigned and Ramsay MacDonald had deserted to the other side.

At the top, only a handful of Labour MPs supported MacDonald's action. Meanwhile, Labour's *Daily Herald* was saying that the crisis was a 'bankers' ramp'. But none of this carried much comfort to its readers, many of whom felt that their cause had been betrayed. As for the active Labour Party members – there were well over a quarter of a million individual members, let alone the millions affiliated through their trade union – their hopes had dissolved, their confidence had gone.

To convinced Conservatives, however, MacDonald's defection brought enormous satisfaction and some relief. There were hardcore Conservatives in all classes of society from the very rich to the very poor – at the previous election when the prevailing wind had veered against them they had nevertheless mustered nearly four votes out of every ten cast. They had been persuaded that disaster faced them if the pound was devalued. Now it seemed that the pound was going to be saved. Everyone had known all along that Labour couldn't govern, they represented uneducated men, quite unequal to the situation. But now the country was going to be in the hands of the right people once more. There was a great wave of congratulation in the newspapers. A selfless decision had been taken by the party leaders to rise above narrow party considerations in the country's hour of need. The *Daily Mail* spoke of the 'new body of men whose mission it is to save Britain from disaster . . . In their patriotic endeavours we wish them heartily God-speed.'³ The mood of thankfulness among the middle class hardened into one of determination, and indeed a certain patriotic fervour, which led them towards the end of the year to respond to calls to 'Buy British' and boycott foreign goods. Meanwhile they accepted without grumbling an emergency budget, announced on 10 September, putting up income tax from 4s 6d in the £ to 5s 0d* and imposing heavier duties on drink and tobacco. Such a mood is infectious – in the weeks of crisis it filtered down to the lower reaches, helping to undermine further the confidence of habitual Labour supporters.

It was sustained by the readiness of the Liberal leaders to accept office, and by the behaviour of the Liberal press, for instance the *News Chronicle*, which was initially scarcely less enthusiastic than the Conservative press. Liberal voters in 1929 had amounted to nearly a quarter of those going to the poll. Among them were many elderly working men whose allegiance really derived from the pre-Labour period and was a matter of habit as much as anything else. There were also professional people and salaried employees who wanted to be radical without being socialist, who believed in social progress but did not find themselves in tune with the manual workers who dominated the Labour movement. There

*The income tax exemption level for single people was lowered from £160 to £125. Out of 22 million odd 'income receivers' it was reckoned that about 8½ million came above this level. But the operation of allowances etc meant that in practice only 3·7 million people were liable to pay income tax.

was traditional Liberal support in many rural areas and from certain national and regional minorities – Scottish, Welsh, Cornish, Jewish. For all these habitual Liberal supporters, the independent Liberal voice seemed to have been suddenly submerged.

It was a situation which was exploited by the Conservative leaders with great skill. Granted that there was an immediate financial emergency which, to their minds, required the ruthless application of orthodox financial remedies, as well as the protective tariffs which the big industrialists wanted. But it all went deeper. The twenties had seen a great upward thrust of militant trade union and socialist endeavour which seemed to offer a long-term threat to the established social order. Forced to manoeuvre and compromise all through the twenties, the governing class now saw its opportunity to re-establish old relationships.

By the second week in September the new government was rushing through economy measures by a process of Emergency Act and Orders-in-Council hardly paralleled before or since except in time of war. They included pay cuts for the forces, teachers, civil servants and others and the expected reductions in unemployment pay. But suddenly in the middle of it all the unbelievable happened – a mutiny in the Royal Navy.

Of all possible reactions to the emergency legislation, a flare-up in the Navy was the least expected. And it carried with it the most ominous implications. The Navy was the symbol of Britain's greatness, the link with her far-flung Empire, the rock on which her status as a great power depended. As though the event was too horrible to look at, a sort of self-imposed censorship descended on most of the newspapers. With one or two exceptions such as the *Daily Herald*, and of course the very young *Daily Worker*, the outbreak of 'unrest' in the Navy was unsensationally and inconspicuously reported. The word 'mutiny' scarcely appeared. The BBC confined itself to the briefest of official statements. Though questions were asked and tersely answered in the House of Commons, no debate was permitted until after the whole affair was over, and even then the word 'mutiny' was carefully avoided by most speakers. As for the sailors involved, they did not use the word 'mutiny' either – they said they were 'on strike'.

The 'strike' was provoked by the news that the basic daily pay of a naval rating was to be reduced from 4s to 3s – a cut of 25 per cent. And though certain additional allowances meant that the all-over percentage reduction was not as great as 25 per cent, it was clear that the cuts in pay for the men would be proportionately much greater than those for the officers.

The main units of the Atlantic Fleet were in Cromarty Firth when the facts about the pay cuts became known. 'We could not stand the cuts', one of the strike leaders said afterwards, 'We were already on the bare minimum required to enable us to support our families.'[4] Resentment was reinforced by the belief that the men had been tricked – the crisis was a pretext for cuts that had been prepared long before. As men came on shore leave on the evening of Sunday 13 September and congregated in the naval canteen at Invergordon, anger was translated into action; volunteers were appointed from each ship to return and test opinion on strike action and to report back the following evening. And at this further meeting on the Monday night, after hearing reports from each ship, it was decided by a unanimous show of hands to strike the following morning when the fleet was due to put to sea on an exercise. The plan was that the crew of the battleship *Rodney* should signal that they were on strike by cheering, and that then each ship should cheer in turn, so that all would know who was in the strike and who not.

On Tuesday morning, 15 September, it all went even better than planned. Just before 7 a.m. the crew of the battleship *Valiant*, which was due to leave harbour first, refused the order to raise anchor. Soon after, the sound of cheers far out towards the sea signalled that the *Rodney* was on strike. And then the men on the other ships could not be restrained, and the whole fleet burst out cheering simultaneously. Twelve thousand sailors were involved.

That day, while the officers were trying to persuade the crews to turn to, the men on the cruiser *Norfolk* drafted a manifesto which was smuggled across to the other ships and endorsed by their crews. It said:

We, the loyal subjects of His Majesty the King, do hereby present to My Lords Commissioners of the Admiralty our representative, to implore them to amend the drastic cuts in pay which have been inflicted on the lowest paid men of the lower deck. It is evident to all concerned that this cut is the forerunner of tragedy, misery and immorality amongst the families of the Lower Deck, and unless a guaranteed written agreement is received from the Admiralty and confirmed by Parliament, stating that our pay will be revised, we are resolved to remain as one unit, refusing to sail under the new rate of pay. The men are quite agreeable to accept a cut which they consider reasonable.[5]

For the whole of Tuesday and Wednesday the fleet was paralysed. A *Daily Herald* correspondent was an eye-witness and wrote:

The scene in Firth has to be seen to be believed ... At the gates between the mountain peaks, *Repulse* stands like a sleeping sentry, not a wisp of smoke from her mighty funnels and her crew below decks. Behind her in the line stretching along the whole firth lie *Valiant, Malaya, Warspite, Nelson, Dorsetshire, Barham, Norfolk, Hood, York, Exeter, Rodney*. From the shore I can see the meetings on the foredecks with the leaders addressing the men from the gun turrets and the cheers and shouts that are picked up and passed on from ship to ship until they fade into the distance.[6]

Every time the men refused a turn of duty they signified their stand by cheering and receiving answering cheers in return. It was later to be suggested that there was something rather sinister about this, since the German sailors of Kiel had used a cheering code during the 1918 mutiny which had precipitated the German revolution in that year.[7] As some of the leaders of the Invergordon action were Communists it is quite possible that they knew about the Kiel mutiny. However, cheering was the obvious method of signalling from ship to ship that the strike was still solid. It had in fact been used in the mutinies of Spithead and the Nore in 1797.

Not many of the sailors involved were conscious of any affinity with socialist ideas. Insulated from the main stream of the labour movement, the average naval rating got his information about civilian life from newspapers like the *News of the World*. His opinions about the Empire, foreigners, the monarchy, were not much different from those of his officers. Moreover, he accepted it as natural that his officers should have a different class background from himself. On the other hand, a battleship is, and was then, a vast industrial complex involving the most advanced, delicate and intricate machinery and a very high degree of training is required of its crew. The men who went 'on strike' were very like skilled engineers, and their strike had much in common with any comparable action taken by their opposite numbers in industry, in that it was well planned, well organized, skilfully led and highly disciplined.

And it was successful. For at Whitehall it was suddenly realized that a serious blunder had been made. At all costs a show-down had now to be avoided. So by Wednesday evening the Admiralty had announced that the exercises were to be abandoned, and that all ships were to return to their home ports where, it was promised, a full investigation would be made with a view to alleviating the special hardships of certain classes of ratings. And there would be no victimization. On this promise the strike was called off and the fleet sailed for its home ports. The upshot was that no individual pay cut exceeded 10 per cent. But though no victimization had been promised, thirty-six ringleaders were subsequently dismissed from the Navy.[8]

Invergordon made a deep impression on the working-class movement. To the left it became a symbol of revolt, rather like the Battleship *Potemkin* – a sign of the common bond between industrial workers and workers in uniform. It also made a deep impression on the governing class, who were to deem it advisable a year or two later to bring in the Incitement to Disaffection Act with the object of insulating the armed forces from subversive influences.

In the short run its impact was not merely ideological. For in spite of the discreet behaviour of the British press, the continental press played it up, creating the impression that Britain was on the eve of insurrection. Confidence in British credit took another dive, and by 21 September Britain was off the gold standard, the preservation of which had been the ostensible reason for the National government in the first place.

The government's emergency legislation had meanwhile run

into trouble from others whose loyal cooperation it could normally expect. Civil servants, post office workers, police, all appeared to be in ferment, and in particular, the teachers, whose contracts were not due to expire until the following March. Now the government was taking power to break the contracts by Order-in-Council so as to impose an immediate 15 per cent pay cut.

The teachers remembered a difficult struggle to achieve unified salaried and professional status. Most of them had come up the hard way. Originally the children of skilled manual workers or the lowest paid clerical workers, they had won free places in council secondary schools. Now, owing to the fall in prices, they were beginning to be able to afford a style of life a little better than that from which they had sprung; in short they had begun to acquire 'middle class' status.

Tempers had not been improved by the report of the May Committee which, suggesting that very substantial salary reductions would be justified, coldly observed that 'the majority of the profession have acquired their qualifications largely at the expense of the public'. Now the government's proposed cuts of 15 per cent – greater than the 10 per cent being imposed elsewhere – led to allegations that teachers were being singled out for attack. The average salary of a certificated male teacher before the cuts was estimated at £333, that of a woman teacher £254, but averages can be misleading. It was said that if the cut went through fifty-three thousand qualified teachers would be getting less than £3 a week, and of these, twelve thousand would get less than £2.[9] So on 11 September, ten thousand teachers were seen marching in procession through the streets of London, and there was much lobbying of MPs.

On 21 September the government retreated, the Prime Minister admitting that there were undoubtedly 'classes of persons who were unfairly affected' and announcing that in all cases – which included teachers, civil servants, police, armed forces – it had been decided to limit pay reductions to not more than 10 per cent.

There remained the central item – unemployment pay. The massive savings involved here made all others look small. It was this issue that had finally divided the Labour cabinet and was the immediate cause of its fall. The overriding argument for the cuts was, of course, that unless the economies were drastic enough to restore confidence the pound would collapse. However, the employers' organizations had been urging cuts in benefit on other grounds, and the Labour Party and the TUC were now claiming that benefit was being attacked because it strengthened resistance to wage reductions.

The Prime Minister argued that the proposed 10 per cent cut in benefit was less than the fall in prices over the past two years, so that the unemployed would be no worse off than they had been in 1929. Moreover, at a time when everybody was being asked to make sacrifices, it would be unjust to ask nothing from the unemployed. Many of the general public were misled by this into believing that a cut of 10 per cent was all that was being asked of the unemployed. Yet this cut was really the least of it. The measures being rushed through the House were manysided and far-reaching – they involved putting about half the unemployed on to a means test for the first time, and the estimated reduction in money payments to the unemployed was nearer 20 per cent than 10 per cent. In the areas of heaviest unemployment there was much anger and bitterness, and many thousands came out on protest marches and demonstrations. But in this case the government made no retreat, and by the end of September the emergency legislation had been completed.

Even before this, the Conservative leaders had decided to force an immediate general election. With the other two parties in confusion, the moment had arrived to press home the advantage of Conservative candidates everywhere appearing as patriotic standard bearers for a 'National' government with MacDonald at its head. The calculation proved correct. In the General Election which followed on 27 October 1931, Conservatives were returned in an overwhelming majority. But the magnitude of their victory in the House was much greater than their victory in terms of votes, and they owed it less to Labour's rout than to Liberal disarray. For the Liberal Party, still officially supporting the concept of a 'National' government, but subject by this time to a three-way split, put up only 160 candidates instead of the 512 who stood in 1929. So that in about 375 constituencies Liberal voters who wanted to support a National government felt they had no alternative but to vote Conservative. 'It is not disputed that about three million Liberals, without surrendering a shred of their disapproval of the Conservative Party policy, for once in their lives and for this time only, screwed themselves up to this unfamiliar form of discharging a patriotic duty', observed the *Liberal Magazine*.[10] The Liberal vote fell from 5·3 million to 2·3 million, and the Conservative vote rose by $3\frac{1}{4}$ million – from 8·6 million to 11·9 million. But the Liberal assumption that it would be a 'this time only' event was not justified. Thereafter more and more former Liberal voters were to feel themselves compelled to choose between Labour and Conservative.

Labour's vote meanwhile fell from 8·3 million to 6·6 million. It was still 30 per cent of all votes. But many straight fights with Conservatives in areas where there had previously been three-cornered contests contributed to a heavy reduction in seats to fifty-two – only $8\frac{1}{2}$ per cent of all seats. Labour's loss of $1\frac{3}{4}$ million votes may have been less a matter of Labour voters switching their allegiance than of a sullen refusal to go to the polls at all. For the total poll dropped by one million, and at only 68 per cent of the electorate was one of the lowest on record.

The apathy shown by habitual Labour voters was an inevitable reflection of the mood of the organized membership, who seemed to have lost faith and with it their crusading spirit. And while many of them were to be involved in the ensuing years in great crusades and great radical movements of dissent, these were seldom to be initiated by the Labour leaders or carried forward behind Labour's banner. In this respect the movements of resistance to the emergency legislation – Invergordon, the teachers, the unemployed – all of which were outside the range of the official labour movement, revealed a pattern which was to dominate the thirties.

For the great majority of those who went to the polls on 27 October, the result was a relief after the scares and terrors of the preceding weeks. 'The electors have declared in no uncertain voice that the insidious doctrines of class warfare cannot make headway against the general desire for national cooperation at a time of national emergency', observed Stanley Baldwin, the leader of the Conservative Party. So the country settled down under a government of unusually old men who, having survived the brief storms of the past few weeks, now looked back longingly to the standards and values of pre-war days.

The National government was to last with minor modifications throughout the rest of the decade. Always predominantly Conservative in composition and support, it became more obviously so when Baldwin took over the premiership from the ageing Mac-Donald in June 1935. After the National government had won another General Election in the autumn of that year (though by a reduced majority and with only 53 per cent of the poll) there was little left of its National Labour and Liberal trimmings, and when Neville Chamberlain succeeded Baldwin in 1937 it was as leader of a frankly Tory administration, though the title of National government remained, and was still there when the war broke out in 1939.

3

The Unemployed
and the Means Test

In August 1931 the unemployed on whom the main weight of the new economies was about to fall officially numbered 2·7 million. This was then a record figure. Nearly one in five of the unemployed had been continuously out of work for more than six months.

The great majority of them were drawing unemployment insurance benefit, which at that time stood at 17s a week for an adult man, 9s for his dependent wife, 2s for each child. An insured unemployed woman got 15s; boys and girls got lesser amounts.

So far as the state was concerned, unemployment benefit was a 'ceiling', not a 'floor'. The unemployed were expected to manage on it – it was meant to cover rent, heat, light, food, clothes and everything else. Some of those newly out of work had savings to help tide them over. Some got a few shillings extra from their trade union or approved society paid over a limited number of weeks. But if the weeks dragged on and these resources came to an end, then indeed the outlook was black unless there were earning relatives to help out.

Unemployment benefit was enough to keep the family from outright starvation, but not very much else. It meant an unbalanced diet dominated by bread and margarine and tea with condensed milk, so that health began to deteriorate. It meant that when clothes wore out they could not be replaced, and breaking a cup or plate could be a minor disaster. After a time it meant pawning blankets and selling off bits of furniture, getting into arrears with the rent and so on. Prices were low in comparison with those prevailing thirty years later, but the 30s a week on which a man, wife and two children had to manage was in real terms about *half* the amount considered necessary for minimum subsistence by the National Assistance Board in the mid-sixties.

'Unemployment benefit is not a living wage; it was never meant to be that' said the Prime Minister, Ramsay MacDonald, in his broadcast to the nation on 25 August, apparently under the impression that this was a justification for his proposal to reduce the benefit even lower.

Not all the unemployed were entitled to unemployment benefit. Agricultural workers and domestic servants and those black-coated workers who earned more than £250 a year were excluded from the unemployment insurance scheme. If they had no private resources or relatives to fall back on when they were out of a job, they had to apply for help to the local Poor Law Authority. The Poor Law was in the hands of local Public Assistance Committees which administered relief paid for partly out of the local rates. The considerable body of uninsured unemployed was to have curious repercussions on the later course of events.

Unemployment benefit itself was financed through a separate Unemployment Insurance Fund, into which workers, employers and the state paid weekly contributions, and out of which benefit was paid.* For the originators of the scheme an important aim had been that it should be 'self supporting' – that is, that the amount paid out in benefit would not exceed the amount coming in in contributions. But during the twenties unemployment had been much higher than expected, and social pressures had forced succeeding governments to make the contribution conditions less onerous, so that benefit in one form or another could continue to be drawn for continuous periods of up to seventy-four weeks or even longer for those who were continuously unable to get work. In this situation the Fund had been forced to borrow from the Treasury and was now deep in debt. So that parallel with the argument on the need for government economies in general there was a subsidiary argument on the importance of making the insurance

*The weekly contributions in mid-1931 were 7d for an adult man, 8d from the employer, 7½d from the state. On 1 October they were increased by 3d, 2d and 2½d respectively.

scheme 'solvent' again – indeed the condition of the Fund was spoken of in rather the tone of voice that would be used about a dickey private insurance company which was about to fail.

The new economy measures passed by the National government began to come into operation just after Parliament dissolved for the General Election. First came the reductions in benefit. The rate for an adult man went down from 17s to 15s 3d, that for his wife from 9s to 8s. Other rates went down too; only the child's allowance of 2s was left untouched. Simultaneously weekly contributions from those at work were increased.

Next came the Anomalies Regulations[1] whose main impact was on married women. They provided that unless a married woman had *since marriage* paid a certain minimum number of contributions (i.e. had been actually in work for a number of weeks) she would be disallowed benefit no matter how many contributions she had paid before marriage unless she could prove that she was normally employed, would seek work and could reasonably hope to obtain such work in the district. Underlying this measure was undoubtedly the prevailing assumption that married women shouldn't work – if they did, it implied a loss of status and a certain reproach to their husbands. Many employers dismissed women on marriage anyway. And indeed, except in certain areas, such as the textile areas, it was relatively uncommon for a married woman to have a job. Less than one in eight did so in 1931.★

The results of the Anomalies Regulations were immediate and drastic. By the middle of November, 5,000 married women had been struck off benefit in Glasgow alone, 2,880 in Liverpool, 1,000 in Bootle, 2,000 in Birmingham. And so the process went on. By the end of the year 134,000 married women had been disallowed.

Last came the most far-reaching economy of all, the Order which provided for the means test.[2] This limited the period for which unemployment benefit could be drawn as of right, to twenty-six weeks, and it also abolished the special arrangements whereby those who had only had a few weeks in work in the

★As compared with more than one in three in the sixties.

previous year had been enabled to draw benefit. All those not entitled to benefit under the new rules – and they comprised all those who had been longest out of work – would in future have to apply for 'transitional payments' which were to be financed by a special grant from the Exchequer and paid out through the Employment Exchange. But before getting the 'transitional payment' the applicant would have to undergo a means test which would be carried out, not by the Employment Exchange, but by the local Poor Law Authority – the Public Assistance Committee – which would investigate all the circumstances and then notify the Exchange the amount of transitional payment to be made. The *maximum* transitional payment that could be recommended was not to exceed the new unemployment benefit scales of 15s 3d for an adult man, 8s for his wife, 2s for each child and so on. But the payment could be much less than this if the local Public Assistance Committee's own scales for relief for uninsured unemployed were less than this, or if the means test revealed household income which could be set against the payment.

The Means Test

The transitional payments order came in force on 12 November 1931, and on that day half a million unemployed faced the immediate prospect of undergoing a means test at the hands of the local Poor Law Authorities. Many of them had never been near the Poor Law before and indeed had hoped and believed they never would. Unemployment benefit was something you paid for when you were at work, and therefore had a right to when there was no work to be had. The new people now being means-tested included skilled men in their fifties who had paid contributions for ten and even twenty years; they included young men in the prime of life with wives and children to support. There were many coal miners among them, there were boilermakers and other skilled craftsmen from the idle shipyards, cotton operatives from the moribund textile industry, bricklayers and carpenters whose chances had gone with the abandoned public works projects, women from the potteries, men from steel works which had closed down, and every type and grade of worker from the engineering industry.

The two hundred Public Assistance Committees into whose hands the work of means-testing was placed also faced a new situation. There was one for each County Borough and County Council and they consisted of elected councillors plus a certain number of coopted persons. Beneath them was a network of relief sub-committees and guardians' committees. Their main concern hitherto had been to distribute relief in cash or kind to the old, the sick, the widows and orphans. Though a few able-bodied unemployed had fallen to their care, it was mainly those in uninsured occupations. Now they were to be involved with a new kind of client, one who was much less accustomed to being pushed around, much more outraged at the indignities of the means test.

The Public Assistance Committees (or PAC's, as they were commonly called) were not to foot the bill for the new allowances, but they had to investigate the case of each applicant according to their own rules and fix his allowance at the level of their existing relief scales for uninsured unemployed. These relief scales varied widely. Many of them fell several shillings below the new reduced unemployment benefit. Some gave only 20s for a man and wife, a few gave as little as 16s.[3] But quite apart from the scale rate, the Public Assistance Committees operated a household means test which meant taking into account almost the entire resources of family and deducting these from the recommended payment. These resources had to be disclosed under threat of prosecution; wages of any earning member were checked with the employer; war pensions, widows' pensions, savings certificates belonging to everyone in the applicant's household were all set against the final payment. People who had savings could be disallowed until they were spent, but this was not the worst of it; the worst was to have your allowance reduced on account of your father's pension or your child's earnings. In some areas where there was no work for skilled adults there was still a certain demand for juvenile labour, albeit in blind-alley jobs. Now young sons and daughters found that the few shillings they earned were taken into account when calculating the allowance of their parents and younger brothers and sisters. A likely lad of fifteen who secured a shilling a week rise found that his parents had had a shilling knocked off the following week. Thus the means test imposed on the unemployed in practice spread much wider and deprived many of those still in work. So began the break-up of the family, as the young people drifted away from home to avoid seeing their parents means-tested on their account, or to avoid being means-tested themselves.

By January 1932 over nine hundred thousand were registering for the transitional payments and undergoing the means test. Hundreds of thousands of others had been cut off altogether either under the anomalies regulations or under the means test itself, so that not more than half the unemployed on the register were still drawing unemployment benefit as of right.

Complaints about the operation of the means test began to grow into a flood. In February 1932 the TUC submitted a memorandum to the Minister. 'People who have not been in touch with the Poor Law before are being subjected to the indignity of a prying enquiry into their domestic circumstances', they said, and complained that 'benefit is refused until savings painfully accumulated over long periods in Post Office Savings Bank or Cooperative Society are withdrawn and spent', and 'investigating officers assume the right to enter houses and make remarks about the furniture'.

Examples quoted at the time showing how the means test worked included an unemployed man, wife and two children whose allowance was reduced to 20s a week because the claimant was living in the same house as his mother-in-law; two young men aged twenty and twenty-five disallowed because their mother had a war widow's pension; benefit for a twenty-three-year-old man reduced to 10s because his mother had a 10s a week old-age pension and his sister earned 23s a week; an unemployed miner with wife and six children cut off altogether because he had £15 saved in the Coop – 'not a case for help so long as this sum was on deposit'.

Some Public Assistance Committees became notorious for their low scales and rigorous implementation of the means test. In Lancashire, for example, less than 16 per cent of the unemployed were awarded the maximum 'transitional payment' rate and 33·3 per cent were disallowed altogether under the means test.

The National Unemployed Workers' Movement was actively organizing local 'hunger marches' and demonstrations to try and persuade Public Assistance Committees with low scales to increase them. The NUWM was an organization under Communist leadership with Wal Hannington at its head. It had considerable support among the unemployed all through the thirties, particularly among the younger men. The prospects for many of the unemployed getting back to work seemed remote, while their present conditions were intolerable. The NUWM attracted those who wanted to get something done, those who wanted action, those who wanted to 'have a go'. Some came to it with a definite conviction that it was the capitalist system which caused unemployment and the degradation and misery that accompanied it; they had a vision of a different kind of world for which they wanted to struggle. Others were simply glad of a chance to be involved in activities which broke the deadly monotony of life on the dole. For all of them the historic Communist slogan 'you have nothing to lose but your chains' seemed true. The Labour Party and the TUC, however, had banned the NUWM as a Communist Party Organization, and the authorities in 1932 regarded it as a red rabble which had to be put down or it would get out of hand, and saw Wal Hannington as the rabble-rouser in chief. The police habitually acted on these assumptions.

The Birkenhead event of September 1932 illustrated the attitudes of those involved. Birkenhead Public Assistance Committee was operating a scale 3s below the maximum permitted transitional payment level – 12s for a man instead of 15s 3d and so on. Several thousand marched to the hall where the Public Assistance Committee were meeting, and sent in a deputation to ask for a 3s increase. The Public Assistance Committee agreed to send a telegram to the government asking for the abolition of the means test and a few days later raised its scales by 3s. But meanwhile on the march away from the hall violent battles broke out between demonstrators and police and continued over a period of four days, during which, it was alleged, the police had raided working-class tenements late at night, dragged people from their beds and beaten them up. Many ended up in hospital.

Some of the Public Assistance Committees had been appointed from Labour-controlled authorities and were bitterly opposed to means testing the unemployed. They began to refuse to operate the means test at all, or did it hardly at all, in their handling of transitional payment claims, awarding nearly every claimant the maximum-permitted allowance regardless of family resources. Thus in Rotherham and Merthyr Tydfil 98 per cent of the unemployed were getting the maximum payment, in Durham County over 90 per cent. The Ministry of Labour took to warning Public Assistance Committees against 'illegal' payments. Among the first to be warned were Durham County, Glamorgan County, Rotherham and Barnsley. But not all rebellious Public Assistance Committees were Labour-controlled. There was Lincoln which was divided between Independents and Labour and Middlesbrough where the Liberals were the largest party. Lincoln Public Assistance Committee began its argument with the Ministry in February 1932 and by September had come out in open defiance, one of its number saying that 'he was prepared to do all he could to get round the means test or through it, because it was a rotten piece of legislation.'[4] Middlesbrough Public Assistance Committee decided to discontinue administering transitional benefit under the Ministry's conditions, saying 'Let the Ministry do its own dirty work'.[5] Even the Conservative-controlled Manchester City Council was in trouble with the Ministry – it had decided to disregard, in its operation of the means test, one-half of disability pensions and up to £50 of capital assets.[6] The resistance to operating the means test as laid down was indeed widespread. Public Assistance Committees who were 'warned' or otherwise in trouble included as well as those mentioned above Barrow-in-Furness, Blackburn, Essex County, Monmouth County, Nelson, Northumberland County, Oldham, Southampton, Stoke-on-Trent, Swansea, West Ham, Wolverhampton.[7]

In the end the Ministry took disciplinary action. Rotherham Public Assistance Committee was superseded in October 1932 by a commissioner appointed from London, with instructions to administer the means test in the approved style. In November Durham County Public Assistance Committee was similarly unseated. The three commissioners installed at Durham which was one of the worst of the Depressed Areas succeeded in reducing the proportion of those receiving allowances at the maximum rate from over 90 per cent to 70 per cent.

One by one the other recalcitrant Public Assistance Committees drew in their horns and appeared to be toeing the line. West Ham made a public statement: 'We were threatened with supersession, and in face of that threat we prefer to keep our poor under our own care and do what we can for them rather than hand them over to an arbitrary Commissioner from whom they could expect little humanity.'[8] Surreptitiously many of these Public Assistance Committees continued to do what they could 'to get round the means test, or through it'.

That same autumn of 1932 the government was also concerned with the fact that a national hunger march organized by the NUWM was on its way to London to present a 'monster petition' against the means test. These hunger marches in which contingents of unemployed spent many arduous weeks on the road, holding meetings to explain their case and to appeal for support in the towns through which they passed, were a special form of demonstration intended to have a national impact. They required many weeks of careful preparation, collecting funds to supply boots for the marchers, enforcing a rigorous medical check to ensure that only those who were fit to stay the course took part. Rejecting unfit would-be marchers was a depressing job in many areas. On this occasion, from the end of September onwards, contingents from Scotland, Lancashire, Yorkshire, the North-East Coast and elsewhere had been moving down the main roads towards London. They were met by great crowds in some towns with well-organized reception committees providing meals and accommodation. In the House of Commons, Conservative members were demanding that the marchers be prevented from entering London, alleging that the march had been 'organized from Moscow'. Labour members were expressing misgivings about the behaviour of the police. 'The tendency has been to get another kind of police in the Metropolis', said George Lansbury, Leader of the Opposition, 'and I read the other day of another sort of police in Birkenhead, I think, where half a dozen on motor cycles charged a crowd as if it were an armed crowd. In London we have these new horse patrols who carry long staves and use them on occasion very effectively.'[9] He went on to describe events in a Lambeth street where mounted police had formed up at either end, charged and met in the centre, so that nobody could get away and many were hurt.

Lansbury's misgivings were justified in the days that followed. On 27 October when the marchers reached Hyde Park and a crowd numbering some hundred thousand was there to welcome them, the mounted police made repeated baton charges, there was bitter fighting and many were hurt. In the days that followed the same thing was repeated in many London streets. The leaders of the NUWM were arrested and the great bundles of petition, which its sponsors claimed held a million signatures, were seized by the police and never reached their destination. It seemed that the authorities were determined on a brutal exhibition of strength.

By the end of the year the Prime Minister was appealing to everyone to help in the work of the National Council for Social Service to give the unemployed something to do, 'teaching men how they may be able to furnish their homes, to make mats out of bits of old rope, purchased for a few pence'. 'Report yourself,' he said, 'join up; contribute your knowledge.'[10]

The Restoration of the 10 per cent cut

The year 1933 opened with the highest figure of unemployed yet known. Including those in Northern Ireland 2·9 million were on the register, but this was by no means a complete figure. For those who had been struck off under the Anomalies Regulations and many others in uninsured categories often did not bother to register for work, preferring to look for it themselves. Indeed at the worst point in the depression the figures of unemployed were probably at their most unreal. Meanwhile one third of those on the register had been continuously out of work for six months or longer.

The 1931 Emergency Measures were due to expire in June 1933, but by the time this date arrived the government had decided that the cuts in benefit must be maintained for a further year yet. Suffering and hardship had never been so widespread, reports of malnutrition among the children of the unemployed were mounting; yet as the Commons adjourned for the summer recess it was reported that thousands of cases of oranges had been dumped in the sea at Liverpool; it would have been 'a loss to land them'.

It was not until November 1933 that the government produced its long-promised Unemployment Bill, Part II of which was to sever the connection between the unemployed and the Public Assistance Committees. The implementation of Part II, however, was still something for the future – as it turned out, the far future – the immediate consideration at the turn of the year was the restoration of the 1931 10 per cent cut in standard benefit. For 1934 was early on heralded as the year of recovery; slowly, patchily, like the thaw after a terrible winter, economic life started up in the last months of 1933 and the first of 1934. But as the ice melted, curious distortions were revealed in the economic landscape beneath. While certain areas in the South and the Midlands were springing into life, others in the North and in Wales, from which life had been ebbing for many decades, now seemed to have died outright. From then on *long-term* unemployment, in the sense of men without work for years as opposed to months, was increasingly concentrated in those areas known as Depressed Areas. So that those who had exhausted their benefit rights and were on the means test were to be found in much larger numbers in such areas than in the rest of the country.

Unemployment as a whole was nevertheless falling. Moreover since the long-term unemployed were no longer a charge on the Unemployment Insurance Fund, the latter had begun to show a substantial surplus. Yet the government was obstinately resisting demands for the restoration of the 10 per cent cut in standard benefit.

Pressure for the cuts to be restored began to mount. By February

1934 the NUWM had another national hunger march under way. The authorities and most of the newspapers began by denouncing the march in much the same terms as had been used in 1932. They found, however, a rather different climate of opinion. Many people, it seemed, even if they didn't support the march, were sympathetic to its aims. Just before the march reached London, a letter to the press signed by a group of writers, lawyers and politicians, announced the formation of a Council for Civil Liberties. The letter expressed concern at the Attorney General's hints of possible bloodshed and the police instructions to shop-keepers to barricade their windows. Recalling police behaviour in the 1932 hunger march, the writers said that they were going to arrange for 'vigilant observation of the proceedings' in the next few days.[11] By 25 February when the marchers reached Hyde Park the police had clearly had different instructions. They behaved with careful restraint towards the crowd – variously estimated at between fifty thousand and a hundred and fifty thousand – which assembled in drizzling rain to greet the march-ers, and with restraint towards the crowds who went lobbying in the next few days. Finally it was announced on 17 April 1934 that standard benefit rates would be restored in July to their old level (17s for a single man, 26s for a couple, 2s for each child).

The ostensible reasons for stringency – the financial emergency and the insolvency of the fund – were long since over. From then on so far as standard benefit was concerned the Unemployment Insurance Fund continued to show a surplus and there were annual debates on what to do with it, with the opposition asking for higher benefits and the government seeking to do something else. What were the motives behind the extreme reluctance to restore the benefit level or to increase it in the later thirties, in spite of considerable public feeling and political pressure? The motives were of course mixed – one factor was the fear that the economy was heading for another slump. But the main consideration was undoubtedly the relation between benefit and wages. Wages were so low in some areas and industries that the benefit rates for a man with children were not all that far below them – indeed if there was only intermittent work to be had on a few days each week, people could sometimes be better-off on the dole. The idea that benefit rates might compete with the level of wages, or circumscribe opportunities of maintaining a low wage level, was one about which the employers were acutely sensitive, and this sensitivity was reflected in Whitehall which seemed positively obsessed with the fear that a man might feel as well-off out of work as in work.

So it was that in spite of all the agitation and evidence about child poverty, improvements were very small and slow in coming. The first improvement came in 1935, just before the General Election, when the child's allowance was raised from 2s to 3s. By the time the war broke out in 1939, standard benefit was 17s for a man, 10s for his wife, and 3s for each child. Prices had risen by this time and the 33s for a family of four was just about the same in real terms as the amount received before the 1931 cuts.

The Coming of the UAB

When those on standard benefit got their increase in July 1934, there were an equal number of unemployed who were not directly involved, since those who had exhausted their benefit rights were still getting 'transitional payments' after a means test by the local Public Assistance Committee. After July 1934 some of the local Public Assistance Committees raised their maximum recommended payments to the equivalent of the new standard rates; others kept them as they were before, and some, as we have seen, were still considerably below standard benefit rates.

Part II of the 1934 Unemployment Act had however provided for a revolutionary change in administration. The arrangements for the Public Assistance Committees to do the means testing while the government footed the bill, which had been introduced in 1931, were a temporary expedient which those in charge were anxious to be rid of. Unlike poor relief which was paid for partly out of local rates, the Public Assistance Committees had no financial responsibility for the transitional payments scheme and yet, as elected bodies were subject to all kinds of local pressures in its operation. The early showdown with Rotherham and Durham

County had been, it was uneasily conjectured, only a symptom of something which was fairly widespread – in many other localities there had been what was officially described as a 'relaxation of responsibility'. And in any case, as Sir Henry Betterton, the Minister of Labour was constantly arguing, the variations in PAC scales from area to area and the anomalies arising therefrom, were quite indefensible.

The solution decided upon was the transfer of all those unemployed now on the means test into the hands of a new central body, the Unemployment Assistance Board, which would settle allowances and operate a means test on a uniform basis throughout the country. Henceforth the Public Assistance Committees would revert to their former prime concern which was to care for the sick and the aged.

The Unemployment Assistance Board was to be an 'independent' body, over which parliamentary control would be very indirect – thus the explosive issue of the means test would no longer be subject to detailed control or supervision by any elected person, whether councillor or MP. There were some misgivings about the implications of this in Parliament, and not only from the opposition, but in the end the Act went through after which it was immediately announced that the chairman of the new Board was to be none other than Sir Henry Betterton, the Minister of Labour who had had the main responsibility for the National government's unemployment policy. He went to the Lords and became Lord Rushcliffe.

The new Board (commonly known to its applicants as the UAB) was due to take over early in 1935. Less than four weeks before the appointed day, the scales which the UAB was to operate were published. It was revealed that some of those who had hitherto been receiving allowances via the PACs at the maximum rate (i.e. equivalent to standard benefit) would have them cut. The UAB allowance for a couple was to be 24s compared with 26s on standard benefit. Moreover, payments for adult sons and daughters were to be much below standard benefit rates. In the Distressed Areas it was not uncommon to find parents and grown-up children all unemployed together. Some such families might be hard hit if the Public Assistance Committee had been operating the maximum allowances permitted. However children's allowances were to be higher than under standard benefit, so that there was a general impression that families with several children would be better off.

Apart from the new allowances, detailed rules were published for operating the means test – for computing resources of all kinds to set against the payment. There was an elaborate list of disregards; for example one-third of the earnings of sons and daughters up to 20s would be disregarded and one quarter of the excess over 20s; the rest would be counted as family resources and used to reduce the applicant's allowance. There was a curiously complex rent rule which almost no one could understand, and a surcharge whereby the total allowance would be reduced by 1s per member for each member in excess of five.

The Regulations went through the House just before Christmas and the Board began to operate on 7 January 1935. Within a few days there was uproar. In one district after another the unemployed found that their new allowances were less than they had been under the transitional payments scheme – in some cases far less. And some were even being cut off altogether. In Wales the vast majority of unemployed families transferred to the UAB had suffered reductions, and protests were growing with every day that passed. The anthracite miners called for a twenty-four-hour protest strike and were followed by a similar call from the Cambrian Combine miners in the Rhondda. The South Wales Miners' Federation called an all-Wales Conference and set up a council of action; three hundred thousand people came out on demonstrations. In Merthyr a demonstration of women smashed the windows of the UAB office.

The protests were not confined to Wales. There were big demonstrations in Glasgow, large-scale protests in Lanarkshire, Renfrewshire, Yorkshire and elsewhere. Some families, it is true received increased allowances, but this was in areas where the Public Assistance Committees had been operating exceptionally harsh scales – notably most of the rural areas.

The House re-assembled on 28 January in an atmosphere of ten-

sion and a good deal of bewilderment among government supporters, who had been led to believe that the Board would
improve the position of the unemployed, and who had never
grasped the significance of the constant allegations of the Minister
of Labour about 'lax administration' by the Public Assistance
Committees. One after another members from both sides of the
House spoke of the appalling results of the new regulations in
their constituencies. Geoffrey Mander, a Liberal MP, quoted a list
of cases from Willenhall, near Wolverhampton: '38s reduced to
25s, 28s reduced to nothing, 26s to 6s 6d, 17s 6d to 10s, 14s to
nothing, 21s to nothing, 16s to 10s 6d, 10s 6d to nothing, 26s to
nothing, 16s 3d to nothing, 13s to nothing', and observed that
'many people who were bitter critics of the public assistance scale
are now obliged to say that it was a model of generosity compared with the treatment that is being received today'.

Robert Boothby, a Conservative, said that the average reduction in the small fishing town of Peterhead was 6s 11d per household and that 'the new administration is brutal. I can use no other
word.' Sir John Wallace, a government supporter, said, 'I did
not contemplate there was even a remote possibility of such cuts
being made as are now operating in the Dunfermline district.'
Kenneth Lindsay, a government supporter from Kilmarnock,
complained that 80 per cent of the applicants in his constituency had had reductions. W. H. Mainwaring, Labour MP
from the East Rhondda closed his speech with a ringing call to
action:

> I hope the working classes of this country will pay heed to what is
> said and done here today and that from now onwards the agitation
> which is at such a height in South Wales (Hon. Members: 'And all
> over') will spread like a flame throughout the country and that the
> English and Scottish working classes will join with the Welshmen and
> make the demand that come what will, these damnable regulations
> must be withdrawn.[12]

The lobbies were crowded; there were outbursts from the public
gallery. Oliver Stanley, the new Minister of Labour, was defensive. The officials were new to their job, he said, so there were

bound to be cases where they were not aware of the way the Board had intended them to use their discretionary powers – an excuse that was to arouse the indignation of the Civil Service.

The debate wore on inside and outside the Commons – so did the movement of protest. At last on 5 February the government announced total retreat; there was to be a standstill order under which applicants were to get either what they would have got under the previous PAC assessment or an allowance in accordance with the Unemployment Assistance Board's new regulations, whichever was the higher. And past reductions were to be refunded. This arrangement was temporary, until the UAB had had time to make further proposals. The bill to operate the 'standstill' was introduced on 8 February – it had gone through all stages and received the Royal Assent by 15 February.

The Standstill Act

The standstill Act was to last for nearly two years, during which the Unemployment Assistance Board was to be involved in one of the most complicated administrative tasks ever faced by a body of officials. Each applicant had to be assessed twice, once according to the Board's own regulations, and once according to the scales for transitional payments which would have been applied to him by the local Public Assistance Committee had the Board not existed. He was then awarded an allowance equal to whichever formula provided him with most. The Unemployment Assistance Board's organization was divided into twenty-eight districts; each district covered the territory of half a dozen or more Public Assistance Committees each with its different scales and rules. Within the area of each Public Assistance Committee were sub-committees or guardian's committees operating with varying degrees of autonomy, sometimes according to rules, sometimes disregarding the rules, sometimes without any rules at all.

Poor Lord Rushcliffe! For so long he had argued against the 'anomalies' and talked of the necessity of establishing 'uniformity'. Now his main job was to *enforce* anomalies. 'The standstill Act involves, as a statutory obligation upon the officers of the Board, the continuance of many of the anomalies in the transitional payments position whose abolition was one of the reasons for the creation of the Board' he wrote in the 1935 Unemployment Assistance Board Report. 'It also requires the Board, in numerous cases to pay allowances to households, ostensibly on the ground of need, which are simply an abuse of public money.'[13]

The Board's officers made heavy weather about the difficulties involved. Thus the District Officer for the Nottingham area reported:

When the Act came into operation the administration of transitional payments in this district was in the hands of fourteen local authorities ... Many of these authorities had adopted outdoor relief scales, some of which included rules governing treatment of household resources but so far as can be observed these rules appear to have been largely disregarded. Others had no formal scales in use and dealt with each case 'on its merits'. The outlook of the appointed Committees appears to have varied considerably and was not even constant in the same Committee at different meetings, and where no definite scale was in force the determinations at different meetings of the same Committee were altered from time to time without ascertainable cause...[14]

The officer from the Norwich district said:

Within the boundary of the same Authority there was often a notable divergence of practice on the part of the respective area Committees and even the composition of a Committee at a particular sitting was a factor, because the presence or absence of particular individuals not uncommonly influenced the amounts awarded.[15]

The officer for the Swansea district observed that 'even when scales had been drawn up or accepted by the governing authority, the sub-committees had in practice unwritten scales of their own'.[16] Allowances in excess of the scales where these existed were common. The officer for the Newcastle district reported that 'it is not unusual to find ... that the actual amounts granted exceeded the scales by sums of from 2s to 5s without any apparent reason'.[17] The Liverpool District Officer reported on the widespread general use of an additional discretionary allowance called 'dignity money'.

The Poor Law had always been an offence to tidy minds, but this of course was not the real issue at stake. The real complaint which was echoed in the reports of every district officer without exception was that so many of the allowances which the Board was now being forced to pay were 'in excess of need'. The biggest discrepancies between the Board's scale rate and those of the PACs occurred where adult sons and daughters were involved. If they were unemployed their PAC allowances had been frequently higher than those laid down by the UAB. If they were earning, their earnings had been quite often disregarded by the PACs when the parents' allowance was being fixed. And if the earnings were not altogether disregarded, they were often treated very lightly. In other words the means test was being operated very half-heartedly in many cases – in some cases not at all. Disregard of household earnings was particularly widespread in Wales.

It transpired that during 1935 the Unemployment Assistance Board was obliged by the standstill order to pay no less than half its applicants' allowances in excess of its own estimate of need.[18] What this really meant was that those local Public Assistance Committees who had received 'warnings' from the Minister about illegal over-payments and who had carried on a sort of running fight with the Minister had only been the tip of the iceberg. Innumerable sub-committees had met and quietly decided that they were not going to administer the means test if they could help it, or at least not in the stringent way expected of them. Innumerable councillors had fought and argued and wangled – and to a great extent got away with it. They belonged to the great body of opinion that was opposed to means-testing the unemployed. They thought, for instance, that if a skilled man could not get work, he should not be forced to live on the earnings of his daughter, and that young adults should not be made to live on their parents or brothers and sisters when there were no jobs to be had.

Months passed and nothing was done to end the 'abuse of public money' which had so troubled Lord Rushcliffe – indeed some Public Assistance Committees had the nerve to raise their own scales for the uninsured unemployed again 'avowedly', said Lord Rushcliffe, 'in order to produce an immediate influence upon the amount of assistance given by the Board'.[19] But a General Election came and went, and still no steps were taken to abolish the standstill. Meanwhile employment was rising and the Board's applicants were falling in number.

At last in the summer of 1936 the government published new draft regulations and it was announced that the standstill was going to be liquidated. The scale rates were marginally improved, the rent rule made more flexible, the treatment of resources, particularly earnings of the applicant's family, was to be made less stringent. The regulations were due to come into operation in November 1936.

Once again the NUWM organized a national hunger march to demand the abolition of the means test. This time no ban was imposed on it by the National Council of Labour and the reception in London was under the auspices of the London Trades Council. The crowd which assembled at Hyde Park to greet it on 8 November 1936 was reckoned at two hundred and fifty thousand. Among the numerous speakers was Clement Attlee. The marchers' leaders had an interview with Ernest Brown, the Minister of Labour, who promised that the regulations would be introduced gradually over a period of eighteen months.

And that is actually what happened. The numbers on the Board were down to a little over six hundred thousand (plus of course their dependants) and about two hundred and thirty thousand who were due for an increase as a result of the new regulations got it at once; the rest stayed as they were. But during 1937 the squeeze was on; bit by bit the standstill was being liquidated. True, there was a let-up in Coronation week in May when a special bonus of 2s 6d was made to each applicant, and in operating the means test the Board disregarded any special gifts from charities or payments to reservists in connection with Coronation duties. That was a week to remember. But after it, bit by bit, category by category, the remainder of those on the Board had their allowances reduced to the Board's own estimate of need. It took a long time in some areas – particularly in Wales, and in the cities of Glasgow and Dundee, and the whole operation was not completed until the summer of 1938.

The UAB's last years

So the government got its way at last and during the last twelve months of its existence the Unemployment Assistance Board was able everywhere to enforce the means test on a uniform basis. The victory came late in the day; there is no doubt that the conditions of the unemployed throughout the thirties could have been far worse had it not been for the prolonged resistance by the Public Assistance Committees in many areas. These Committees were elected bodies and they were on their way out; the break-up of the Poor Law, long heralded as a desirable and progressive goal, had begun. It is a curious fact that the Poor Law authorities, objects of traditional loathing by the poor over a century, nevertheless acted in some measure in their final years as protectors of the poor against their rulers. That was one reason why they were on their way out. The process pioneered by George Lansbury in the early twenties when the elected local body refused to reduce poor relief scales to the level required by the central government had made a deep impression. Now in the thirties a less dramatic but much more widespread and diffused challenge was offered by many Public Assistance Committees who had put up resistance to the means test by every means open to them for many years. Small wonder that the solution for the government of the day was to take the whole thing over and put it in the hands of a 'responsible' centralized body.

The Unemployment Assistance Board in its later days became increasingly preoccupied with the attitude of mind and behaviour of its applicants. For example it worried about the foolishness of applicants who insisted on spending their savings, despite the fact that the rules provided for the safeguarding of capital of up to £300. As early as 1935, the Board's Birmingham District Officer had reported disapprovingly of a man who had received £300 workman's compensation (for an industrial accident) and who 'immediately spent £100 on furniture and clothing'; and of another who had received a legacy of £320 and who 'immediately took his whole family for an expensive seaside holiday, lent money and lived on a scale disproportionate to his position. Attempts on our part to induce him to be prudent failed, and he was given a nil assessment until the money was exhausted.'[20]

Somehow the applicants had an attitude that was unsatisfactory. If they were well dressed they might have undisclosed resources; if too badly dressed they must be improvident; if they sent their children to school with inadequate shoes, this might be a case of indifference or careless household management.

The Unemployment Assistance Board carried out elaborate surveys into the attitude of mind of young men and girls to whom no work had been offered, in order to discover whether there were any 'obstacles of an individual or personal character'.[21] It worried about 'the problem of those who would probably accept work if it were offered to them, but have fallen into such a condition of mind and body that they make no personal effort to obtain it'.[22] It worried about the young men who wouldn't leave their own district and who 'claimed that work should be found for them at or near their homes'[23] and about the 'idleness and irresponsibility of young girls' who were unwilling to consider domestic service or move away from home.[24] It thought that young people ought to be made to recognize their duty to keep themselves fit in mind and body in return for the receipt of a public allowance,[25] and in this connection was concerned in trying to persuade young men to attend courses at the residential instruction centres and camps. These courses were not designed to enable men to learn a skill, and seldom led to a job at the end; they were intended to restore and maintain 'employability' and those participating were set to work on unskilled tasks in drainage, afforestation and road-making while living under a regime of strict discipline, somewhat analogous to that in the army, with ex-army officers usually in charge.

These centres were separate from the training centres (dealt with in the next chapter). They were opposed by the NUWM on the

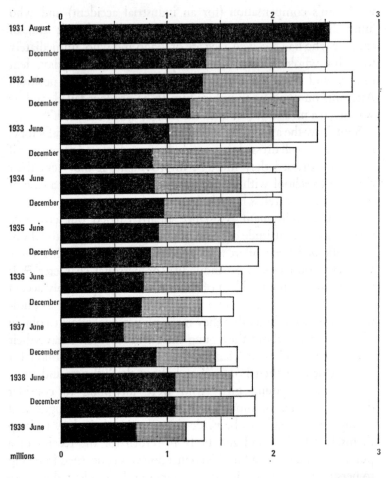

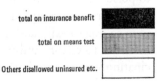

total on insurance benefit

total on means test

Others disallowed uninsured etc.

Fig. 1 Numbers unemployed in Great Britain: Total unemployed on Register. (See appendix on page 341 for the tables on which the figures are based.)

grounds that the inmates were being forced to work without wages on jobs that should be paid for at trade union rates, and on the whole there was very great reluctance to volunteer for them. Lord Rushcliffe was anxious that compulsion should be used. So was *The Times*, which had published correspondence from influential people in praise of the compulsory labour camps in Nazi Germany and which alleged in a leader that there were:

hundreds and thousands of young men who do not show any disposition to bestir themselves to get out of unemployment into employment. They are content with a life of laziness . . . there is a slackness of moral fibre and of will as well as of muscle . . . Salutary action is necessary beyond dispute . . . the breakdown of morale can only be made good by applying compulsion.[26]

Actually the government had power to apply compulsion under the 1934 Act, but its compulsory powers were never openly used, though it was constantly alleged that the pressure put on by the UAB to persuade men to go voluntarily was not far off compulsion. But in this, as with so many things, the UAB met with prolonged passive resistance.

When the war broke out the Board's name was suddenly changed to 'Assistance Board' and it was put in charge of bombed-out and war-distressed persons to the mutual astonishment of both parties. For the old-style method of treating the unemployed was somehow inappropriate for the new customers. The family which had lost everything in an air-raid did not expect to be dealt with like malingerers, and the Board had to begin to mend its manners. As for the household means test, it received a death blow under the 1941 Determination of Needs Act, and has never again reappeared except as a shadow of its former self.

4
Industrial Graveyards

The Decline of the Basic Industries

All through the nineteen twenties the old industries which had made Britain great in the nineteenth century – coalmining, iron and steel, shipbuilding, cotton textiles – were fighting a losing battle. Most of them never again reached the output levels of 1913, even before they were overtaken by the world crisis in 1930–1. At the same time mechanization and technological change were reducing the number of workers needed to produce a given output.

These older industries were concentrated geographically in the North and West of Britain. Primarily their location had been determined by the coalfields. The heavy industries were also producing largely for the export market, and were therefore attracted towards the seaboard (iron and steel and shipbuilding on Clyde, Tyne and Tees; heavy engineering in Clyde, Tyne and the Manchester/Liverpool area). Long hauls to London and the wealthy South-East were cheapened by the tapering system of railway charges, which reduced the cost per mile over long distances.

This concentration meant that the post-war depression, instead of being evenly felt over the whole country, hit the people of these areas with far greater force. Already in 1927 Neville Chamberlain had said: 'The devastation in the coalfields can only be compared with the war devastation of France.'

Meanwhile wholly new science-based industries were growing (though more slowly than the old industries declined); electricity supply and all kinds of electrical and radio equipment; aluminium; cars and aircraft; road and air transport; rayon; synthetic dyestuffs and fertilizers; food canning; film-making and cinemas. Building (with related industries like furniture and wallpaper, as well as building materials) was also rapidly expanding. But by far the greatest increase in employment was in distribution, hotels, and catering and various service trades (laundries, cleaners, hair-dressers, entertainment), and these, like the newer manufacturing industries, were already concentrated in the South East and the Midlands, and continued to grow there. This was the main cause of the growing economic prosperity and increasing population of these districts.

Two technical developments made industry free to develop away from the old declining areas – electric power and road transport. Once electricity was available it was no longer so important to have coal near at hand, and new modernized works were built close to their main markets. As the relative importance of exports declined, industry was attracted less to the ports and more to the great wealthy population centres of the home market, especially London. When the shipbuilding industry lost customers abroad and fell into decay, innumerable engineering and fitting trades which had been concentrated around Glasgow, Liverpool and Newcastle declined too, while new ancillary trades grew up round the motor factories in the Midlands and the South. Competition from road transport undermined the system of tapering charges on the railways, and more and more exceptional rates were quoted to keep the shorter-distance traffic; this gave an increasing cost advantage to firms nearer their home market. Meanwhile coal faced growing competition from oil, above all for fuelling ships.

By the nineteen thirties British capitalism was coming to accept that many of the pre-war export markets were gone for good. The policy pursued by heavy industry, inspired by the banks, with strong support from the government in the form of protective tariffs, was to amalgamate the main firms in each industry or form them into some kind of a cartel, so that production could be restricted and prices maintained at the most profitable level. Whether growing monopolization took the form of outright merger or agreements on prices and production quotas, the effect on the workers was much the same. Instead of works continuing to run at a reduced output, as had normally happened in previous depressions, a large proportion were closed down altogether so that the rest could produce at a profit. Many towns lost their only industry overnight, and got nothing to replace it.

Cartelization made this situation rigid and lasting. Thus attempts to *expand* efficient modernized production of cheap steel in the Distressed Areas were successfully opposed by the British Iron and Steel Federation and the banks. Richard Thomas met innumerable obstacles to its low-price strip-mill scheme at Ebbw Vale, and eventually was forced to join the cartel and produce at its price.[1] A scheme by a syndicate outside the industry for a new integrated steel plant at Jarrow was so strongly opposed by the Federation that it had to be dropped.[2] To protest about this was one of the main motives of the famous march to London by the Jarrow unemployed.

Following a similar pattern, National Shipbuilders' Security Ltd was formed in 1930, with the banks and most of the shipbuilding firms as shareholders, to buy up and close down 'obsolete or redundant' shipyards out of the proceeds of a levy on those still at work. The sites were placed under restrictive covenants to make them unusable for shipbuilding, and might (but usually could not in practice) be disposed of to other industries. By 1934 National Shipbuilders' Security had purchased and scrapped some 137 berths, or two-fifths of the industry, and more were acquired later. In 1937, although rearmament and increased world trade had brought some increase in orders, Glasgow was still producing only half its output of 1929-30, the Tyne about one-third, the Tees and Liverpool little more than half.

In coalmining, although a good deal of cut-throat competition continued, the trend was towards amalgamations, and the permanent closure by each combine of its older and less profitable pits. The Coal Mines Act of 1930 was intended to assist this process. The exporting coalfields were the worst affected. In the narrow valleys of South Wales, the urbanized moorlands of Northumberland and Durham and Central Scotland, many villages and townships had no work at all.

For cotton and woollen textiles such 'rationalization' proved much more difficult. In these industries, made up largely of a mass of small firms, each carrying out only one of an immense variety of processes, amalgamation and cartelization was only partial. Cut-throat competition and attrition over a period of years, rather than the planned and permanent shut-down of a whole district, was here the pattern of decline for most of the decade.*

In all these schemes the stress was on reducing productive capacity rather than on modernization, the aim being to make existing plant (frequently obsolescent) profitable to run. The resulting stagnation left these key industries technically well behind world standards, as a series of government Commissions and Working Parties found when they took stock at the end of the Second World War.†

The conversion of the proudest industrial centres of the nineteenth century into Distressed Areas, or Depressed Areas, or (a beautiful euphemism, devised by the House of Lords) Special Areas, was not a development of a year or two. The thirties merely continued and intensified the tragic failure of the twenties. The areas officially scheduled as distressed had a population of some four million, and this excluded Lancashire with another five million, and many large towns and cities in the old industrial regions such as Newcastle and Glasgow, where unemployment was almost as bad. Anything from a fifth to a quarter of the population was living in districts which remained severely depressed until the very end of the decade.

Migration and 'Distressed' Areas

The shift in industry drastically altered the structure and balance

---

*Nevertheless in 1933 the woolcombing firms formed a company called Woolcombers' Mutual Association, analogous to that in shipbuilding, to buy up and dismantle plant, and the Lancashire Cotton Corporation, backed by the Bank of England, bought up 140 mills and was in process of scrapping 80 by 1936, while in 1936, under the Cotton Spindles Act, spinning mills still at work began to pay a compulsory levy to purchase and scrap redundant plant.

† Indeed over all manufacturing industry (not to speak of mining and agriculture) 1931–3 were years of net disinvestment – investment did not on balance suffice to replace obsolete plant. (See C. H. Feinstein, *Domestic Capital Formation in the UK, 1920–38.*)

of the main communities in Britain, and its effects on every aspect of social life were deep and lasting. It is estimated that over a million people between the ages of fifteen and forty-five emigrated into the South-East alone in 1923-38, and there was a fairly large influx into the Midlands and South-West as well. Between 1931 and 1938 alone, the population of Greater London increased

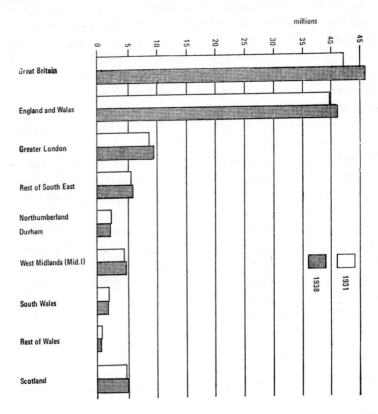

Fig. 2 Movement of population within Great Britain 1931-8 (in thousands).

by nearly half a million, while that of Northumberland and Durham fell by thirty-nine thousand and that of South Wales by one hundred and fifteen thousand.

Over the period 1932-7 the insured population in London increased by as much as 14 per cent. In Lancashire over the same period it declined by 1 per cent, in Northumberland and Durham by 0·7 per cent and in Glamorgan and Monmouth by 3 per cent. In the main migration was a spontaneous, unplanned movement.

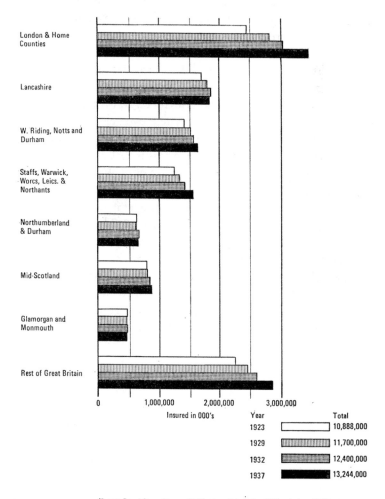

(Source Royal Commision on Distribution of the Industrial Population, 1940)

Fig. 3 Geographical distribution of working population (persons insured under Unemployment Insurance Acts).

It provided the expanding industries with the cheap semi-skilled labour they needed, but did not solve the problem of unemployment and decay in the old industrial areas. Indeed by taking away the youngest and strongest (for most of those migrating were between sixteen and thirty-five), and by further cutting purchasing power, it gradually intensified the poverty and dereliction. The depressed areas had more than their share of old people, fewer of working age; this made it harder to provide social services for those who remained. Rates rose far higher than in the rest of the country, and became a further deterrent to industrialists who might have set up factories there. As the public assistance rates rose and the value of property fell, even elementary services like road mending and drainage were perforce neglected.

An extreme yet representative story was that of the once proud County Borough of Merthyr Tydfil in South Wales, the cradle of the British iron industry. The Cyfarthfa ironworks, the biggest in the world in 1803, were closed in 1910, operated for a short time during the war and finally dismantled in 1928. The Dowlais works of Guest Keen and Nettlefold were extensively modernized after the war, but this did not prevent the company in 1930 from transferring their operations to new works on the coast at Cardiff and Port Talbot. A Royal Commission described the scene in 1935:[3] 'Merthyr Tydfil has many sites of decaying ironworks, the most modern of which stands like a gaunt memorial to past prosperity on the hillside at Dowlais.' The number of people made destitute by this change was far greater than the three thousand steelworkers directly thrown out. As the Mayor of the town pointted out:

When the works were in full employment, a large number or elderly men were employed as watchmen, signalmen, gatekeepers, and on other light work, who are now regarded as unemployable and in receipt of Public Assistance, but if the works were still going they would still be in employment. Similarly, elderly men and women who had small shops and were independent by this means when the industries were in commission have since had to close down because of the reduced purchasing power of the inhabitants, and become chargeable to Public Assistance. Women who kept lodgers, or who went working days cleaning and washing for workers' families who are now unemployed, or parents who were dependent on sons or daughters who have removed from the area, are also in receipt of public assistance.[4]

The pits in the Merthyr area, which had employed twenty-four thousand in 1913 and sixteen thousand in 1924, were down to eight thousand in 1935. Miners were desperately seeking work at distant collieries; over a thousand were reported to be travelling twenty to twenty-four miles a day to and from work, at a cost to themselves of 7s a week. A hundred Dowlais steelworkers who had managed to get jobs at the new Cardiff works were paying 9s a week in fares; they left home at 4 a.m. and got back at 7.30 or 8 p.m.; yet if they were married men with fair-sized families, they would have been financially far better off unemployed as most of their neighbours were. Out of nineteen thousand insured against unemployment in the Borough in 1934, twelve thousand or 63·6 per cent were unemployed.

As a result of the heavy cost of public assistance and the slump in the value of property (for who would buy houses or shops in a ghost town?) rates in Merthyr were abnormally high (28s 5d in the pound in 1935), and this, together with the gloomy and forlorn aspect of the place, was bound to deter new industries. The council and local organizations asked the government to take over the public assistance costs so that rates could be lowered: to resite part of Woolwich Arsenal in the old steelworks; to manufacture Post Office equipment there. None of these proposals was acted upon. The only result of the Royal Commission's deliberations was that Merthyr was deprived of its County Borough status because of the financial breakdown. A responsible estimate by PEP in 1939 showed that it would be cheaper for the taxpayer to rebuild the whole town on a new site on the Glamorgan coast or the Usk valley than to pay £1 a week (over and above the 27s 6d local rate) to keep each Merthyr family alive in Merthyr.[5]

Social Conditions in the Areas

Communities in these areas suffered a sort of twilight existence which was new, at least on this scale. The social effect was different from that of 'normal' unemployment which periodically affected most workers in times of bad trade, and which fell most heavily on the unskilled or casuals, the weak, the disabled and those past middle age. This unemployment involved virtually the whole working-class community, including the most skilled and highly organized – for those still employed, apart from a handful in neighbouring pits or ship yards, were mainly running public services and shops for the terribly shrunken demands of a town on the dole. Few of these were in skilled jobs or brought in anything above a low fixed rate of wages. Many were youngsters who were likely to get the sack at eighteen. It was common in mining areas to see fourteen-year-old boys, with black faces, plodding wearily home from the pit while their fathers stood unemployed on the street corner. Wages even in the basic industries were pulled down by competition for jobs and the fear of victimization.[6] Thus the Pilgrim Trust in 1936 investigated the position of seventy-six families in Tonypandy and found that normal wages were very little above unemployment allowances, and that men with three or more children probably were worse off financially by working.

In some ways all this made the position of the unemployed less intolerable than in a relatively prosperous town. To be out of work did not carry the stigma of being a failure and inferior to the neighbours.* On the other hand, men lived for years without even the hope of a job. The run-down of all trade and social services in the areas meant that the people existed in an environment of un-relieved shabbiness and deprivation outside the home as well as in it, with no financial help from relatives or friends. Shops, public houses, welfare halls, schools, all came to look grubby and worn-out for lack of funds to maintain them or even keep them clean. One could go for miles through the streets and never see a freshly-painted building. One investigator in 1934 counted twenty-three shops closed and whitewashed in the village of Tonypandy alone.[7] Because of their poverty the areas got few of the new cheap stores

* Indeed it was sometimes the employed worker who was suspect. Where so many were out of work, a man with a regular job under the local authority might have used bribery or relationship with a councillor to get it and a miner still employed in the pit must surely be considered by the management as one who would give no trouble.

such as Woolworth's and Marks and Spencer's which were opening in the high streets of more prosperous towns. The shops that stayed open were often poor and ill-stocked, with notices in the window 'PAC vouchers taken'.

J. B. Priestley described the scene in Jarrow: 'Wherever we went there were men hanging about, not scores of them but hundreds of thousands of them. The whole town looked as if it had entered some penniless bleak Sabbath . . .'[8]

The landscape was generally one of industrial squalor and ruin. Thus in North Lanarkshire the difficulty of attracting new industry was officially blamed on 'the accumulated waste of industrial depression – unsightly industrial rubbish, derelict building, neglected amenities, all representing the debris of a passing industry',[9] while in Cumberland the eyesores formed by buildings and workings abandoned by industry 'are likely to prove deterrents to industrial enterprise or tourist traffic'.[10]

Despite depopulation there was much overcrowding, even while many houses stood empty. Poverty and arrears of rent* forced the unemployed to sublet, and small working-class houses built for one family were made to hold two or more.

A strong cultural and educational tradition existed, especially in the mining districts, but it was being eroded by poverty.† For example, public libraries and those in miners' welfare halls and institutes, which had long been the workers' main means of self education, had been unable to buy any new books for years. Not only had the areas more than their share of slum schools. The Medical Officer of Health of Abertillery reported that most children had no boots; they went to school in plimsolls and many therefore stayed at home in wet weather. The Rhondda teachers even raised their own fund to provide their pupils with boots.

Malnutrition was general and ill-health with it. In Jarrow, for instance, the tuberculosis death rate was double the national rate

---

* Many families in the thirties still had £50 or more of rent arrears as a result of the nine months miners' lockout in 1926, which continuous unemployment since had made it impossible to pay off.

† The Pilgrim Trust investigators in the Rhondda were struck to find unemployed men who discussed philosophy or read Balzac. At Newport the Chief Librarian reported that 50 per cent of the unemployed read books on economics.

and infantile mortality 112 per thousand births, almost double the national rate. In 1938 the Board of Education wrote to the Jarrow Council, pointing out that there was serious malnutrition among schoolchildren, and requesting that something should be done to increase the number of free meals. But the following year the increased provision had to be cut again, along with the supply of cheap milk for expectant mothers, because the Council could not raise the sum required from the rates.*

Instead of regular paid employment, men spent much of their time adding a little in kind to their family's subsistence by various sideline methods that could escape the calculations of the means test man, such as allotments, boot-repair schemes, and working the neglected colliery outcrops for house-coal. J. B. Priestley at Hebburn-on-Tyne ('a stranded hulk of a town') found an active social centre 'in a couple of huts by the side of a derelict shipyard ... There were places for carpentering and cobbling, a tattered library, and a newly finished hut for their twopenny whist drives and dances.' He was proudly taken to see an old ship's boat in which the unemployed went out to catch fish to distribute among workless families:

> To get there we had to cross the derelict shipyard, which was a fantastic wilderness of decaying sheds, strange mounds and pits, rusted iron, old concrete and new grass ... Down the Tyne we could see the idle ships lying up ... fine big steamers rusting away in rows.' And he commented: 'These men, who were once part of our elaborate industrial machinery, but have now been cast out by it, are starting all over again ... out at sea with a line and a hook. And it will not do. These are not simple fishermen, any more than this island is one of the South Sea Islands. They are the skilled children of our industrial civilization ... and every time they go out and fumble frozenly with their lines and hooks, they declare once again the miserable bankruptcy of our system.[11]

Of the Rhondda valleys, where almost half the insured men in

* A penny on the rates in Jarrow produced only £350–450 (whereas Holborn with about the same population collected £6,000 and Bedford £1,500), says E. W. Wilkinson in *The Town That was Murdered*. See also Chapter 16 for a comparison of health statistics with those of more prosperous areas.

a population of two hundred thousand were out of work in the mid-thirties. Arthur Horner, long an unemployed Rhondda miner and later the first General Secretary of the National Union of Mineworkers, wrote in his autobiography *Incorrigible Rebel*:

> Most of the men had allotments and that would enable them to provide themselves with vegetables, but few had more than one – or at the most two – meals a day. We used to walk over the tips collecting lumps of coal. It was a point of honour never to buy anything if you could get it in other ways. We took wood from fences without any sense of shame. We would steal timber from the pit heads. And if a sheep could be enticed from the hillside, it would be killed and the meat divided among the people of the village. We shut the doors and windows while the mutton was cooking and we buried the fleece. We were not ashamed because we were being made outcasts by those who owned the means which could have given us a livelihood.[12]

Coal picking was indeed universal in South Wales.* Coal might be taken legally from disused tips or outcrops beyond the colliery boundaries, but it was illegal to take it from trucks in sidings or from outcrops on colliery land, even those which the company was admittedly never going to work. Coal stealing was one of the commonest 'crimes' of the period, and miners were continually being taken to court and fined for it. The disused tips at closed collieries had mostly been picked bare, some even mined for the scraps of good coal; so the miners would climb in their pit clothes a thousand feet or so up the mountain, to scramble for bits of coal among the slag as it was discharged down the steep unstable tip. A day of this weary work – as hard as a day in the pit – might fill a hundred-weight sack worth 1s 3d, while under the valley floor the rich seams remained unworked. The process was recorded for incredulous posterity in a feature film, *Proud Valley*, made in the Rhondda by Paul Robeson.[13]

The Distressed Areas had a strong tradition of trade unionism and were rich in local organizations of many kinds. This led to a degree of solidarity and organization among the unemployed unparalleled before or since, made possible by the concentration

---

* So much so that the Pilgrim Trust investigators lowered the cost of their minimum 'poverty line' budget for South Wales to allow for it.

of unemployment and the fact that local leaders of the labour and trade union movement were out of work along with the rest. The habit of organization persisted, and Labour Party and Communist Party, social clubs, trade unions continued to be strongly supported (more than a third of the Rhondda unemployed, for example, continuing to keep up their trade union membership). Churches and chapels, though losing members during the thirties, were still powerful if impoverished institutions. Demonstrations and protests against the means test and for increased unemployment benefit (led initially, as a rule, by the NUWM) involved at peak moments almost every organization from the local council and the union to the male voice choir. On some of the biggest literally half the population took to the streets. Undoubtedly it was this continuing organization which prevented Mosley and his Fascists from making serious headway in these areas, despite repeated efforts.

But the very conditions which helped solidarity also meant isolation. This great movement of protest was tucked away in narrow valleys and remote moorlands, invisible to the prosperous part of the country. If the streets of the mining and shipbuilding towns were packed with marching people, who was there to see it? The hunger marches represented an attempt to break out of this isolation, and to impress the needs and the fighting spirit of the areas on the attention of an indifferent Parliament and capital city. But they were, of course, on a token scale. The threat to the established order was limited, and the degree of suffering never fully understood outside the Depressed Areas themselves.

Industry locates itself

The government and business interests alike took the line that to compel industrialists to locate new factories in the Depressed Areas was out of the question. The national interest and those of businessmen were assumed to be identical: and the businessmen alone were to be the judges of where industry could grow and flourish. Not unnaturally, they and their financial backers decided, almost to a man, that it was cheaper, pleasanter and more convenient to build new plant on the outskirts of London or Birmingham, where rates were low, the general setting clean and cheerful, and the managers' families could enjoy West End shopping and theatres, good schools and upper middle-class social life. Only foreign businessmen wishing to extend or establish factories in England – most of them at this period German-Jewish refugees – were directed to the Depressed Areas or other heavily unemployed districts such as Lancashire; some one hundred and ten such enterprises had been set up in the Special Areas by 1938. The fact that a number of these relatively small-scale enterprises were successful in establishing themselves in the areas suggests that there was no reason at all why British capitalists should not have been able to do the same if similar pressure had been applied.

Fear of working-class militancy seems to have played some part in the employers' attitude. The official government investigator in the North-East, Captain Euan Wallace, MP, wrote in 1934: 'The fact that the local administration of County Durham is now generally regarded as a stronghold of Socialism is unlikely to prejudice industrialists in its favour.'[14] This despite the fact, which he also recorded, that the Durham strike record was far below the national average. Sir Malcolm Stewart, first commissioner for the areas, in 1935 again listed 'fear of industrial unrest' as an argument frequently used by unwilling employers,[15] although Oliver Stanley, Minister of Labour, had already officially declared the survival of this idea to be 'quite unjustified'.[16]

Special Areas Legislation: Too Little and Too Late

It was not until 1934, when economic recovery was under way in the rest of the country, that any special legislation was attempted in order to deal with the appalling social and economic breakdown in the Distressed Areas as a whole. The great hunger march of that year helped to bring their suffering home to people in London and other towns through which the marchers passed. A month afterwards the government appointed four special investigators to make confidential reports on conditions there. When their main findings were published they revealed a horrifying picture of suffering and waste.*

However, although two full-time Commissioners for the Distressed Areas (one for England and Wales, one for Scotland) were appointed in 1934, they were never given sufficient powers to make much impression on the vast problems. To begin with, the Distressed Areas Act provided for the government to advance only £2 million initially to the Commissioners, a sum which was plainly too small to get any large-scale action going, even though Ramsay MacDonald suggested with characteristic vagueness that more might (or might not) be forthcoming if necessary:

It would have been sheer folly for us to have said twenty million, fifty million or one hundred million pounds ... The business-like way is to say: 'The problem is now clear. You go down. You visit. You deal with it. You spend money on it and I will stand by you.'[17]

The demand of the unemployed and the local authorities was for large-scale schemes of public works, which would both employ

---

* Cmd 4728 1934. The report of Captain Euan Wallace, Conservative MP, on Durham and Tyneside showed that at the time of his investigation there were still 165,000 unemployed in that area: of these 63,000 had been out of work over two years, 40,000 over three years, 18,000 over four years and 9,000 over five years. Since anything over three days' work counted as breaking a spell of unemployment, the number of long-unemployed who had had only a few days' work in three or four years was certainly much greater.

Lieutenant-Colonel Sir Wyndham Portal, reporting almost entirely on the eastern area of South Wales, found the unemployment percentage there 44·5 per cent. Many mining villages, especially those on the worked-out seams in the North of the coal-field such as Blaina, Bryn Mawr and Merthyr Tydfil, he described as 'derelict', with over two-thirds of the workers unemployed. Of 50,000 miners unemployed, 76 per cent had had no work for a year, 56 per cent for over two years, and 35 per cent for over three years. Miners were willing to travel long distances to collieries that were still working – some were travelling as much as twenty miles each way – but for most the work simply was not available. Even in the more prosperous Western area, the anthracite coalfield, unemployment was 28·6 per cent.

In the Depressed Areas of Scotland, Sir Arthur Rose considered there was a permanent surplus of something like 64,000 men, not counting one hundred thousand partly unemployed: while in West Cumberland the Hon. J. C. Davidson found that out of a total of 33,800 men insured, no fewer than 10,500 were registered as unemployed, in addition to those unregistered.

large numbers of men directly and improve the conditions of the people living in the areas. Indeed, there was a great deal to be done merely to bring roads and drainage up to national standards. But the government was quite determined that the Commissioners were not to spend their money in extensive public works. Grants towards such schemes, which had made some small contribution in the twenties towards absorbing those out of work, had been deliberately abandoned as a matter of government policy in 1931, and this policy was persisted in. The aristocratic Oliver Stanley, Minister of Labour, declared in opening the debate on the Distressed Areas Bill:

We want to prevent the Commissioners simply acting as men pouring out money on regular statutory work . . . The direct advantages to be gained by public works are quite extremely limited in their scope, while the indirect implications may be almost unlimited in their reaction.[18]

In practice, the Commissioners' powers, like their finances, turned out to be very restricted indeed – as many MPs had pointed out from the beginning. For one thing, they could not act independently even within the limits of the finance allocated to them, but were subject to continuous control by the government. Moreover, they were not in fact charged with the duty of relieving unemployment by providing work. Any scheme they wished to support was to be judged on the contribution it would make, when completed, to the economic development of the area. Levelling slagheaps or planting them with trees, for instance, usually failed to qualify. The Commissioners were forbidden to supplement a grant already being given by any government department. Thus if a hard-pressed local authority was receiving 60 per cent government grant for a new road, but could not find the other 40 per cent from its rates, the Commissioner could do nothing to help. Nor could he give a grant to a project eligible for a government grant but not receiving it. The Commissioner might initiate plans to prepare sites for new factories, but could not provide them with roadways because that was another Department's business. And so on.

Many important schemes with a bearing on future prosperity were turned down. The scheme for a Severn road bridge, which would have brought South Wales more closely in touch with inland markets, was stopped because it interfered with vested railway interests (it was finally opened in 1966). A fish quay for Sunderland harbour, a Welsh National Park with roads and camp-sites designed to attract tourist trade, were among the still-born projects. A large-scale drainage plan for the Welsh coalfield, to reduce risks to mines and safeguard coal reserves, came to nothing because of divisions among the coalowners.

Such action as the Commissioners were able to take to provide work remained on a small scale. For example, they laid out indus-trial estates to provide sites (and in some cases factory buildings) at low rents and rates to industrialists willing to start up in the areas; but these were a drop in the ocean. The estates at Hillingdon (Scotland), Treforest (Wales) and Team Valley (Durham) pro-vided by 1939 only some 7,400 jobs between them, mainly for women and girls.

Resigning from his office as Commissioner in 1937, Sir Malcolm Stewart put his frustration on public record:

> It has to be admitted that no appreciable reduction of the number of those unemployed has been effected. This, however, was not to be looked for, seeing that the Special Areas Act makes no direct provision for this purpose . . . It is difficult to see how the office of Commissioner can be usefully continued unless it is endowed with authority to take independent action.[19]

Although from January 1935 to August 1937 the unemployed in the Special Areas of England and Wales fell from three hundred and sixty-one thousand (36·8 per cent of the insured population) to two hundred and seven thousand (21·7 per cent), the rate re-mained throughout double what it was in the country as a whole.

The Social Service Movement

The restrictions on the Commissioners' powers meant that in practice a great part of their efforts was devoted to supporting the social service movement. Though not prepared to spend money on providing the unemployed with work, the authorities were prepared to spend something, even if not much, in an endeavour to keep them busy.

So in the Distressed Areas unemployed clubs and occupational centres were set up if they did not exist already, usually under the auspices of the National Council for Social Service or some other voluntary body like the Society of Friends. The TUC early on decided not to be associated with this work, accusing the government of 'attempting to shelve their responsibility for the welfare of unemployed workers by placing it upon the shoulders of a voluntary organization with a paltry grant'. However, the TUC did not oppose activity of this sort by local trade unions and trades councils, who participated in many areas with varying results. The money allocated rose – in 1937–8 alone, the National Council for Social Service got over £300,000 from the Ministry of Labour and the Special Areas fund: 100,000 men and 35,000 women were reported as belonging to clubs in 1938.

As well as organizing recreation and classes, many clubs helped to promote schemes of 'self-help', boot-repairing, carpentry, allotments and the rest. These schemes were usually controlled and managed by people of a very different social class and background from those they were intended to benefit. And this added to the resentment felt by the unemployed themselves at having to go to what were in essence charitable organizations to get the benefits of subsistence work schemes. They would have preferred to get whatever help might be available through their own working class organizations, especially the trade unions. Meanwhile the trade union movement continued to express fears that the schemes would become a means of cheap production by semi-skilled workers, undercutting the work of trade unionists in the industries concerned who were paid a proper rate.

It was common practice for social service organizations, or more prosperous areas in the South East, to adopt a town or village in the Depressed Areas. Thus Surrey 'adopted' Jarrow, and Hertfordshire adopted six distressed Durham villages. University students ran summer camps for the young unemployed, or volunteered to work as leaders in the 'settlements' under the National Council of Social Service, in much the same spirit in which they collected for Oxfam or joined Voluntary Service Overseas in the nineteen sixties. Such activities were well meant; they were not always received, however, with unalloyed gratitude, and their impact on the problem itself was of course largely irrelevant.

Opposition to transference

The main official remedy for the Distressed Areas, and the old industrial areas generally, was to transfer people out of them – a remedy which was in general bitterly opposed by those involved. The government's special investigator reported from West Cumberland:

> The Cumberland miner has been a failure in Kent, partly because of his independence, but partly also because of the deep roots which he has struck in his native village . . . Many Cumberland miners left jobs in Kent even though they had to walk home. Many returned before they had worked more than a few days.[20]

And he reported the chairman of a Parish Council as expressing the typical feeling: 'We are up against transference. We do not want to see our community breaking up. We know that there is abundant wealth under our feet, and we want to work that coal.'

From all the Distressed Areas the same feeling was recorded: workers were willing to move house or to travel long distances to work within their own region, but generally unwilliing to accept that they must move outside it to get work, and liable to return home later if they did move.

The Commissioner for the Special Areas in 1935 had written to five thousand eight hundred firms asking them whether they would consider establishing factories in the areas, but with negligible success (only seven were prepared to consider it at that time). He had no power to do more, and accordingly tried his best to persuade the people that it was idle and sinful not to migrate. But he found it a hard job, as his reports show:

A man puts his roots down in the place where he works and lives. It is a hard thing to tear up those roots. It is one of the many fine characteristics of mining communities that their personal associations, their communal life is strong ... It appears at first sight harsh to tell such communities that removal must be the policy which governs their future life. Yet it must be recognized ... Large numbers of persons in these communities are living upon money received but not earned.[21]

A vivid impression of the conflicts engendered by this policy is given in the Commissioner's account of his discussions with local leaders:

I feel that too many of the unemployed miners, knowing that the coal lies beneath their feet and seeing the winding gear ready to turn, cannot realize that nothing can be done to put them back to work to bring the coal to the surface. Habit of mind influences them ... If they live in despair it is despair tinged with expectation ... In one district I visited, particularly hard hit by closed mines and works, I met the local representatives. They were convinced something could be done to restore prosperity. Could not the government establish factories or the commissioner take the situation in hand and reopen closed pits and works? I told them frankly that the first thing to be determined was whether their district was on or off the industrial map, and, if they were off, there was probably no power that could in their lifetime, restore its industrial activities.[22]

For the older workers who were so reluctant to move, it was not usually a question (as it has been in the fifties and sixties) of moving to the certainty of a job in London or Birmingham, but rather of moving from a permanent dole queue at home to the back of the employment queue in a strange place. A miner with no trade outside the pits would have to leave a relatively cheap colliery house and neighbours he knew, on the outside chance of unskilled work among strangers.

A few workers from heavy industry were able to find work at their old trades in new regions. Stewarts and Lloyds, while closing down several works in Scotland, built a large new integrated plant on the Northamptonshire ore field, where one-third of the four thousand employed in 1936 were transferred Scots. In the new, expanding Kent coalfield, one pit was manned mainly by immigrants from Scotland, another from Wales. Scots and Welsh miners took the tradition of militant trade unionism with them; it was a Scottish immigrant, Mick Kane, who played a leading part in the Harworth strike which ended company unionism in the Notts coalfield. But for the majority, the move at best meant unskilled or semi-skilled work on building sites, in motors and light industry, or in distribution and catering.

Some people were retrained at government training centres. These centres (not to be confused with the instruction centres mentioned in the last chapter), some of which were residential, gave courses in various trades – building, furnishing, vehicle building, engineering. Admission to the centres was open to unemployed men who lived in areas of heavy unemployment, though not confined to them. The centres were geared to the needs of industry and the entrants were carefully selected. By the late thirties some fourteen thousand men a year were passing through them, the majority obtaining employment at the end.

But in practice transference proved an unsatisfactory solution for the men over thirty-five, especially those with families. Out of ninety thousand men transferred under Ministry of Labour schemes of assisted transference in 1930–7, over forty-nine thousand were known to have returned home.[23]

A large proportion of those transferred were young boys and girls, many of whom were given training for domestic service in official or semi-official centres. For example, the Rover scouts set up camps to train young men from the Depressed Areas as footmen, butlers and chauffeurs; this scheme was heavily subsidized by the Ministry of Labour. In Durham, the Hon. Mrs Headlam established a highly successful agency to move boys and girls to 'mainly domestic' employment in London and the South of England. This agency, supported by voluntary contributions and fees from employers wanting servants, had already moved some seven thousand boys and girls by 1934, and received a £1,000 grant from the Commissioner for the Special Areas in 1935, by which date nine thousand eight hundred workers trained for domestic service at the Ministry of Labour centre had also been successfully transferred. 'Durham girls have now acquired such an excellent reputation as domestic servants that the demand exceeds the supply', reported Captain Euan Wallace, 'and in some villages it has been found that almost every girl over the age of fifteen has left the village and found employment elsewhere.'[24]

In other areas, such as Scotland and Wales, families often had a 'conscientious dislike' of the girls going into domestic service, or the boys into the Forces, for which they were sternly reproved by the authorities: 'The acceptance of money from public funds should create in the mind of the recipient a sense of obligation to the state in return for the protection it gives.'[25]

Hotel work and catering were other branches for which youngsters were trained. Others again went to jobs in factories – either direct or with some rudimentary preliminary training. In general, parents in the Depressed Areas were reluctant to let their sons and daughters leave home, not without reason. Few of the young people transferred earned enough to be fully independent in their new surroundings, away from the help and company of family and friends. And while there was plenty of low-paid work for juveniles in the South and the Midlands, they were in danger of being sacked when they were old enough to demand an adult wage. Juvenile transference through the Ministry reached a peak figure of 16,000 in 1936. By 1938, when industry in general was falling into recession once again, and the rearmament programme had at last brought some additional work to the Distressed Areas the figure fell to under 10,000 and many of those who had transferred were returning to their homes in the hope of getting work.

The Damage Recognized

Towards the end of the thirties there was a growing realization at Westminster that the officially encouraged movement in search of work was having dangerous consequences, both in the further impoverishment of the Special Areas and in the growing congestion of London and the South East. Sir Malcolm Stewart still maintained that compulsory location of industry would be 'unnecessary and dangerous' because 'economic considerations must in the main determine the location of industry'.[26] But while the government was not justified in saying where industry *should* go, was there not good ground for directing where it should *not* go? He recommended an embargo on further factory construction in Greater London, and inducements to industrialists (in the form of income tax relief, relief from local rates, and low-interest loans) to set up in the Special Areas. Arising from this, the government, while it stood firmly opposed to compulsory location, in July 1937 appointed the Royal Commission on the Distribution of the Industrial Population to go into the whole matter. Its report, completed in August 1939, provided striking evidence of the need to halt the drift to the South East and to provide new types of employment in the old industrial areas. But by that time much irreversible damage had been done: and compulsory location was still blocked by the opposition of the organized employers.

In retrospect, it seems to have been fortunate for the British people that transference was not still more successful. In 1936-7 strategic considerations led the government to do what they had never been willing to do on social grounds, and place new armament factories in the Distressed Areas so as to disperse the targets for enemy bombers. Already the coalowners (like the cotton mill-owners) were beginning to complain of a shortage of boy recruits, caused not only by the transfer of young workers to other districts, but by the fall of the birthrate in mining villages in the years after 1926. In Scotland and South Wales mine-managers were obliged to take on older miners who until then had been regarded as unemployable. By the time war production was in full swing in 1941, there was an acute and continuing shortage of manpower in the pits, so that in the latter years of the war boys had to be conscripted for the mines as they were for the army; and this shortage remained serious for years after the war.

Indeed the scars left by the thirties were so deep that after more than twenty years of relatively high employment from 1941 onwards, they were still plainly visible. In the sixties the former Distressed Areas still suffered a lower standard of buildings and social services, had less than their normal share of young and strong people and modern factories, and were the first hit when recession led mining and other industries to cut back production.

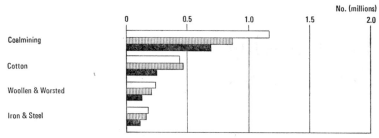

No. (millions)

Coalmining

Cotton

Woollen & Worsted

Iron & Steel

Fig. 4 Number of insured persons employed – above: industries showing marked decreases; below: industries showing marked increases.

June 1923

June 1929

June 1938

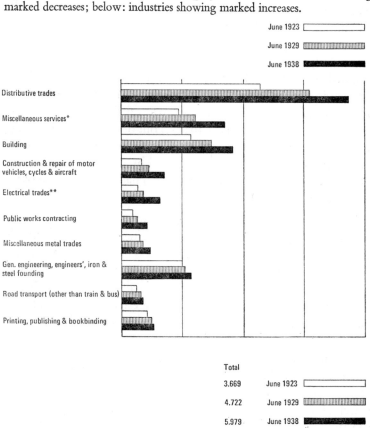

Distributive trades

Miscellaneous services*

Building

Construction & repair of motor vehicles, cycles & aircraft

Electrical trades**

Public works contracting

Miscellaneous metal trades

Gen. engineering, engineers', iron & steel founding

Road transport (other than train & bus)

Printing, publishing & bookbinding

Total		
3.669	June 1923	
4.722	June 1929	
5.979	June 1938	

* Entertainments, sport, etc. hotels, laudries, dyeing & dry cleaning, professional services.

** Electrical engineering, electrical mining & contracting, cables, apparatus, lamps, etc.

5
The Growing Communities

While the older industries declined, newer industries were rapidly expanding, although for some of these the 1931–3 economic depression temporarily slowed down growth. The main areas of expanding industry were London, some smaller towns in the South-East, such as Reading, Slough and Luton, and the West Midlands, particularly around Birmingham and Coventry. It was towards such areas that population was shifting from the North and Wales. In the five years 1932–7, out of a *net* increase of 644 factories in Great Britain, 532 were in Greater London. Almost two-thirds of the employment afforded by new factories in Great Britain was in Greater London, though it had only one-fifth of the population.

These centres of expanding industry were themselves in a state of flux, with population and jobs moving outwards from old congested central areas. Thus London was being ringed with new suburban factories. To the West the existing industrial belt was growing fast at Park Royal, Hayes, Southall and along the North Circular Road, Great West Road and Western Avenue. Another large new industrial area was developing to the North of London and another at Dagenham. Much new industry – for instance aircraft, cars, and electrical engineering – was being established in outer London. At the same time old-established firms which wanted to use new mass production processes moved outwards in search of space for development. Thus many firms emigrated from the West End to West Middlesex or from the East End to the Lea Valley.

It was not only factories which were migrating to the outskirts. Great suburban housing developments – both private and municipal housing – were biting into the surrounding countryside. In particular the London County Council, faced with appalling congestion in the centre and an insatiable housing demand, had embarked on the construction of great out-county estates. There was, however, no planned connection between housing and jobs. The new municipal estates were commonly referred to as 'dormitory estates' precisely because you could sleep in them but do little else. It was only as an afterthought that Fords came to settle at Dagenham in 1930. The LCC's great Becontree and Dagenham estate had been started long before in the twenties when there was practically no work available locally at all, and people had continued to work in the East End factories or docks as before.

Much of the suburban housing spread was, however, occupied by office workers who formed a high proportion of those who commuted from the outer suburbs to the city and West End. Travellers to the centre already numbered 1,700,000 a day by 1937. Meanwhile many of the big new factories on the outskirts drew their industrial labour from people still living in the old crowded working-class streets at the centre. The extension and electrification of London's suburban railways, together with more bus services, made it possible for people to live farther from their work than they had ever done in earlier decades, but it also meant millions travelling daily not only in and out, but even across great parts of a huge conurbation. It added anything from an hour to two hours to the working day – exhausting hours strap-hanging in packed bus or underground. By 1937, when overtime was common, many workers were spending twelve hours a day away from home. Since cheap workmen's fares were only available up to eight o'clock in the morning, typists and office boys commonly arrived at their London terminus half to three-quarters of an hour before their offices opened and did not leave till after six. The *average* expenditure per family on fares in London was officially estimated at £15 per annum or about 8 per cent of the average income of working-class families.

In the Birmingham 'outer ring' comparable developments were going on at Longbridge, Solihull and other suburban districts.

The council estates were being built almost entirely on the outskirts, and 70 per cent of council tenants travelled over two miles to their work.[1] Already in Birmingham by 1936 the average spent on fares per family was estimated at £8 17s per annum.

Here again there was little attempt to coordinate houses with industrial development – indeed any such attempt was unusual. Among the few exceptions were Wythenshaw (Manchester) and Speke (Liverpool) where enlightened councils set out to establish factory areas (assisting employers by loans, or renting out factory space) as an adjunct to their housing estates.

The worker who migrated to London or Birmingham from one of the older industrial areas found a social pattern quite different from the one he had left. In the mining village or mill-town or shipbuilding port the workers had lived close to their workplace, probably going home to dinner. In many mining villages and some other 'company towns' even the houses were built and owned by the employers. Workers shared leisure time pursuits with the people they met at work. A whole street had a common interest in a wage claim or a strike, and youngsters still at school knew that their lives were likely to be spent in the same industry as their parents. Much of the work was skilled, and the workers had a strong interest in organizing to maintain wage rates since they expected to remain in the same trade until they retired. It was a drab life with little freedom of choice, but one in which solidarity and organization flourished.

But in the expanding industrial areas this strong sense of a close-knit community was lacking. Workers living in the same street were unlikely to have much of their working life in common – they travelled to work all over Greater London or Greater Birmingham or Greater Manchester to innumerable different districts and workplaces and industries. They were no longer tied to one workplace and, apart from those in the old skilled occupations, many were not even tied to any one occupation or skill, for the new industries offered a wide range of semi-skilled or unskilled jobs, usually with little training required or given. Instead of settling down to work half a life-time for the same employer, workers expected to change jobs fairly often, and tended to move from one light industry to another as employment offered. They gained in having more choice of employment, and, so far as the new factories were concerned, more space and better working conditions in the workshop itself. And this variety of choice meant that they were less liable to long-term unemployment.

The new pattern, however, undermined the old sense of solidarity and community. It also presented great difficulties to the trade union movement, traditionally based on separate crafts or skills, and organized in branches meeting in the evening. To attend a trade union branch where he worked a man would have to miss his transport home and his evening meal. And if he attended one where he lived (as most trade unionists did) he might not find one other worker employed by the same firm, and discussions would seem remote from his own problems. The trade union structure, indeed, seemed poorly adapted to the new industrial conditions, and until the later years of the decade most of the new industries remained 'black' except for the small handful of highly skilled men on toolroom or maintenance work.

The sense of belonging to a community was particularly lacking in the new housing estates on the outer rings. For at least in the old drab central areas people had grown up together, been to the same school, met one another in their leisure hours in the old way, even if they worked for employers far afield. But in the outer suburbs they had as yet no roots and many of the things to which they were accustomed were still lacking. Apart from the fact that expenses were higher than before – in particular the rent and cost of transport which often meant less money for food for the family – communal services and buildings, churches, schools, libraries, clinics and public meeting places were slow in coming: on some of the newest estates even the shops were a long way away, let alone the bus services. The community centres, officially or unofficially provided on some estates in an attempt to fill the place taken in older industrial communities by workmen's clubs and 'locals', usually suffered from being also a long way from the houses. 'Near a bus garage, and that's about all it is near', was how a Dagenham resident described the civic centre on the edge of the estate.[2]

The giant cinemas were going up in the suburbs, together with

D

giant pubs. Mitchell and Butler, the brewers, ringed Birmingham with their vast tied houses, each in a distinctive and anachronistic style of architecture, mammoth thatched cottage, mammoth Tudor, mammoth Dutch Colonial. But a formal expedition once a week to such attractions was no real substitute for the corner shop or the corner pub where you could pop in for a quick one or attend a meeting of the local darts club. There were few sociologists in the thirties studying the social and psychological problems of these new communities. But it did not take statistical sampling or years of family interviewing to make clear that loneliness and isolation were bound to be common, especially among the women.

In the mid-nineteenth century capitalists had dignified the industrial towns in which they made their fortunes with the self-advertising glories of civic halls, museums, neo-Gothic churches, libraries and chapels. Thus in the nineteen thirties Birmingham's city centre still stood as a monument to Joseph Chamberlain – the Town Hall, the art gallery, the three big metropolitan-looking shopping-streets and even much smaller Lancashire and Yorkshire towns had something of the kind. But the new industrial areas and the urban development of the thirties enjoyed no such embellishments. The new generation of employers preferred to spend their money well away from it all – either in London or in exclusive but countrified suburbs like Four Oaks or Barnt Green near Birmingham, where top executives built large villas standing in their own grounds, and their daughters rode ponies and bred spaniels – a smooth pastiche of the life style of the county families of earlier epochs without its agricultural roots. In the same way the managers and employers of Slough lived in county style at Amersham, Maidenhead or Denham.

The thirties was the last decade when outer urban sprawl went virtually unchecked. The London County Council did make some attempt from 1935 onwards to preserve a green belt round outer London. But in general the very suggestion that the location of industry should be controlled was contrary to the dominant philosophy of the period, which held that interference with the freedom of the individual industrialist would handicap initiative and threaten prosperity. And at a time of unemployment and insecurity few councillors on the smaller local authorities were prepared to put obstacles in the way of any potential employers who might bring employment to an area and trade to the local shopkeepers. So as a Royal Commission observed at the time, the movement of industry:

has proceeded with little or no regard to the fact that it necessarily involves heavy expenditure by the community for the provision of such necessary facilities as new roads, housing accommodation, water supply, sewers, gas and electric mains, schools, churches, increased transport . . . This expenditure, moreover, has to be undertaken at a time when facilities of a similar character are already available in the older industrial areas, where they must be maintained in spite of the fact that much of the labour in the new areas is drawn from the older ones, whose authorities, because of the loss of working population, become progressively less able to support the services for their remaining population.[3]

The owners of the new factories called the tune. They could go where they liked, and the industrial derating act in 1929, which relieved industry of three-quarters of its liability for local rates, meant that to a large extent they could do so on easy terms and partly at others' expense. For example, the cost to Dagenham's ratepayers of Ford's sewage disposal was greater than Ford's own contribution to Dagenham's local rates. In many of the new industrial areas, of which Slough was a typical example, the expense of the new factories forced up local rates quite disproportionately.

On a broader view, the unplanned movements in the conurbations were to throw up terrible problems for later generations and start trends which were going to be very hard to reverse. Moreover, most of the development was unbeautiful to say the least. As J. B. Priestley wrote of a bus ride from Coventry to Birmingham in 1933: 'Did all this look like the entrance into the second city in England? It did. It looked a dirty muddle.'

6
Inside the Workshops

The new technology altered not only the map of industry but the working conditions inside the factory itself. For technical reasons plants opening up in the new industries were often very large, notably in motors, gramophones, radios, chemicals and electrical equipment, where for the first time single factories were employing ten to twenty thousand workers or even more. Work previously done in small country factories could now be done more cheaply in large ones, and distributed by road transport over a wide area. Generally these new works were healthier places than the old. Most were single-storied and electrified with good lighting, heating and sanitation; and some had cloakrooms, rest-rooms and trained medical staff.

Such new factories, however, still employed a minority of industrial workers. An authoritative survey of factory buildings made during the war in Birmingham and the Black Country, for example, showed that factory buildings so bad as to justify immediate replacement ('slum factories') covered about a quarter of the factory space in central Birmingham, and in central Wolverhampton 30 to 40 per cent. These were found most often in the central areas, and were usually converted houses, narrow small-windowed workshops with low ceilings and timber floors, or newer but ramshackle buildings, badly maintained. It was estimated that as many as 20 per cent of the workers in Birmingham and the Black Country were still employed in factories of this type, despite the large amount of modern factory building there.[1]

In the older factories working conditions in the early thirties were still much as they had been in Victorian times. Until electric motors with individual drive for each machine were installed –

and in many industries this was only coming in gradually during the decade – the power was conveyed from the engine to the machines by a maze of transmission belts, a very frequent cause of accidents since workers' hair or clothing could easily get caught in them. Few factories had canteens – a Leeds millowner who installed one in 1930 was told by his fellow-employers that it would never be a success. Even the now-familiar trolley bringing tea and cocoa to workers at their machines was still being hailed as an innovation in 1931.

By the end of the decade canteens were common in large firms, but many of the older and smaller works had not even a mess-room, and food was eaten among the machines. The Chief Inspector of Factories in 1937 drew a typical contrast between two neighbouring works, 'in one of which the workers may be seen enjoying a nourishing and appetizing meal at a reasonable price in a bright airy canteen, while in the other the worker toasts his bread and fries his sausage at the furnace on his stoker's shovel, and eats it squatting on the ground'. Factory inspectors in one city in 1936 found 'conditions of extreme discomfort for workers who came from a distance and could not afford to patronize restaurants. Out of ten factories only one had facilities for heating food, and none had a messroom or even a proper table for meals.' In another factory 'workers were found sitting for a meal on the floor of a dusty woodworking shop'. During the 1939–45 war, when some factory canteens were made compulsory, a very great number of firms had hastily to improvise their facilities.

Accidents at Work

From 1930 to 1936 the number of industrial accidents was steadily rising, especially among young workers, although the new factories were more spacious and better-lit than the old, and might therefore have been expected to be safer. This appalling toll of death and injury (it reached one hundred and seventy-five thousand accidents in all in 1937, with twice as many fatalities as in 1967) was attributed by the factory inspectors to speed-up, longer hours, and the lower standard of training given to young people as the apprenticeship system declined. Indeed, there was virtually no improvement in the accident rate compared with 1900. Improved safety precautions were more than offset by the greater speed of machinery. Accident rates dropped in the slump years, when employers could pick and choose among young, strong and alert workers, but rose again in the boom.

'I am afraid that a rising toll of death and injury must still be regarded as a penalty to be paid for increased prosperity', said the Chief Factory Inspector in his report for 1936. The increase was due, he thought, to the employment of more new workers, including many coming into industry after long unemployment which had undermined their health and alertness; to the employment of new machinery with unknown risks; and to longer hours and the greater speed of machinery. In 1937 he had to report a further 9 per cent increase, caused partly by the employment for the first time of unskilled or half-trained people because of the shortage of skilled and semi-skilled labour. Among the 'indirect' causes of the rising accident rate among young workers, he suggested, was the decline of the skilled trades to which many boys were formerly apprenticed, and the lack of choice of job for them in many areas; this led to boredom and inattention, and hence to tragedy.*

The 1937 Factories Act did something to strengthen and codify the law in relation to safety, and gave the inspectorate power to require that where possible safety devices (such as guards) should actually be incorporated in the machines. Some dangerous working conditions, hitherto largely untouched by the law, were covered by requirements that, for instance, floors and staircases must be soundly constructed, lift wells and hoists encased, and fire precautions tightened up. Minimum standards for ventilation, temperature and lighting were laid down, seats required for women workers, and firms on dirty or dangerous processes might be required to provide washing facilities and cloakrooms. Moreover, no young person was to work at a dangerous machine

* Statistical comparisons with the sixties are almost impossible to make, because of changes in compilation and definition. However, fatal accidents in factories were more than halved between 1937 and 1967, in spite of a much larger labour force, which is some indication that safety standards in the thirties were much lower than today.

unless he 'has received a sufficient training . . . or is under adequate supervision by an experienced person'. Women and young people were forbidden to clean prime movers or machinery in motion, or to carry excessive loads.

However, for 1938, the first year of operation of the new Act, progress in implementing it was officially reported as 'rather slower than seems necessary', and in 1939 war led to a temporary suspension of many of the new requirements.*

Hours

Working hours had in practice been much reduced in the great majority of factories during the twentieth century, and trade union agreements usually provided for a normal 48-hour week. It was still legal, however, even for women and young people to work up to 60 hours in non-textile factories ($55\frac{1}{2}$ in textiles), and as much as 600 hours' overtime in a year. It is impossible to say how many employers actually worked their employees such hours, but in a minority of ill-organized firms it was certainly done. The Chief Inspector of Factories in 1935 reported that:

> The improvement in trade has resulted in a tendency to increase the hours of women and young persons in a wide variety of industries. Many cases of such hours ($55-57\frac{1}{2}$) are reported from all over the country, although the adverse effect of such long hours is sometimes realized when employers admit that their workers, like their machines, may reach a fatigue point. (p. 64.)

In times of depression when retailers and wholesalers in clothing and similar trades were nervous of holding large stocks, it was common for them to place small orders for delivery in a hurry.

* The new legal requirements, though the employers complained of their cost, had some unexpected compensations: 'It is recorded that an objection to cleaning floors caked with grease was raised, the reason given being that safety under the old conditions was better than when new grease was dropping on a clean floor. But good comes out of evil – one firm removed several tons of grease from the floor and sold it at a good price as a fertilizer.' (J. C. Bridge, Chief Medical Inspector of Factories, 1938.)

This meant periods of feverish overtime alternating with short-time and unemployment. Certain seasonal industries regularly worked very long hours for part of the year. From the Motor Show in the autumn until Easter, hours for women in the motor and cycle accessories and forging trades were reported to average 56 weekly. The Whitechapel clothing trade was still not organized on the basis of a 48-hour week at all – there were periods of slack trade and of intermittent working, but 'in the rush seasons before Christmas and the various holidays, the weekly limit is often that set by human endurance and the visits of inspectors'. Hours in the Midlands motor accessories trade were particularly long – 12 hours a day was not unknown:

A distressing fact about these long hours in the Midlands is that they are generally worked by the least physically fit portion of the population. The best workers tend to go to the best employers, and the weakest to drift to the factories with the longest hours and the least good conditions. Some of the night shifts consist entirely of youths from eighteen to twenty years of age. Sometimes in the same works men in an organized trade are found to be working 48 hours weekly, while women and girls over sixteen on another class of work are working up to the legal limits. In one case they were found to have been employed for more than three months on presses making domestic hardware for 60 hours weekly.[2]

These long hours – which suggest the nineteenth century rather than the twentieth – were made even longer because new factories were commonly larger and farther from the workers' homes. A survey in the late thirties showed that at the Austin Motor works less than half the workers lived within five miles of the factory. At Carreras in London, a third of the workers left home more than an hour before starting work, and 83 per cent had to allow half an hour or more for travelling. At Standard Telephones in Southgate, 60 per cent of the workers had journeys taking half to one hour, and 10 per cent over an hour.[3]

The Factories Act of 1937 reduced maximum legal hours for women and youths under eighteen to 9 a day and 48 a week, with not more than 6 hours' overtime a week and a limit of 100 hours a year (except in trades subject to sudden pressure, where women might be allowed to do up to 150 hours). These exceptions, however, still allowed employers in the seasonal trades to work women a 60-hour week for half the year – as much as they had been doing before. For young workers under sixteen the rules were more stringent: they must not work more than 44 hours a week unless special permission was given for 48, and could not be employed on overtime or shift work. Hours for young shop assistants were limited by the 1934 Shops Act, which came into force at the end of 1936, to 48 a week between 6 a.m. and 10 p.m. Here again, exceptions might be made for seasonal work, in catering and so on.

The abundance of exceptions allowed under both Acts, as the TUC protested, not only allowed hours which were admittedly too long for the needs of health and education: it also made enforcement more difficult. There was no statutory provision for annual holidays, and normal working hours were still 47 or 48, even though in France the 40-hour week and paid holidays had been achieved by the organized workers in 1936.

Paid holidays remained the exception until the end of the decade, which meant that only a minority of families could afford to go away on holiday. At the time of the Holidays with Pay Act, 1938, only some three million wage-earners were entitled by collective arrangements to such a holiday. A year later, when Agricultural Wages Boards and Trade Boards had been given power by the Act to fix holidays with pay, and there was increased pressure for similar concessions from private employers,* some eleven million workers had already become entitled to paid holidays, usually of one week. The first commercial holiday camp was opened by Butlin's at Skegness in 1937, and in the next two years enough commercial camps were opened to accommodate half a million people; but it was still a minority who took a holiday away from home. On the whole, Britain still lagged

* The Amulree Committee on Holidays with Pay considered that all workers should have one week's holiday, but the Act did not make it compulsory by law. If voluntary agreements proved inadequate the Government proposed to introduce compulsion after three years.

behind other countries, notably France, in the matter of holidays both for families and for school children.

Speed-Up and Efficiency systems

Speed-up and intensification of work was one of the most acute grievances of industrial workers in these years, and it is not hard to see why. Capital investment during the slump was low; few firms in established industries were willing to take risks with completely new processes and to scrap outdated plant was often considered prohibitively expensive. Reduction of output and price maintenance was the method favoured. The earlier part of the decade accordingly saw little technical or scientific innovation except in the new industries. Employers tended rather to concentrate on getting the maximum out of the labour power they paid for, the conveyor belt being a popular way of doing this. The knowledge that there were plenty of unemployed workers outside the gate often made it possible to increase the individual work-load, at any rate in an unorganized factory, without causing resistance.

The factory inspectors, who were not sentimentalists, repeatedly drew attention to this speeding-up, and expressed concern that the health of the workers might suffer. Noting the rapid introduction of conveyors into the Leeds clothing industry, the Chief Inspector in 1935 warned that 'to avoid fatigue and overstrain the speed of the conveyor requires careful adjustment, and enquiry into this aspect is being made.' The Chief Medical Inspector expressed more general anxiety: 'The hurry and bustle of manufacture at the present differ widely from the quieter conditions of the past, and long hours of employment under such unnatural conditions must in the main be disadvantageous to the adolescent.'[4] And again:

Speed is the essence of present-day industry, as exemplified in the conveyor system, such as exists in the clothing trade, wherein a single operation is performed, minute in minute out, throughout the working day. It is too early yet to judge of the results of this system on the health of the workers concerned, but some apprehension cannot but be felt as to its ultimate effects.[5]

Mass production meant further subdivision and specialization of semi-skilled and unskilled work, the gearing of the worker's speed to that of the machine, and with it an even more deadly monotony. 'To work for a living in employment giving interest is a healthy occupation', commented the Chief Inspector in 1934, 'but the monotony and tedium of so many forms of work in modern industry makes one wonder how it is carried out so zealously.'

Intensification of work took different forms in different industries. In cotton, weavers were required to work six looms instead of four. In mining, piecework rates were cut, conveyors brought in, and the yardage of coalface each man had to clear was lengthened. In light engineering, motor factories especially, the speed of the conveyor belt determined the time the worker had to complete his operation; by speeding up the belt the operative could be compelled to work faster. This method is immortalized in two brilliant films of the period, Chaplin's *Modern Times* and René Clair's *À Nous la Liberté*, both of which dramatized the plight of the 'little man' trying to keep up with the merciless conveyor. In real life, workers complained that often no relief worker was provided, and if one felt ill or wanted to go to the toilet one could not do so unless the whole line were stopped. It was even reported that workers were known to relieve themselves at the side of their machines.

Ordinary day-work jobs were being converted to individual systems of payment-by-results, and time-and-motion study experts and consultants specializing in incentive systems of wage payment were increasingly employed. The best-known firm, and in trade union circles the most notorious, was Bedaux, an American concern introduced into Britain in 1926, whose chairman, Charles E. Bedaux, was a friend of the Prince of Wales.

The penetration of such systems into British firms was met at first with a good deal of hostility and unrest among the workers. They felt that in the name of science they were having unlimited speed-up and rate-cutting imposed upon them without negotiations, and that they could neither calculate nor control their own earnings. A number of strikes resulted.* The TUC instituted a special enquiry, and its report stressed the urgent need for trade union control of such systems.

The resistance was most acute in the slump. Later, in the boom years, when bonuses were perhaps more generous and the threat of unemployment less, there seems to have been less opposition to the introduction of such systems provided there was trade union consultation.†

In organized factories, of course, the 'scientific' timing of jobs became more or less openly a form of bargaining or trial of strength between workers and employers. The management had naturally an interest in keeping the timing of jobs as tight as possible, allowing a minimum of time for rest and relaxation, and assessing as 'normal' the effort of the fastest worker in the shop. Equally naturally the workers, especially in organized shops, used their ingenuity to combat this particular advance of 'science' in the workshop.

* Among the strikes were those at Wolsey Hosiery, Caledonian Linoleum Works, Henry Hope (Metal Windows), Venesta Plywood, Joseph Lucas, Elliots Engineering. It is significant that some of the largest and most determined, as at Lucas (motor accessories) in Birmingham, were by unorganized women workers. At some firms, such as Rover Motors and Hornes (Clothing), the system was tried and abandoned because of opposition by the workers concerned. At a wire manufacturing firm workers brought an unsuccessful legal action against the Bedaux firm on the grounds that the stop-watch men were affecting their nerves and hindering their piecework earnings (1935).

† A publicity brochure of Bedaux issued in 1936 listed 240 firms operating the system, including ICI, Joseph Lyons, Carreras (cigarettes), Crosse and Blackwell (canning), Hoffman Ball Bearing, Mullard Radio and Kodaks. They gave details of results said to be typical – thus in a large cycle and motor-cycle firm productivity rose 122 per cent and operator earnings 18 per cent and labour costs fell 38 per cent. At a teleprinter and radio firm productivity rose 171 per cent, earnings 15 per cent and labour costs fell 57 per cent.

7
Industrial Workers: Backs to the Wall

The trade union movement, though weakened by the slump and by conflicts of policy and aim, continued to be by far the largest organization involving working people, with $3\frac{1}{2}$ to $4\frac{1}{2}$ million members. If this was a minority of those employed it was at least a sizeable one.

British workers had traditionally looked more to their old-established trade union movement than to political parties for improvements in their standards. It remained their principal means of exerting influence and expressing their common interests. But trade union strength and customs varied enormously from one industry and region to another. It was in the old industrial areas, which were hardest-hit by the depression, that the movement was strongest and most cohesive. In the new mass production industries and the expanding industrial areas of London and the Midlands it was as yet relatively weak and scattered. This problem was never fully resolved in the years before the war.

Trade union membership had reached a peak in the brief boom after the First World War, when it touched $6\frac{1}{2}$ million. Thereafter it fell, with growing unemployment and the withdrawal of women from industry, to 4·3 million on the eve of the General Strike. The defeat of 1926 was followed by growing unemployment in mining and other basic industries, and by victimization and discrimination against active trade unionists. Many workers regarded as ringleaders were never taken back after the strike. The Trades Disputes Act, passed by the Conservative Government in 1927, struck a further blow, splitting off the unions in government service from the Trades Union Congress, restricting picketing and outlawing sympathetic strikes.

By 1930, therefore, membership affiliated to the TUC had already fallen to 3,744,000. As the full impact of the slump hit industry, membership fell not only in mining, shipbuilding and textiles, but in almost every sector of the movement. By 1934 it was down another 450,000 at 3,294,000, half the 1920 figure and the lowest level since the end of the war.

The twenties had been a time of great industrial conflicts – not only in the mining industry, but also in engineering, shipbuilding, textiles and railways. In the thirties, in contrast, there were comparatively few large-scale strikes. Only in cotton in 1932 was there an industry-wide official strike. The London bus strike of 1937 (which began official and became unofficial later) and the engineering apprentices' strikes in the same year (beginning unofficially and later made official) were the only large-scale disputes which received national union recognition. A growing proportion of trade union action at job level was 'unofficial', unsanctioned and often opposed by the union leaders, and remained localized – though often with wider effects. This was not merely the result of weakness, but a deliberate redirection of aims and policy by the leaders.

Strikes involving 5,000 or more workers: duration in working days (in thousands)

1924	5,430	1931	5,865
1925	5,749	1932	5,055
1926	160,316	1933	127
1927	316	1934	—
1928	740	1935	402
1929	6,650	1936	421
1930	3,697	1937	1,552
		1938	52

The majority of top leaders of the TUC after the 1926 débâcle had made up their minds at all costs to avoid in future any such large-scale and terrifying conflict with the employers. 'The approach to a new industrial order is not by way of a social explosion', Walter Citrine, secretary of the TUC, had written in 1927. They saw the way forward in collaboration with the employers to reorganize industry, an idea elaborated in later discussions (1928) between the General Council and a group of twenty big employers headed by Sir Alfred Mond, founder-chairman of Imperial Chemical Industries. This policy, later known as Mondism, was in the words of the General Council 'for the trade union movement to say boldly that not only is it concerned with the prosperity of industry, but it is going to have a voice in the way industry is carried on. . . . The unions can use their power to promote and guide the scientific reorganization of industry.'[1] The General Council and the employers' group moreover held that the tendency to rationalization and trustification in industry 'should be welcomed and encouraged'. To trade unions with this outlook the employers were ready to concede recognition as 'definitely in the interests of all engaged in industry'. Trade unions as monopolists of labour supply could enter into partnership with the monopolists of capital, the aim being 'a concerted effort to raise industry to its highest efficiency'.

Although the talks produced little immediate practical result, the employers' organizations not being willing to set up the permanent joint machinery suggested, they did much to encourage the TUC leaders to seek advance not so much through hard bargaining backed by the threat of industrial action, but rather through cooperation with the more approachable employers (usually the big combines), and with any government, whatever its political colour, that would recognize their claim to speak on behalf of an essential section of the community.

The main spokesmen for this policy in the TUC throughout the thirties were Walter Citrine, Secretary of the TUC, and the leaders of the general workers' unions, especially Ernest Bevin, leader of the Transport and General Workers. Bevin himself was much impressed by the rationalization and efficiency of American industry. In his own industrial bargaining he frankly preferred to deal with 'one or two big companies which could afford to take long views'.[2] And he made it clear that as one whose job was the large-scale organization of labour, he felt himself in many ways akin to the growing managerial profession. 'We look upon ourselves as the labour side of management', was his phrase.

Thus the majority of the TUC leadership came to look to 'nationalization' of industry (in default of nationalization) as the best available solution for poverty and unemployment. In a few cases where the employers were wealthy and the labour force small, as in flour-milling, and here and there in the gas industry, the unions were able to negotiate compensation and resettlement for men made redundant by monopoly reorganization. But in the major industries, in steel, shipbuilding, wool and cotton, where far more workers were involved, no compensation was payable, and unions approving rationalization were reduced to passive spectators of unemployment and speeding-up among their members.

Certain unions, however, and especially the general workers, did extend their field of negotiations in the late twenties and thirties largely by agreement with a few very large concerns. Thus when Imperial Chemical Industries was formed, and Mond decided to establish a network of works committees at all plants, he agreed to do so on a trade union basis, the National Union of General and Municipal Workers being the principal union concerned. Once assured that the committees would not become an anti-union device, and convinced that the employers would help it to recruit members, the union cooperated. In some chemical plants the union was empowered to collect dues at its own office inside the factory. In the cocoa and chocolate industry, where the leading firms were Quaker family businesses, notices were posted explaining that while it was for the individual employee to decide whether or not to join a union, the firm believed it to be desirable in general that he should do so.

For the left, the lesson of 1926 was entirely different. In their view, the General Strike had not failed: it had been betrayed. The miners had been disowned, left to fight alone, and the millions who solidly answered the strike call had not even been safeguarded against victimization. The leaders had the power to compel the capitalists to retreat but were afraid to use it. What was necessary, therefore, was to get rid of such leaders, and to build trade union organizations that would understand the need, in the next great struggle between capital and labour, to carry it forward without weakening.

Many of the left, moreover, believed that British capitalism was facing an insoluble crisis, and their aim must be not to stabilize it and palliate its evils, but to get rid of it altogether and establish socialism, whether by parliamentary means or by revolutionary overthrow of the existing order. Accordingly they considered agreements merely as a truce in war, where they were not an outright betrayal by the leaders, and they regarded co-operation with the employers in rationalization as treachery. They believed that only through direct action would the employed and unemployed workers gain the organization and confidence necessary for them to end the capitalist system.

Hostility to the 'industrial peace' line was strong in some districts of the Miners' Federation (whose secretary, A. J. Cook, had unsuccessfully opposed the Mond talks on the General Council and in Congress); but the miners' union was weakened, impoverished and divided after the nine months' lockout. There was also opposition from the Amalgamated Engineering Union, the railwaymen, the Amalgamated Union of Building Trade Workers and some of the craft unions, all suspicious of any joint working with the employers and acutely afraid of the effects of 'rationalization' on their members. But in the TUC the Mondist line carried the day.

The left, meanwhile, was increasingly divided. The Communists and the Minority Movement, the most forthright and extreme opponents of the Mondist policy, had played a leading part in the strike in many areas and were hard hit by the victimization and unemployment that followed it. A determined effort was made by the General Council at this time to root them out of the unions altogether;* and the attitude of the left itself gave the General Council some assistance.

* Harry Pollitt, then a TUC delegate of the Boilermakers and in the running for secretary, was barred by a union decision banning Communists and Minority Movement members from office. He later became secretary of the Communist Party. The NUGMW introduced a similar rule, having disbanded branches which were likely to oppose it at the conference.

Up to the General Strike the Communists and the Minority Movement had worked publicly and not unsuccessfully within the unions to influence them, and through them the Labour Party, for a militant policy. After 1926, in the face of mounting bans on left-wing delegates and activities and with the bulk of their leading members unemployed, they concluded that it was hopeless to win over the 'reformist unions' as such, and increasingly counterposed the aim of independent leadership, exercised through factory committees of unionists and non-unionists (though they continued to contest elections within the unions). This brought them into conflict not only with the right-wing leaders who stood for Mondism, but with former left-wing allies (for example A. J. Cook), whom they now criticized as 'so-called lefts' who misled the workers by continuing to support the Labour Party. The 'class against class' line of 1929, strongly influenced by the leftward turn of the Communist International at this time, meant opposing not only MacDonaldism but the Labour Party right, left and centre.[3] Even unions which had taken an anti-Mondist position, notably the AEU, were held to be deceiving the workers thereby, since their real aim was to cooperate with capitalism. The readiness of the workers for strike action, especially political strike action, was often seriously overestimated – for example in 1927, when the Minority Movement called for a general strike against the Trade Disputes Act, in a situation where almost any strike action was impracticable.[4]

This line was never carried in Britain, as it was elsewhere in Europe, to the length of creating an alternative system of revolutionary or 'red' unions.* Nevertheless it helped to divide the left

* Only two such cases arose, neither of them in a planned way, and both remained localized (the United Mineworkers of Scotland and the United Clothing Workers in London). In the case of the United Mineworkers it was the left-wing leaders who were duly elected, and the right-wing officials who refused to operate democratic procedure and 'broke away', thereafter receiving Miners' Federation of Great Britain recognition. The United Mineworkers, after an active existence of seven years, was voluntarily dissolved in 1936 in the interests of unity, by agreement with the Miners' Federation of Great Britain. In 1937, some years after the Minority Movement had ceased to exist, a section of militant London busmen formed a breakaway union, the National Passenger Workers' Union, which was opposed by the Communist Party. The natural inclination of the

well into the thirties, and thus strengthened the position of those who wished to see the trade union movement make sacrifices to stabilize British capitalist industry. As another result, some of the most experienced trade union talent in the country went into organizing direct action by the unemployed (a field which the TUC had failed to tackle), and with conspicuous success.*

Honours and Black Circulars

Conflicting attitudes to trade unionism were highlighted in 1935 when Arthur Pugh and Walter Citrine, secretary of the TUC, accepted knighthoods from the National government. Citrine still had many years of active union work ahead of him, and there was no question of the title being one to retire with. 'It was a generous admission', said the *Daily Telegraph*, 'that those also serve who oppose the government of the day.' David Low in the *Evening Standard* of 10 June 1935 published a cartoon, depicting Citrine entering a gilded hall with footmen ushering him into a group of bewildered Tolpuddle Martyrs as 'Sir Walter Citrine, KBE'; underneath there was a caption 'A hundred years' progress in trade unionism'. Citrine, however, felt that the knighthoods were an important way of improving the image of the movement:

What had been the result of 1926? We had been regarded as revolutionaries. There was no doubt in my mind that considerable damage had been done to the Labour movement because of this. People did in

* Wal Hannington, Secretary of the NUWM, was a former AEU shopsteward and during the 1939–45 war became National Organizer of the AEU. Arthur Horner and Will Paynter (later general secretaries of the Mineworkers), Leo McGree (Woodworkers), Abe and Alec Moffat (later Presidents of the Scottish Miners) were likewise prominent in NUWM and hunger marches.

British Communist Party leaders, in fact, seems to have been to continue to work in practice within the existing trade unions, whatever they thought about their leaders – partly perhaps because some of the best-known leaders of the Party, such as Pollitt, Horner and Hannington, had grown up in the trade union movement as well as in the unofficial shop stewards' and Miners Reform Movements.

fact suspect that we were aiming at destroying the Constitution, despite our disclaimers.

We now had the position that the man who had been the chairman of the TUC at that time (Pugh) was a knight. The acting secretary had received similar recognition at the hands of the State. In effect, through us, our movement had been proclaimed, both by King and Government as one whose members were citizens deserving of one of the highest honours that the State could convey. How could this fail to affect the minds of the thousands who know little about trade unionism, and to enhance its status and prestige?[5]

The acceptance of the honours was, of course, sharply attacked by the left (notably by Jennie Lee in the Independent Labour Party's *New Leader*). At the 1935 TUC a motion was moved* objecting to trade union leaders accepting honours 'at the hands of a government which is not established in the interests of the workers'. Congress, however, rejected the resolution after hearing Citrine's personal statement, though with a large minority supporting it.

It was the same congress, logically enough, which endorsed (though by a much narrower margin) the two circulars issued by the General Council requiring affiliated trades councils to ban delegates who were Communists or had any associations with Communists, and requesting unions to modify their rules so as to exclude Communists from any office. If the leaders' primary aim was to show that the movement had no revolutionary aims, but was prepared to work loyally for the prosperity of privately-owned industry, this decision was as logical as the other – and much more far-reaching in its effects. It was, however, carried only by 1,869,000 against 1,427,000 – one of the narrowest victories for the platform in the whole decade – against the expressed opposition of the AEU, clerks', railwaymen's and miners' unions, whose leaders declared themselves quite capable of dealing with any disruptive activities in their unions without depriving members of their democratic rights.

The TUC had, of course, no power to compel its constituent

* The mover was Miss B. A. (later Dame Anne) Godwin of the Women Clerks, later chairman of the TUC and by no means a left-winger.

unions to ban Communists from office, and many of them ignored or rejected the advice. The miners, engineers, builders, railwaymen and many others continued to elect Communist officials; and the Transport and General Workers, though it was reported that a last-minute switch of its vote had enabled the 'Black Circular' to carry the day, did not in the thirties amend its own rules accordingly. In certain big unions, however, notably the steelworkers and the General and Municipal Workers, as well as many smaller ones, the ban was applied; and many trades councils were pressured into operating it by the threat to withdraw TUC recognition and set up an alternative council in their area.

The policy of Communists in the unions was by 1935 far less narrow and self-isolating than it had been in 1930–3.* Trade unions, even under right-wing leadership, were no longer considered merely as reformist bodies, but as organizations commanding the class loyalty of the industrial workers, within which the left must work and prove itself if it ever wished to obtain their support and initiate united action. There was, indeed, a good deal of practical unity on the left from 1935 until 1939. But the gap between right and left within the movement was never closed.

Backs to the Wall: textiles

The full brunt of the depression and the loss of purchasing power fell on the older textile industries. In the years from the General Strike to 1934, two-thirds of all working days lost in strikes were in textiles. It was here, nevertheless, that the trade unions suffered the greatest losses in membership and strength.

The wool textile workers in the West Riding had already suffered a two-months' lockout in 1930, and further wage-cuts after a strike in 1931; they entered the decade with their central organization greatly weakened and a virtual breakdown of collective bargaining in the industry, which was not restored till 1936. In cotton

---

* This change of emphasis seems to have antedated, though it was endorsed and assisted by, the decisions of the seventh World Congress of the Communist International. The dividing line appears to have been the advent of Hitler to power in 1933.

the issue was yet to be fought out in the greatest and most bitter industrial conflict of the thirties. The spirit of resistance shown by trade unionists was the more remarkable, considering that politically the Lancashire textile towns had swung overwhelmingly to support of the National government in 1931.

Actual production in cotton was little over half potential production in 1931. The effect of the crisis was intensified by the success of Japanese competition in export markets, with more up-to-date machinery and lower wages than the British. Such recovery as there was came later than in other industries and faded sooner.

The industry was fantastically backward both in technique and in organization. A modern mill in Lancashire meant one built since 1900, and the machinery was almost as antiquated as the mills. A survey in 1930 showed that 42 per cent of the looms and 30 per cent of the mule and ring spindles in use had been built before 1900. It was still predominantly an industry of many small firms, though big combines had recently been formed with the support of the banks (Lancashire Cotton Corporation and Combined Egyptian Spinners). Most firms were heavily loaded with bank debts contracted in the speculative boom after the First World War. The banks, already deeply committed to unprofitable investment in cotton, were not anxious to involve themselves further, and firms were short of cash to install ring-spinning or automatic looms. In order to get at least some cash to meet their creditors' demands, millowners accepted orders at cut-throat prices, and tried to keep within them by speed-up and competitive wage cutting. The workers, organized in local and sectional unions federated on a county basis, resisted these attacks with extraordinary determination.

The policy of the banks and the big combines was to amalgamate the small firms, to buy up and scrap the weaker mills and concentrate production in those remaining; and some of the union leaders believed this offered the only hope for the industry. Reorganization on these lines, however, proved slow and ineffective.

Meanwhile, although Lancashire was never officially designated as a Distressed Area, over much of the thirties poverty and suffering there was as bad as in any of them. Cotton wages were generally among the lowest in any major industry, though the work was skilled. In weaving, men and women worked side by side on the same piece rates, and women's wages tended to set the standard. Men mule spinners were better paid, but their assistants (the so-called big and little piecers) received only youths' wages. In the nineteen thirties there were few opportunities for promotion to spinner, and grown men with families had to struggle along on big piecer's money or be out of work. Indeed most Lancashire workers depended on a family wage to keep the home going, and it was traditional for married women to continue at work (which was not common in other industries at the time). Unemployment for either husband or wife often brought the family below subsistence level; and unemployment in Lancashire had reached 38 per cent at the end of 1932.

Weavers also suffered severely from various forms of underemployment. A worker on four looms might have one or more idle if orders were short; in that case his wages would be cut though he would still have to be at work the full 48 hours. Many employers tried to cut costs by using inferior raw material; this led to frequent breaks, so that the weaver had more work to do in joining broken ends of thread, and was fined if there were imperfections in the cloth.

Since there was no other work in the smaller cotton towns, workers were desperately keen that their local mills should remain open. Many accepted worsened conditions below union standards in the hope of avoiding a shutdown. Some employers frankly cut wage rates. Others required their workers to 'invest' in shares in the mill as a condition of employment, or even issued envelopes along with the pay-packet for the workers to enclose 'gifts' of 6d per loom to keep the mill going.

Already in 1929 wages had been reduced after a three weeks lockout. In January 1931 the conflict came to a head again over the employers' attempt to get the operators to work six or more looms in place of the traditional four, and thus increase profit margins without any extra investment. An attempt to introduce the system piecemeal in Burnley caused a strike; the employers retaliated by locking out first the Burnley weavers and then the whole of the weavers in Lancashire. For the time being, however, they were forced by the determined resistance of the unions to postpone the attempt at six-loom working, the Weavers' Amalgamation General Council firmly rejecting the advice of its leaders to agree to a 'scientific experiment' with the more-looms system.

In 1932, however, the employers resumed the attempt to introduce six-loom working in some districts, notably Burnley, without agreement with the unions. Usually six looms per weaver were worked in the 'knobstick' mills for little or nothing above the wage formerly paid for four. This meant increased effort and strain for those continuing in employment, and loss of jobs for a third or more of the operatives.

When the Weavers' Amalgamation once again rejected the 'experimental' more looms agreement proposed by their leaders in February 1932, the employers determined to fight. As one member of the Central Committee of the Cotton Spinners and Manufacturers' Federation put it: 'It is now clear we shall only get from the operatives what we can force from them, and we shall have to plan our campaign accordingly.'[6]

Throughout 1932 the struggle went on mill by mill. The 'advance guard' of mills breaking away from trade union agreements, cutting wage rates and introducing six-loom working was followed up by the denunciation by the master-spinners and weavers of all their agreements with the unions, including that for the 48-hour week.

With the existing agreement due to terminate in time, the Northern Counties Textile Trades Federation then took a ballot which showed a majority of four to one for strike action. A second question on the ballot paper, however, allowed the leaders to continue negotiations meanwhile, and no strike was called. The employers demanded cuts amounting to about 14 per cent of earnings: and the county leaders (though not the local unions) were prepared to concede about half this, considering resistance to be hopeless. But meantime notices announcing cuts without agreement were being posted in mills all over Lancashire. In this situation the whole of the Burnley weavers, faced with a 12½ per cent cut, struck work.

The strike was conducted by the workers with extraordinary tenacity and spirit. The Burnley Committee had advised the strikers to keep away from the mills, but their advice was disregarded. There was mass picketing, and thousands of strikers rallied on the streets leading to the few mills which tried to keep working. Although police were brought in to protect them, 'knobsticks' (blacklegs) were chased through the town. In three days the Burnley strike was solid with twenty-five thousand weavers out.

During August, the General Council of the Weavers' Amalgamation (the county union) first decided to continue negotiations and then to call a Lancashire strike.* But by the end of August the vast majority of weavers, led by their local unions, had already struck in support of Burnley. Within a few days one hundred and fifty thousand weavers were out, and the big weaving towns were closed right down. Mass pickets of thousands, marching out from the big centres, were bringing weak spots in outlying townships into the strike. Buses conveying blacklegs were stoned, and mill managers had to be escorted home under strong police guard, followed by booing crowds.

There were many baton charges of police against strikers, police being imported from all over Lancashire and the West Riding. The Trade Disputes Act of 1927 was continually invoked against pickets, who were charged with obstruction, disorderly behaviour and assault; and leaflets urging mass picketing and solidarity were treated as illegal. The state also took a hand against the strikers' families. The Burnley Guardians received a report that there was widespread refusal of relief by relieving officers, and instructed them to give it in all cases of destitution in future. 'I have never known quite so many people in Nelson as there are at the present time absolutely without food', declared Alderman Smith of that town.[7] Public Assistance Committees in some

---

* The county leaders were doubtful: Tom Shaw, a veteran cotton leader, wrote in the *Daily Herald* (24 August 1932): 'Nothing but disaster could come of a protracted stoppage. No amount of trade union action whatever under present conditions can get more than it is humanly possible to give.'

towns refused to give food and coal vouchers to strikers' families, and would issue nothing but tickets for the workhouse. Nevertheless the strike continued solid for a month (and almost two in Burnley).

Meanwhile the Master Spinners' notice to their two hundred thousand workers of 2s 9d in the pound wage cut had been met by the Spinners' union with a twenty-to-one ballot in favour of strike action; whereupon the notices were postponed, and the cut later reduced to 1s 6½d in the pound. Andrew Naesmith, the cotton operatives' representative on the General Council, told that year's TUC (held during the dispute) that the response of the workers had been far greater than the leaders had believed possible:

> We thought that the spirit of resistance among our men and women had been broken, but they have responded in a remarkable manner, which indicates, I think, both to the employers and the citizens of this country, that there is a limit to which the working classes can be driven.

Lancashire delegates gave the TUC a vivid and bitter account of their strike experience. A weavers' delegate from Great Harwood told how his whole district had been stopped within three days, despite the police protection given to blacklegs. 'I went to a little village with only a population of about eight hundred. We took five hundred demonstrators from Great Harwood, and when we got there we found fifty police and a Black Maria.' The issue, to his mind, was not only one for the cotton operatives: it involved the very existence of the trade union movement. The delegate of the Burnley weavers, himself a striker, made a bitterly moving appeal for support so that reinstatement without victimization could be achieved:

> I am one of those men who come from a town that has been fighting for seven weeks . . . I am one of those men who have been knocked and kicked about by the police for the last few weeks . . . I was running six looms for a matter of 35s a week, and I had five bellies to fill out of that wage. Now the employer has come along and says he wants 3s 4d out of that. Is not that enough to get any man's back up? We have got eight thousand people in Burnley fighting on 12s 4d a week, and they

are as firm as a rock . . . Do your best to assist us, and let us achieve the reinstatement of every man jack who answered the call of the trade union.

Congress resolved to organize 'all possible moral and financial support' to the cotton workers, and Ernest Bevin took the lead in launching an appeal for £500,000, but by the next congress only £58,000 had been subscribed. It was a far cry from the General Strike, and the cotton leaders (unlike thousands of their members) were not prepared to prolong the strike in the hope of a better settlement.

After intervention by the government, a settlement of the weavers' dispute was reached at the end of September, which in general went in the employers' favour, though they had to make some concessions. It imposed a wage cut of 1s 8½d in the pound (less than the employers had originally announced, but more than the unions' offer), allowed the six-loom system on some cloths and on certain conditions, and included a reinstatement clause which in practice was largely ignored by the employers.

Following this defeat, workers' conditions continued to worsen. Where under the old piecework list the weaver had got 36s for running four looms, under the new system he or she was supposed to get 41s for running six – 5s extra for a 50 per cent increase in work. Many six-loom weavers, however, failed even to get the 41s. The looms were not slowed down as promised in the agreement, and poor raw materials, causing breakdowns and lost earnings, were not improved. In many places four looms were run at the reduced six-loom rates; and although there was supposed to be a fall-back wage of 28s for weavers who had looms stopped for lack of work or material, it was frequently not paid in practice.*

By 1933 a Ministry of Labour report showed that the agreement was not being generally operated, and the employers admitted that not all the offenders were unfederated firms. 'The Lancashire weaver has been betrayed', wrote the *Daily Express*.

---

* The unemployment benefit for a man, wife and three children was then 29s 3d.

Such expert students of the industry as Daniels and Campion commented in 1934:

Perhaps it may be that a period of attrition is necessary if the industry is to settle down to a new and more stable basis. Unfortunately there has been a large number of cases of firms breaking away from existing wage agreements, and of operatives acquiescing in lower wage rates and new working conditions, particularly in the manufacturing section.[8]

By 1934 the system of agreements and trade union enforcement of them had largely collapsed, and uncontrolled wage-cutting was widespread. The unions therefore were reduced to demanding that payment of the collectively agreed wage rates be made legally compulsory. But the employers, while assenting to this, held that the breakaways from agreed wage rates showed these rates to be too high. When in 1934 the Cotton Manufacturing (Temporary Provisions) Act made a new wage list legally binding, its general effect was still further to reduce wage rates on four looms, though raising them somewhat on six looms. In 1935 average earnings for all workers (according to the Ministry of Labour figures) were only 31s 6d a week, compared with 33s 6d in 1932 before the 'more looms' agreement began to operate. The *Cotton Factory Times* reported that thousands of underemployed weavers were going home with a wage of 15s to 25s week after week, and had to swallow their pride and go to the Public Assistance Committee[9] for food tickets.

At the end of 1936, during a brief period of boom, the operatives claimed the restoration of the 1929 and 1932 cuts, and strikes were only narrowly avoided. A compromise settlement left rates still well below their 1929 levels, and the employers still refused to put into effect the fall-back wage of 30 to 35s demanded by the weavers' union.

By the late nineteen thirties there had developed in Lancashire, as in some of the coalfields, the paradoxical situation of heavy unemployment alongside labour shortage. The industry was finding it difficult to recruit boys as spinners – and no wonder. Since each spinner employed two boys or youths as piecers, for many of them the cotton industry must be a blind-alley occupation as well as an ill-paid one. The supply of little fingers, out of which Lancashire millowners had made their fortunes since long before Dickens' day, was running low, as the new arms factories were built and youth sought better paid employment with more prospects.

For the trade unions it was a disastrous period. In cotton, membership fell by over a third (from 282,000 in 1931 to 182,000 in 1939). There was a similar fall in other textiles (from 155,000 in 1930 to 105,000 in 1939).

Backs to the Wall: Coal-Mining

If miners' wages did not fall very much in the slump, this was mainly because the cuts made after the General Strike had already reduced them in many districts to something close to a bare subsistence level. In Scotland and South Wales, however, there were still further cuts in 1931. Whereas in building and engineering money wages in 1938 had reached over double the 1900 level, in mining they were only 39 per cent higher than in 1900. In real terms, while over industry as a whole wage standards had risen during the century by some 14 per cent in mining they had gone down by 20 per cent. The difference is striking enough to override detailed problems of statistical treatment. There can be no doubt at all that employed miners, even at the end of the thirties, were living worse than they had done before the First World War, although productivity over the period 1933–9 was some 11 per cent higher than it had been in 1900.[10]

The miner in employment was accounted one of the lucky ones compared with the long-unemployed living in the same community. By comparison even with the recent past, however, or with other industries, his was a life of intense hardship. In most districts short-time working was the rule, and often he could earn his miserable paypacket (averaging 9s 3d a shift, including piecework, in the early thirties) only on four or five days in the week, so that he took home only a little more than the unemployed. Moreover, many miners, as late as 1933, still owed debts accumulated during the 1926 lockout.

Average weekly cash earnings of mine workers

1930	1932	1934	1936	1938
43/9	42/1	44/6	50/6	55/11

After the lockout the owners had successfully destroyed the system of national wage negotiations and agreements won after the war, and enforced a return to district wage agreements, with severe wage cuts in most districts. Throughout the thirties the owners remained obdurate against any national minimum wage or national settlements of any kind. And when the Labour government established a National Industrial Board under the 1930 Coal Mines Act to examine and report on wages and conditions, the employers declined to nominate representatives, even though the Board had no power to regulate wages.

Thus the bargaining strength of the miners in the more favourably placed inland coalfields like Yorkshire and Derbyshire could not be used to assist the men in the hardest-hit exporting areas like Durham, South Wales and Scotland. All were tied by separate district agreements expiring at different times; each coalfield was compelled to negotiate on its own. There was cut-throat competition between different districts at the expense of wages, and friction between different districts in the union as a result.

Miners' wages were nominally tied to sliding scales related to the 'ascertained pithead profits' in each district. But in most districts there were no ascertained profits, only ascertained losses. Though the industry was depressed, it was obviously not as depressed as all that, or more companies would have had to go out of business. The union argued that many of the new amalgamations sold coal to their own allied companies in steel, chemicals or distribution at uneconomic 'transfer prices', so that profits were removed from the mining companies, and shown instead as steel or chemical profits where the miners' agreements did not cover them.

Outside the Midlands and South Yorkshire, the miners were reduced to the minimum subsistence wage, which in most coalfields was desperately low. The weekly earnings already quoted included the relatively better pay of the pieceworkers and crafts-men. But the minimum timeworkers' wage, which was all that some 40 per cent of the men had to exist on, was far lower. Ebby Edwards, MP, the miners' leader, tried to convey to the House of Commons on 6 July 1931 what these standards meant in human terms. He quoted the Northern coalfield where two-fifths of the workers had to exist on the minimum rate of 6s 6½d a day. Since, on average, men were only able to work five shifts a week because of short time, their subsistence earnings amounted to 32s 8d a week – after deductions, a maximum of 30s cash:

Allowing, for the two adults in the house, three meals a day at 6d a meal that means 3s, so that there is 1s 3d left for all the rest of the family, and if there are three children, that amounts to less than 2d a meal. That is not allowing anything for clothes, there is no question of household utensils, nor of anything for the church collection – there is nothing even to buy newspapers.

It can be understood that the men in the mining areas are not only down physically, but down morally . . . it is no wonder that there are cases where men wish that God would take away the spark of life he has created, so that the misery may end.

Hours of work, which had been lengthened (on a temporary five-year basis) from seven to eight a day after the 1926 lockout, and again reduced to seven and a half by the Labour government in 1929, were not restored to seven despite repeated demands by the miners. In 1932 the National government introduced new legislation to continue the seven-and-a-half-hour day indefinitely No provision was made for any legal guarantee of wages, or for a national minimum wage.

Unemployment increased the calls on the wretched earnings; 40 per cent of the miners were unemployed in 1932, and even in. 1937 the figure was still as high as 19 per cent. Young men were often kept on at the pit while the older men were sacked, and then the means test man would cut the father's dole because his son was working and could help to keep him. As mines closed in their own village, men desperate for jobs were prepared to travel farther and farther at their own expense to find employment at another colliery.

In the pits the work intensified and became more dangerous. The mines were technically backward compared with those of competing countries like Germany, Poland, Holland and the US, which had developed new technical methods after the First World War when the British industry was stagnant. British pits were old, and the seams were becoming more difficult and expensive to work by the old methods every year, but money for new investment was scarce. So the type of mechanization introduced in the thirties tended to be the cheapest available. This meant new coal-cutters and conveyors crammed into old confined workings, rather than new and more spacious lay-outs underground which would have involved greater expense.

Thus the miner, instead of working at his own pace with a boy helper (often a relative) in his individual stall, had to work at a pace set by machines, as one of a gang shovelling his stint of coal on to a conveyor. Standards of roof support and safety suffered in the drive for low-cost output. The noise and clatter underground made it harder to hear cracks in the timber, the new machines brought added risks of electric sparks igniting gas; mechanical cutters without improved ventilation produced more dust and more lung disease. The men dared not resist the speeding up of the job for fear of the sack. Power-loading, already used for 18 per cent of the coal in American mines in 1937, was as yet virtually unknown in Britain.

The longer hours and lower wages resulted in a higher accident rate, as men and management tended to skimp safety precautions. The rate was highest among the young workers, who no longer went underground under the supervision of father or uncle, but as part of a gang where they could learn only from their mistakes.

Proposals in 1932 for strike action to secure a national minimum wage and the seven-hour day were rejected, the majority feeling that the union was now too weak for a strike to succeed. In 1933, however, the Miners' Federation of Great Britain executive was empowered to instruct all the districts in the Federation to terminate their agreements together, so that united pressure could be brought on the owners. Failing to secure a national minimum from the government, the Federation nevertheless resolved on strike action if necessary to prevent wage reductions in any district.

By 1934 the first faint signs of improvement were seen; small increases were secured in Scotland and South Wales;* and in 1935 the Federation launched a national campaign for a 2s a day increase – the first such movement since 1926. A ballot in the coalfields showed 93 per cent of the miners in favour of strike action to secure it, though in Nottinghamshire the 'non-political' union (in effect a company union) held sway and instructed its members to work on through a strike. In January 1936 the miners were once again offered and accepted district settlements, ranging from 6d a day in Northumberland and Durham to 1s a day in Lancashire, Leicester and South Derbyshire. Wage standards had at last begun to rise – but at the price of the distressed exporting areas lagging still further behind the prosperous 'inland' coalfields. In 1938 earnings in Durham and Northumberland were 27 per cent lower than in Nottinghamshire and North Derbyshire. The employers still refused national negotiations, and there was no national agreement.

* The increases were 2d to 8d a day, and the minimum rate for daywagemen in South Wales became 7s 8d a shift.

8

Industrial Workers: Recovery and the Fight for Trade Union Organization

From 1933 onwards TUC affiliated membership once again began to increase – slowly at first, then more rapidly with the boom from 1935-7, and slowing down again as recession was felt in some industries in 1938-9. The most striking proportionate advances were those of the general workers' unions, the Amalgamated Engineering Union and Electrical Trades Union, and the Tailors and Garment Workers. In the rapidly expanding building trades the unions made relatively far less headway.

On the outbreak of war in 1939, however, the membership of all unions was still 2 million below the 1920 peak, and TUC affiliated membership still 1·8 million below 1919. This reflected the great difficulties caused by unemployment and the determined hostility of large sections of employers.

Immediately after the First World War it had seemed as if the long battle for the rights of collective bargaining had, at any rate in the main industries, been decisively won. In the late twenties, as we have seen, some big employers at least had come to realize that recognition of appropriate trade unions might benefit them by keeping the peace in industry. But in the early thirties it was clear that many employers, taking advantage of heavy unemployment, were once again refusing union recognition and using every means to prevent trade union membership among their workers, or in some cases to impose what were virtually company unions.

The mine-owners, in particular, made a determined effort after 1926 to destroy the Miners' Federation. In certain coalfields, especially Nottinghamshire, and at some pits in South Wales, they aided the establishment of so-called 'non-political' unions and put pressure on their workers to join them and leave the Federation – a difficult thing to resist at a time of heavy unemployment and intense competition for jobs.

Even more serious, in the newer industries many employers developed their factories, especially in the Midlands and the South of England, on a strictly non-union basis. While such employers were sometimes prepared to tolerate trade union membership among the small minority of highly skilled workers (in the toolroom or on maintenance), and to pay the union rate or more to this minority, they firmly refused to recognize even the skilled unions, or to sanction any spread of membership among the majority of semi-skilled and unskilled production workers. Skilled trade unionists who tried to organize the production workers were faced with the sack. Thus John Parker, Labour MP for Romford, reported:

If there is little chance of ventilating common grievances outside working hours, there is still less inside. There is no doubt that a number of firms carry on assiduous spying which leads to victimization of employees suspected of organization. In some large firms, such as Ford's – and this policy is by no means exceptional – the workers are subjected to wholesale regimentation from the moment they enter the factory gates. They must at all times wear the firm's badge. They may not talk or congregate in groups, or enter other departments. Visits to the lavatory are limited in number, and smoking or talking there is reported.[1]

Nor was it easy for organizers to approach the workers from outside. In Birmingham, for example, trade unionists distributing recruiting leaflets on behalf of the Trades Council outside unorganized factories, such as Austin Motors, were regularly interfered with by the police, under the direction of the local Watch Committee, and arrested for obstruction or causing a breach of the peace.

It was not uncommon in the newer industries, such as the rubber industry, the cinema industry, some sections of distribution and insurance, for employers to compel their workers as a condition of employment to sign a document declaring that they would not join a union.

Miners Defeat Company Unionism

It was not until 1935, when there was a slight measure of economic recovery and the miners were beginning their campaign for increased wages, that they felt strong enough to organize large-scale resistance to the 'non-political' Industrial Union. For this purpose the rank and file developed a new weapon, the stay-down strike, which proved particularly effective in a struggle that turned on excluding blacklegs from the pits.

The owners at Nine Mile Point colliery, in the Welsh anthracite area, were attempting to replace their Miners' Federation men with blacklegs (imported from all over the coalfield by special train), who were prepared to join the 'Industrial' union. One evening the day shift of Federation men refused to come to the surface, and next day villagers went round to the shops collecting food and demanded the right to send it down the pit. As the company sent blacklegs down to one part of the pit, more Federation men went down to garrison another. The miners underground had the support of a left-wing trade union leadership locally, including Arthur Horner, who had recently been elected miners' agent for the anthracite district.* Eleven more collieries held stay-downs in support, while at other pits the men decided on a stay-out till the Industrial Union was cleared out. At Mardy and Merthyr the railwaymen's branches refused to man trains transporting blacklegs. After spending more than a week underground the Nine Mile Point men achieved their main objective – local negotiations with the Federation and the safeguarding of their jobs.†

Another dramatic stay-down, involving 1,500 men, occurred at Parc and Dare collieries in the Rhondda. Here the Federation men

---

* His Miners' Federation lodge at Mardy had previously been expelled from the Federation for supporting him as a Communist Parliamentary candidate against the union's decision. In 1932 he had been sentenced to fifteen months' hard labour for resisting eviction of a miner's family.

† This strike was the subject of *Stay-Down Miner,* a play by Montagu Slater, afterwards librettist to Benjamin Britten, and one of the most talented left-wing writers of the time.

on strike were joined by non-unionists and by others believed by the company to be 'non-pols', who, in fact, were also secret members of the Federation. The management tried to prevent food going down, and the union warned that if that were done it would mobilize the women to attack the pithead, and would hold the safety-officials underground as hostages. After a thirteen-day stay-down which caused lasting damage to the eyesight of some of the strikers, the management gave a written undertaking that men would be permitted to join the union of their choice. The overwhelming majority voted for the Federation and negotiating rights were won. A little later the union was able to sign an agreement with the South Wales owners liquidating the 'non-political' union throughout the coalfield.

The hatred when the battle was on was terrible to see (wrote Horner later.) Even the children were affected by it. But it was understandable because the workers in the pits knew that their only hope of regaining a decent standard of living lay in the strength of their trade union. On the other hand I had a feeling of pity for the men who joined the breakaway union ... The struggle for work in those days was so bitter. Men often were forced into the breakaway union, in order to get a job, by pressure from their wives, who could not understand how a man could stay out of work when a job was waiting for him, just because he had to join another union.[2]

The main battle against the 'non-politicals', however, was in the profitable Nottinghamshire coalfield, where the owners had more to offer and a number of the leaders had gone over to the 'Spencer' union,* after making a separate agreement to end the lockout in 1926. Here the owners would only employ men who would agree to join the 'non-political' union and have their contributions deducted at the colliery office. Although an independent ballot showed that the men overwhelmingly wished the Federation to represent them, its officials were barred from the colliery office at every pit in the coalfield, and men were afraid to raise grievances on wages or even carry out workmen's safety inspections for fear of dismissal. When the Federation threatened strike

* So-called because it was founded and led by George Spencer, a Labour MP and Nottinghamshire official opposed to Federation policy in 1926.

action in its national campaign for a wage increase in 1935, the Industrial Union men in Nottingham were told by their officials to work on.

The turning-point here came in 1937, when miners at Harworth who had overwhelmingly voted to join the Federation were compelled by the company to continue to subscribe to the 'non-pols'. In this strike over a hundred police were drafted into the village to protect blacklegs. Six miners, including the union branch chairman, were sentenced to terms of hard labour for picketing offences under the Trade Disputes Act of 1927, and strikers were threatened with eviction from their company-owned houses. The bitter atmosphere between strikers, blacklegs and police was vividly described to a special conference of the Miner's Federation by a Nottinghamshire delegate, Val Coleman, in a splendid understatement:

When the nightshift goes to work the men are organized at a certain point for the purpose of going to work, and they are preceded by a police car. They then take the middle of the road, and there are policemen on either side of the road. Then a few yards behind them there is a line of police directly across the road standing shoulder to shoulder and keeping back the crowd, who are calling out to them 'left right, left right', and other expressions that colliery men and their wives and families make use of. Then at a certain point the line of police turn round and push back the crowd, and it is at that point where differences of opinion are expressed and objections made, and as a result we now have six men in prison.[3]

The Nottinghamshire coal-owners in this battle saw themselves as standard-bearers against the unions – one of them, Captain Muschamp, forcefully declaring: 'We want to adopt the German idea. If the government is to check future trouble, it must put its foot down. . . . This district can take credit to itself for having smashed the national strike.'[4]

There were protests in Parliament about the behaviour of the police, which had been carefully recorded by observers from the National Council for Civil Liberties. But only after the Miners' Federation had voted for national strike action to enforce recognition in Nottinghamshire was an agreement finally reached, with the assistance of the TUC, based on re-absorbing the company union and its officials into the Federation, which now became the negotiating body. Substantially this was a victory for the Federation.

The fight against the company union was a life-and-death issue for the Federation, which accounts for the bitterness with which the strikes were fought out. Dual unionism remained localized – but it might very well have spread. Despite heavy unemployment, which made the inducement to blackleg very strong, the union was so successful in re-establishing its authority that by 1939 it was organizing a slightly higher proportion of those employed than in 1926. This strength in adversity was the foundation for the advances in miners' conditions won during the war, and the nationalization of the mines which followed.

Problems in the New Industrial Areas

The new industrial areas presented great difficulties for trade union organization. Not only did most of their workers lack the long trade union tradition of the industrial north, but they lived widely dispersed from their factories. Those who had some experience of trade unionism were often immigrants from the Distressed Areas, many of them thankful to have a job and regarding any kind of regular wage, especially on piecework, as untold wealth after years of the dole – and hence very unwilling to risk it by taking the initiative in trade union activity. More important still, the majority were classed as semi-skilled and unskilled workers, machine operators or assembly-line workers with dexterity and adaptability but no recognized skill transferable from one factory to another, and many of them were women and youths.

The trade unions, which were organized not on an industrial basis, but predominantly as craftsmen's and labourers' (or general workers') unions, were not well adapted to meet the needs of workers who strictly speaking were in neither category, and who did not expect to remain permanently in one industry or occupation. The existing agreements normally provided only for craftsmen and labourers, and the vast body of semi-skilled workers on new highly productive processes were not covered by them. The Amalgamated Engineering Union in the late twenties opened its ranks to these grades of workers (though not to women till the war), but many craft unions refused to recognize their existence.

Moreover, it was difficult for the members once recruited to participate in the life of the union and become active in it. Union branches were commonly on a residential basis, so that a worker might work in a factory with several thousand employees and still find no other workers from the same factory in his union branch several miles away. Even if the branch was factory-based (as was common in the TGWU), in big cities long journeys and the rush to get on to bus or tube at factory closing time prevented all but the most enthusiastic from attending branch meetings.

Many of the large new firms, especially perhaps those of American origin, were prepared to spend money to create an atmosphere of anti-union paternalism in which the worker would feel no need for trade union organization. Personnel officers could take the place of shop stewards, and company sports and social clubs provide the enthusiastic and public-spirited with an outlet. Indeed trade union organizers sometimes advised militants to get appointed as sports club collectors, so that they could move freely from one department to another to spread trade union organization.

Organization Grows Slowly

Thus the mass-production industries were almost entirely unorganized at the beginning of the thirties. As economic recovery made conditions for recruitment easier, the situation seemed to call for a crusade, something on the scale of the 'new unionism' of the eighteen eighties, to bring the new army of production workers into the unions. In the US and France in comparable conditions something like this did in fact happen, as new or reorganized trade union centres campaigned for all-grades demands such as the forty-hour week and paid holidays, capable of uniting all sections within an industry, and brought workers flooding into the movement. In Britain, however, a concerted drive by the whole movement to publicize its aims and organize the unorganized was never achieved.* At no time did the TUC or the separate unions make available large-scale national funds and manpower to tackle the problem. In so far as the new industries and areas were organized, it was mainly through the initiative of rank-and-file trade unionists at local and district levels, sometimes assisted by local trades councils.

'The unions', to quote Dr H. Pelling, 'were slow to take advantage of the opportunities in the new areas, and often it was a rank-and-file movement, not infrequently led by Communists, which led to the "capture" of new factories.'[5] Many trades councils undertook intensive publicity and recruiting campaigns with some success. A dispute in an unorganized factory – often over some form of Bedaux or new bonus scheme – would be supported with finance, publicity and advice by the local trade union movement with the aim of recruiting the strikes. Thus the Birmingham Trades Council supported an anti-Bedaux strike by ten thousand unorganized women at Joseph Lucas' motor accessories factory in 1932, and collected food and money and supplied official organizers in support of strikers at Hope's Metal Windows at Smethwick in 1933. At a number of key factories it was Communists who led the drive for organization, notably at Firestone Tyres and other factories on London's Great West Road, at Ford's at Dagenham, Pressed Steel at Oxford, and Lucas' in Birmingham. A contemporary expert, Professor H. A. Marquand, commented:

> In many such cases strikers have joined the appropriate trade unions, and the effect of Communist leadership has been in some cases to induce the employers to consider the desirability of entering into agreements with the regular union leaders, who will undertake to protect them from sudden stoppages or infractions of the agreement.[6]

The problem, however, was not only to enrol members but to

* At the 1934 TUC, the president, Andrew Conley, of the Tailors and Garment Workers, called for 'simultaneous presentation to employers in all industries of a carefully planned programme of wage increases and a standard of working hours' in place of piecemeal wage movements, sporadic and uncoordinated. Nothing, however, came of this.

hold them. Workers who joined a union under militant rank-and-file leadership in a strike, and then found that the next time they came out they were breaking an agreement and were ordered back to work by the union organizer, were apt to tear their cards up in disgust, without gaining any further experience of trade union principles or trade union democracy. The only effective means of *holding* membership was the combination of a strong workshop organization with union officials and district committees prepared to support it over a period against pin-pricking by anti-union managements. This was to some extent achieved in the aircraft industry in the armaments boom (though here the proportion of skilled workers was unusually high), and in a minority of plants in the motor industry. Similarly in road passenger transport the rank-and-file movement, the main base of which was the left-wing garage branches in London Transport, helped to spread organization to busmen in the provinces in the strike movements of 1937.

Nevertheless, success was limited. The London secretary of the AEU at the end of 1936 recorded that it would be difficult to find a dozen 100 per cent organized factories in London's industrialized outer ring. There were thousands of workers there who had never heard of trade unionism and had not yet won established basic rates and overtime payments, the forty-seven hour week or trade union recognition. The AEU had only 27,000 members in Greater London at this time, whereas Ford's at Dagenham alone employed from 20,000 to 35,000 workers according to the season. In Birmingham the AEU doubled its 1935 membership to 12,000 by 1939, but that was about half the number of workers at Austin's Longbridge factory alone.

Engineering and the New Techniques: Rise of the Shop Stewards

As mass-production techniques became more important in the new motor, radio, electrical and arms industries, the engineering unions realized that the old type of agreement for skilled craftsmen was quite inadequate to deal with the new conditions of production. The complex operations formerly carried out by skilled fitters and turners were broken down into a series of simpler ones, which could be carried out on the new types of semi-automatic machines. The proportion of engineering workers classed by the employers as 'skilled' had accordingly fallen from 50 per cent in 1921 to 32 per cent in 1933 : the proportion classed as 'semi-skilled' had risen from 30 to 57 per cent. The machine-man rated as skilled, however, earned on average a quarter more than one rated as semi-skilled. Thus in a period when productivity in, for example, the motor industry had more than doubled, wage standards for the producers as a whole were being undermined by highly-productive specialized machines which did not require a time-served craftsman to run them.

The 'machine question' thus dominated engineering negotia-tions in the later thirties. The AEU pressed for a national agree-ment to establish grade rates for particular machines, irrespective of the grade of worker operating them. They wanted planers, millers, capstan and turret lathes to carry the full fitters' and turners' rate, and some other machines 90 per cent of it. They argued that if a turner's skill on the lathe was not fully used on a particular job, that was the responsibility of the employers. But although progress on these lines was made in certain districts, the employers nationally refused to agree, insisting that the rate in each case must take into account the type of machine, the grade of worker and the product being made.

Thus the general level of earnings in engineering, and especially in the new sectors where technical advance was most rapid, came to depend less on national agreements and more on what the organized workers, factory by factory, workshop by workshop and machine by machine, were able to extract from a particular management. This meant that strong workshop and shop steward organization, covering all grades, was at a premium. It is signi-ficant that as the AEU increased its organization in the mass production industries, it came to depend more and more on its shop stewards, official payments to whom in 1935–8 were nearly three times as great as they had been in the previous four years.[7] The method of wage payment encouraged a lively and active membership in the workshop, since the daily argument and bargaining with the rate-fixer kept stewards on their toes, and there was a considerable measure of local autonomy. In a strongly-organized shop, earnings well above the minimum piecework percentage would be negotiated as a matter of course. On the other hand, it meant that in many factories, where only a few skilled departments such as toolroom and maintenance were strongly organized, the new highly-productive machines would be run for only a few pence above the labourer's rate – a continuous threat to the standards built up elsewhere.

Hence the exchange of information between shop stewards' committees, and the organization of solidarity by one factory for another, became an important part of the effort to raise wages. Organizations of shop stewards, convened officially through the union district committee, or linked up nationally through unofficial inter-union bodies like the Aircraft Shop Stewards' National Council (especially strong because skilled men were still at a premium in aircraft), came to play a key part in the industry and initiate many of the national movements on wages and conditions.

The change in techniques and decline in the proportion of skilled men also radically changed the status of the boys who formed a growing part of the labour force. Young workers in engineering and shipbuilding were largely paid as apprentices, and the unions had been trying unsuccessfully for forty years to get the right to negotiate rates for them. Although the industry was highly skilled, boys' earnings were lower than in most other industries. The number of true apprentices was diminishing and relatively small, but the low wages were supposed to be justified by some undefined training. In many firms boys were being used as cheap labour rather than trained (some firms employed three boys to one skilled man). For many apprentices wages started as low as 8s a week, reaching 20s after five years; for those who were not apprentices wages were somewhat higher, but in the worst cases started at 10s and reached 30s to 35s after five years.

In 1937 the young workers rebelled. An unofficial strike on the Clyde spread to other parts of the country, until thirty thousand boys were out with the backing of the district unions, and an

Apprentices' Charter demanding a wage scale of 15s to 30s a week and trade training was drawn up. Although many of the strikers were unorganized, the unions supported them, and in many districts gave strike pay to boys joining during the dispute. By October a delegate conference of the young workers was in a position to threaten a national stoppage unless their demands were met by the employers. The following week the employers agreed in principle to recognize the unions' right to negotiate on behalf of the boys. Wage concessions of varying amounts and new wage-for-age scales were established in different parts of the country. This was the most important advance by the workers in engineering during the thirties.

The engineering unions towards the end of the nineteen thirties were perhaps the most strongly-placed section of the movement in view of the heavy demand for their labour to speed the rearmament programme, and they made important gains in holidays with pay and the shorter working week in many factories. Right up to the war, however, the unions nationally rejected all requests by the government to help the arms programme by allowing 'dilution of labour' (the use of less-skilled men on work formerly done by craftsmen) and relaxation of trade union privileges and customs in the workshops, until such time as all unemployed engineers were absorbed in production.

Industrial and General Unionism

Many in the trade union movement believed that only industrial unionism – one union for one industry – could give the workers the nationwide strength and solidarity needed to deal with trustified and increasingly organized employers. The miners, AEU and NUR, for example, held this view, and aimed to organize workers of all grades in their industries. It was opposed, however, not only by some of the skilled craft unions, who had been first in the field and were able to exact higher rates for time-served craftsmen, but also by the general workers' unions – the TGWU and the NUGMW, whose massive votes were becoming decisive at the TUC.

The TGWU, in particular, functioned more or less as an industrial union in road transport and docks, but by 1938 transport accounted for less than half its membership. The rest depended on the right to organize the unskilled in almost any industry, on which the general workers' unions, which already had small groups of members in a variety of industries, tenaciously insisted. An unskilled man, they argued, would frequently change his job from one industry to another, and if he were attached to an industrial union this would mean a change of union every time and corresponding instability of membership. A scheme for a single union for all forms of transport, sponsored by the NUR, was firmly rejected by Bevin and the TGWU, since it would mean breaking that union in half by splitting the transport workers from the rest.

In the US a similar conflict of views led in the thirties to the formation of the Congress of Industrial Organizations (CIO), organized as industrial unions in rivalry with the craft-based American Federation of Labour. In Britain, though there was no split, there was considerable friction between the unions. This was only partly resolved by the existence of federations of unions in each industry for bargaining nationally with the employers,* and by joint shop stewards' committees on engineering and building jobs. Differences between the unions could still arise to the advantage of the employers' side.

The absence of strong industrial unions on the face of it made stable organization of the semi-skilled and unskilled much more difficult. In a big engineering factory, for example, the people who were best placed to organize it were the small group of skilled and experienced craftsmen – toolmakers, maintenance men and machine-setters – whose union membership was of long standing and who, being scarce, were less readily dismissed. But if they made members among machine operators or women workers, as often happened when a particular grievance arose, they could not

* Some, like the National Federation of Building Trades Operatives, were fairly comprehensive though never wholly united in their attitudes. In the engineering industry the Confederation of Shipbuilding and Engineering Unions throughout the thirties was without the AEU, the largest union in the industries concerned, which strongly insisted on industrial organization.

enrol them into their own union, but must pass them on to another organization, often with no experienced cadres in the factory itself. As likely as not, once the immediate dispute was over, the new recruits lost interest.

Hence the turnover among such members tended to be very high, and stable membership was only created where a strong and efficiently organized shop stewards' committee was able to collect dues and hold essential meetings inside or close to the factory. Because of the fear of victimization and unemployment, however, it was uncommon for this privileged position to be reached before the war created a general labour shortage.

In motors, light engineering and light industries generally, the mass-production workers remained in the main unorganized up to the war. The same was true of building labourers, who were not officially organized by any of the skilled unions; the Federation stewards on the job might get them to take out a card in one of the general unions, but they often let their membership lapse as soon as the job finished, and were then recruited again next time they went to an organized job. In the TGWU, 80 per cent of the building labourer membership lapsed every year, and over 40 per cent of the membership in metal and engineering (in contrast with the docks where only 10 per cent lapsed).

In the middle thirties the building employers complained that the craftsmen's unions were recruiting semi-skilled men who had never served an apprenticeship: hence the union ticket no longer guaranteed that a worker would be fully trained and competent. The unions replied that if the employers insisted on employing half-trained labour in the hope of getting craftsmen's work done more cheaply, the unions in self-defence would have to organize them. Thus many of the craft unions in the thirties were becoming less rigidly 'crafty', but without developing into industrial unions in the full sense. For example, the workers who operated the new immensely productive machines which were coming widely into use in building and contracting towards the end of the period, such as bulldozers, trenchdiggers and concrete mixers, were still classed as labourers and earned only a penny or two above the labourer's hourly rate.

In many of the mass-production industries, such as tobacco and chemicals, sharp conflict developed between the general workers and specialist unions – for example the Chemical Workers' Union (originally a breakaway from the distributive workers, which as a result was prevented from affiliating to the TUC throughout the period) and the Tobacco Workers' Union. As the new rayon industry expanded at the expense of cotton, the textile unions lost members and the general workers gained them not without inter-union disagreements. In the building industry the TGWU and National Union of Public Employees competed for the labourers, who remained overwhelmingly unorganized. And rank-and-file delegates to the TUC continued to report that the scramble between different unions at the factory gates was a major obstacle to getting organization at all. The unions, however, remained unwilling to sacrifice their long-standing and tested organization to any more orderly scheme. The report, *Disputes Machinery of Congress*, adopted by the TUC in 1939 (the Bridlington Agreement) came out against any union attempting to organize workers at an enterprise where another union already had negotiating rights: this freezing of the *status quo* was as far as general policy on unity went.

Power of the General Unions

In 1931 the Miners' Federation and the AEU, which were most of the time on the left,* had seven hundred and fifty-four thous-

---

* Not, of course, without qualification. The majority of the MFGB leadership under Herbert Smith, for instance, accepted the hopelessness of further trials of strength with the coal owners after 1926, and there were sharp conflicts between the MFGB and the left-wing United Mineworkers of Scotland formed in Scotland in 1929, after elections returning a left-wing leadership had been set aside by the Scottish officials. A period of dual unionism followed. It was not until after Ebby Edwards, MP, became MFGB secretary, that this breach was healed by the dissolution of the UMS in 1935. What is certain is that the MFGB, like the AEU and NUR, had a constitution providing for election of officials and frequent consultation with the members, and this tended to make the leadership responsive to any widespread desire for action among the membership. In the AEU, a number of left-wingers were expelled in 1932 for circulating material opposing Executive policy, but were later readmitted on appeal.

and members between them, as against six hundred and forty thousand in the TGWU and NUGMW. By 1938, however, although the miners retained many of their unemployed members on reduced dues payments, the Miners' Federation and AEU together had only nine hundred and seventeen thousand, as against one million, fifty-one thousand in the two general workers' unions. This shift had very important effects on the official policy of both the TUC and the Labour Party.

The two great general workers' unions – the TGWU and the NUGMW – had come into existence through multiple amalgamations in the early twenties, but it was in the thirties that they came to exercise a dominating influence in the movement. Both were originally based on the militant new unions of the unskilled in the eighteen eighties (on the dockers and gasworkers respectively) and in 1926, 60 to 65 per cent of the members of the TGWU were still transport workers – dockers, busmen, tramway men, road haulage and taximen. But after further amalgamations with the Workers' Union and Builders' Labourers in the late twenties and early thirties, the TGWU branched out more widely to organize non-craftsmen in a great variety of expanding industries, some of them already catered for, at least in theory and sometimes in practice, by other unions; and by 1938 less than half of its greatly enlarged membership were in transport. Parallel developments took the NUGMW far beyond utilities and public services to become, for example, the main union catering for women in the metal and engineering industries.

As the official historian of the NUGMW puts it:

Business unionism is an American expression, but it is a fair description of a great deal of the work of the NUGMW. As one union officer has put it, 'it is the business of the union to sell labour, and to get as good a price as it can. . . . The most successful businessmen keep on good terms with their customers, and the union must do so too.[8]

Indeed, the general unions were quite aware that one of the advantages they could offer an employer prepared to 'do business' with them was that it was easier for their officials to settle an agreement, because, unlike the more democratic craft unions, they provided no constitutional means for the rank and file to repudiate it. On this basis: 'The union has found that, at least in some instances, the desire of the employer to be a good employer has been of as much value to them as the strength of their members' support.'[9]

While in the nineteenth century the craft unions had been the centre of conservative ideas and the unskilled unions the focus of socialism, in the thirties the general workers' unions usually constituted the main strength of the right. It was their votes that were decisive for 'industrial peace' and cooperation with the National government; that turned the scale in favour of the anti-Communist Black Circular, and that prevented moves to reorganize the British unions along industrial lines. A trade union of the unskilled could not, like the craft unions, keep up standards by making its labour scarce through restricting admission to the trade; it had either to use the threat of militant action, or to work by agreement with well-disposed employers and government departments as a substitute for industrial pressure. In the thirties the general unions consistently followed the latter course.

Many explanations have been put forward to account for this apparent paradox. The unskilled workers in the thirties, it has been suggested, were more satisfied with the *status quo* than the skilled men, because they had improved their living standards and relative position, at any rate where former labourers had been promoted to semi-skilled work: whereas the craftsmen were militant because the depression had undermined their former security and privileged position.[10] Or it is suggested that the less skilled were inherently less interested in trade unionism and less gifted at managing their own union affairs (though this is hardly borne out by the history of the dockers or the Smithfield Market porters). Another factor, noted by Professor H. Marquand[11] and Dr H. Pelling,[12] was the high proportion in both general unions of Irish Catholic labour, which while often industrially militant gave powerful support to specifically anti-Communist policies.* Or again, the consistent right-wing trend has been attributed to the

---

* The Catholic Church was much more undeviating in its anti-Communist outlook in the thirties than it became in the sixties, and its members formed a well-organized political pressure group within the trade union movement.

powerful personality of Ernest Bevin as secretary of the TGWU.

No doubt there was something in all these explanations at particular times and places. The most important factor, however, was probably not the attitude of the rank and file (who seem to have been as militant as most and a good deal harder-up than some), but rather the exceptionally powerful position of the General Secretary and full-time officials in these new amalgamations, and the great difficulties attending democratic control by the membership. These features were not simply the result of vast size. The Miners' Federation, for example, was larger at the beginning of the thirties, but its officials were bound by the rules frequently to consult the members through coalfield and national conferences and ballots, as were those of the AEU. The difference lay rather in the great variety of interests represented in the general unions, the spread over many industries and occupations, and some aspects of their constitutions.

The dockers, busmen and drivers who formed the core of the TGWU included some of the most active groups in the trade union movement, with their own democratic traditions and, at least in the bus garages, a lively branch life. Road haulage drivers, because of their irregular hours, were a much less closely-knit section. The dockers, though not great attenders at branches, kept to their own custom of well-attended mass-meetings on the job to decide on industrial issues. But at the national level of executive or biennial conference, representatives of one of these relatively stable and united sections could be outvoted by representatives of other groups, including the much more loosely-organized general workers' sections, where participation in branch life was notoriously low or non-existent.* Such votes were effectively deter-

---

*The exact membership in the large branches of such sections was difficult to ascertain. In the TGWU, annual lapses varied from 11 per cent in docks to 40–50 per cent in engineering and chemical, 40 per cent among general workers and 84 per cent among builders' labourers. In the late thirties some 20 per cent of members were over thirteen weeks in arrears and 80 per cent of members at any time were ineligible, because of short membership, to hold official positions. Paper membership was brought into line with realities by lapsing large numbers every few years (V. L. Allen, *Power in Trade Unions*). In the NUGMW separate records are available of 'members' and 'financial members' the latter category (dues-paying) being some sixty-five thousand or 15 per cent less than the former in 1938

mined by full-time officials, who were appointed from above and not elected, as they were in most unions (with the exception of the General Secretary, who was elected for life). Members dissatisfied with the service or policy they got from full-time officers had no opportunity to change them, although there was considerable democratic discussion by lay members within the trade groups. Indeed the Glasgow docks section actually seceded in the early thirties and formed the Scottish TGWU* because it was refused the right to elect its full-time officials operating on the waterside.

Officials were not always men who had come up from the rank and file. In the NUGMW in particular, it became a common practice for existing leaders to employ their sons or nephews as office assistants; after some years' experience they might offer themselves for selection as district officials. Among those who came forward in this way were T. Williamson (later elected as General Secretary, 1948) and J. Cooper (the next General Secretary).†

* Which is still active today.

† 'One feature of the union (NUGMW) which became firmly established during the process of reorganization was the prominence of certain families in its affairs. District secretaries had control of the appointment of their own office staffs and several of them appointed sons or other relatives to clerical posts on their staff. If they had spirit and ability, such lads, after some years of experience, would run for a full-time organizer's post. When a vacancy occurred they would submit their names and take their chance of being selected by the district committee. Thus Tom Williamson (the last General Secretary) was the nephew of the former Liverpool district secretary. After twenty years in the office, during which he rose to the post of Chief Clerk, he was appointed a temporary District Officer, and two years later was confirmed at an unopposed election. Tom Eccles, son of Fleming Eccles, was already an officer in the Lancashire district. In 1932 he was joined by one of Dukes' nephews, Jack Cooper, who had previously worked in the district office. Next year Arthur Hayday's son Fred was promoted from the Midlands district office to the post of Temporary Organizer. Jack Cooper is now General Secretary, and Fred Hayday is a National Organizer along with a third-generation Eccles and a second-generation Bassett.

'Such a practice has obvious dangers. . . . But those who became organizers were necessarily tested in the exercise of a responsible office, and most of them have survived the test with honour.' (H. A. Clegg, *General Union in a Changing Society*, p. 141).

(H. A. Clegg, *General Union*). The union was affiliated to the TUC on the basis of thirty thousand *more* than its financial membership for 1938.

Hence the General Secretary could be fairly sure of carrying the day in the last resort even in a case where the majority of active lay members were opposed to his policy. In practice they were rarely so united, because of the variety of trade groups and interests involved and the lack of information, close communication or solidarity between them.*

Busmen and the Balance of Power

In the NUGMW the conflict between left and right was muted by the rule banning Communists from office throughout the thirties. The storm centre of the TGWU, where the tussle between right and left influences on its policy – and hence on that of the TUC and Labour Party – was fought out, was the London bus section. The London busmen formed 'a compact body of twenty thousand men highly organized in garage branches, with a strong sense of group solidarity and an equally strong tradition of industrial democracy'.[13] They were already strongly organized before the amalgamation, and their Central Bus Committee had been granted the exceptional status of a national trade group, with its own full-time secretary and direct access to the Executive Council.

At the beginning of 1932 the London General Omnibus Co. demanded wage reductions similar to those already imposed on the railways, together with redundancy for eight hundred men. When official negotiations failed to get the company to withdraw,

---

* The inactive branch life in some sections of the TGWU and the tendency to bureaucratic structure has been examined at length by S. Goldstein in *The Government of British Trade Unions*. It has been suggested that the same picture would hold for all large unions; but without overestimating the degree of democracy in most industrial or craft unions, it seems clear that it was generally greater. Many unions required contributions to be paid in the branch, thus guaranteeing a measure of attendance: and most had elected officials and annual delegate conferences. Trades council secretaries always knew where to find the local secretaries of printers' or engineers' or bricklayers' or plumbers' branches affiliated to them, or the busmen's for that matter; but general workers' branch affiliation fees were often paid by officials through district office, and some of their branches were not known to meet at all.

a powerful unofficial rank and file movement among the London busmen, based on delegates from the garages and led by Bert Papworth, Bill Jones and Bill Payne, organized mass meetings to oppose the new agreement. An official ballot showed a four to one vote against accepting it, whereupon the union's Central Bus Committee called for a strike.

The company and the union leadership both had to take note of this fighting mood among the men. As Alan Bullock, the official biographer of Ernest Bevin, puts it: 'Bevin set to work to cut the ground from under the unofficial committee's feet by re-opening negotiations.' The company, no doubt fearing that the militants might take control completely, abandoned their claim for wage cuts, reduced the maximum working time from nine to eight hours per day, and guaranteed that when new and faster schedules were introduced there would be no redundancies. This was accepted, with the Rank and File Committee 'claiming – with some justice – the credit for the improvement in the new agreement'.[14]

In 1933, new and more onerous schedules of duty (accepted officially by the union) caused an unofficial strike which rapidly spread to some thirty garages, with a threat of sympathetic action by underground railway workers; and this was successful in securing the reopening of negotiations. The Rank and File Movement, with its lively paper *Busman's Punch*, continued strongly to influence the policy of the union's central bus section. It was not only the open existence of the Rank and File Movement, but assistance given to its propaganda by well-known Communists like the Marxist economist and author Emile Burns, which angered Bevin: 'an internal breakaway', he called it. But it was only after another four years of agitation that he 'brought the issue to a head and broke up the dissident organization inside the London bus section'.[15]

In the 1936–7 boom, the London busmen felt the time was ripe to demand shorter working hours to offset the greater speed and intensity of their work, and put in a claim for a seven hour working day (later modified on the advice of their union leaders to seven and a half hours). The London Passenger Transport Board, with a heavy burden of interest charges on compensation to the former owners to meet,* refused to consider any reduction in hours. The union's central bus section was overwhelmingly for strike action, the Executive Committee sanctioned it and notices were handed in. On 30 April 1937, though Bevin advised against it, the twenty-six thousand central busmen struck work, just as London was crowded with visitors on the verge of the Coronation celebrations of George VI. On that year's May Day demonstration, thousands of busmen marched in their white summer uniforms behind a banner which declared 'Twenty-five thousand Busmen Can't Be Wrong'. A Rank and File Movement pamphlet called *London Busmen demand the Right to Live a Little Longer* placed the busmen's case before the travelling public.

The men made their case primarily on the grounds that the strain and stress of their work was seriously affecting their health and endangering the public. They were driving more miles per duty than in 1932, in traffic conditions which had become much more tricky, with traffic lights, Belisha crossings, request stops and speed limits to observe. Buses were bigger (seating sixty instead of thirty-four) and faster (thirty mph instead of twelve). Expert medical evidence showed that busmen suffered more gastric illness than any other section of workers, probably because of irregular mealtimes and working hours and the nervous strain of trying to keep to a rigid timetable whatever the traffic conditions.

A Ministry of Labour enquiry into the dispute found that the men had established a case for investigation on shorter hours. When the London Passenger Transport Board thereupon agreed to set up a joint enquiry with the union – though without any definite undertaking to reduce hours – the National Executive recommended the men to return. The Central Bus Committee and the strikers overwhelmingly rejected this, and instead asked the Executive to call out the tram and trolleybus sections, who, though also in the TGWU, had been instructed to remain at work

* The chairman of the London Passenger Transport Board was Lord Ashfield, former chairman of the London General Omnibus Company, to which the bulk of the interest on compensation was payable.

and were carrying much of the normal bus traffic.* The Executive, however, refused, Bevin arguing that it would mean imperilling gains the union had previously secured for the tramwaymen. The busmen picketed Transport House, but in vain. Attempts by Papworth and the Rank and File leaders to get the tramwaymen to declare an unofficial strike failed. According to Bullock 'Londoners found other ways of getting to work . . . and the Rank and File Committee were left flailing the air'.[15]

In the fourth week of the strike Bevin played his ace. The TGWU executive revoked the powers of the elected Central Bus Committee to conduct the strike, and ordered the men back to work on the terms they had already rejected. The seven-and-a-half-hour day was not achieved. Thus the biggest official strike in any industry since 1932 ended in defeat for the workers – a setback not only for the busmen, but for the whole movement towards a shorter working week.

Following this the Executive declared the Rank and File Movement a subversive organization with Communist connections, membership of which was incompatible with membership of the union, and expelled three of the leaders, A. F. Papworth, by now a member of the Executive Council, W. Payne and J. W. Jones. These expulsions were endorsed by the biennial conference.

This was not, of course, the end of militancy among the busmen. Payne and some of the Rank and File leaders established a breakaway union, which lasted for several years. The majority of the Rank and File Committee, however, including Communists like Jones and Papworth, were strongly against this move as a splitting one, and indeed bore the brunt of the public campaign against it among the men. The bulk of the membership remained within the TGWU, and the Rank and File leaders put their weight behind the demand for 100 per cent membership, which the LPTB was eventually compelled to introduce by agreement.

Jones and Papworth themselves were later readmitted to the

---

* The underground men, NUR members, also remained at work. An NUR proposal for one united transport union had been rejected in 1934 on Bevin's advice.

union, and both maintained their influence among the busmen, Papworth eventually becoming one of the union's representatives on the TUC General Council and Jones vice-president of the

Membership of TGWU by Trade Groups, 1938
(in thousands)

Docks	87·5
Waterways	8·0
Road Passenger Transport	150·8
Road Commercial Transport	79·99
General Workers	171·0
Building Trades	32·4
Metal, Engineering and Chemical	96·0
Admin., Clerical and Supervisory	9·2
Power Workers	28·7

NUGMW Membership by Industries, 1937*

Textiles	18,000
Building and Constructional	43,500
Heavy Engineering	40,500
Shipbuilding	9,000
Docks	9,000
Claystone, Brick etc.	7,500
Chemicals (Paint etc.)	13,500
Quarrying	12,000
Iron Ore Mining	8,000
Coal Surface Workers	8,000
Gas	40,000
Electricity	14,000
Municipal Service	146,000
Food, Drink, Tobacco	24,000
Factories, General and Miscellaneous	27,000
	420,000

* Figures prepared for 1938 Conference. (Source: H. A. Clegg, *General Union*.)

union. But this was after the thirties had ended. For the time being, Bevin and the policies he stood for were firmly in control.*

Trade unions and Government

The trade union leadership was gradually drawn into consultation as state intervention in industry became more frequent under the National government. The textile unions were associated with plans to reorganize the cotton industry by legislation in 1936 and 1939, and the TUC was consulted in the appointment of advisers on the fishing industry in 1935 and 1938. The General Council in 1931 was represented on only one government committee (on juvenile employment), but the number increased year by year until in 1938–9 there were twelve, most of them dealing with matters which directly affected the interests of labour. This gave institutional form to the Bevin–Citrine policy of relying on co-operation through constitutional means with government and employers, rather than on militancy and the threat of industrial action as the movement had done in the twenties.[16] And it prepared the way for the much more throroughgoing involvement of the trade union movement with state administration during and after the Second World War.

The new and intense constitutionalism of the leadership was also reflected in the discussions as to whether the unions should take industrial action to stop transport of war materials to aggressors† or should resort to a general strike in case of war or threat of war. The International Federation of Trades Unions had asked its affiliated bodies to consider these questions. In 1934 the General Council rejected both ideas on the grounds that the trade union movement alone ought not to carry the responsibility for stopping war, and that any attempt to stop munitions would rapidly

* Bevin's practice of securing that policy was determined primarily by the officials of the union seems to have continued under his successors in the leadership, A. Deakin and H. Tiffin. Later leaders of the union such as Frank Cousins, Jack Jones and Harry Urwin have reversed this trend and declared in favour of greater responsibility by the lay membership in policy making.

† London dockers did unofficially take action to stop certain war cargoes to Japan in 1938.

develop into a general strike, which would be illegal. In 1938, when there was strong feeling in congress in favour of taking some practical action to help the Spanish government by securing removal of the ban on arms shipments, Citrine strongly opposed it:

> I raised the issue of the justification for taking industrial action for a political objective. . . . I tried to show that it was not for the trade union movement, which had repeatedly attested its belief in democracy, to strike a blow at its institutions. We ought not to give the Fascists encouragement by ourselves trying to change by force the views of a democratically-elected Parliament. . . . I pointed out that it was a moral certainty that if any decision for strike action or an embargo on arms (which would lead to the same result) was taken, the Attorney General would move in the courts for an injunction to prevent the use of union funds or machinery in support of such a decision.[17]

Accordingly the resolution eventually carried by congress, which called on the leaders to determine steps to secure a coordinated policy for the removal of the arms ban, 'was discreetly allowed to lapse'.

Summing-Up

A detailed analysis of membership and employment towards the end of the decade[18] showed the trade union movement still at its strongest in proportion to numbers employed in the coalmines and steel works, on the railways, in the printing, cotton and boot and shoe trades, and in the skilled sections of the engineering, metal and building trades. The miners, cotton operatives and shipbuilding workers had been memorably successful in maintaining their organization in face of prolonged depression, bitter strikes and shrinkage in the numbers employed, and so had the steel workers, despite the mechanization which likewise reduced employment. In railways and printing, too, all grades were strongly organized.

Among semi-skilled workers in engineering and among builders' labourers, however, trade unionism was still very weak despite the fairly high level of organization among skilled men.

The outstanding weaknesses of trade unionism were still in

distribution and service trades; among clerical workers; in agriculture; and among women workers. Less than one-sixth of

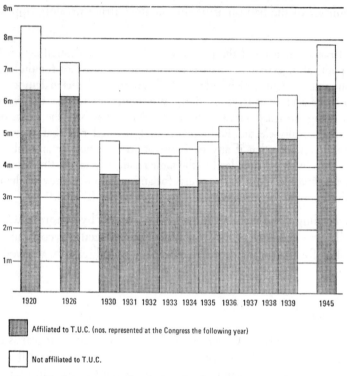

Fig. 5 Trade union membership in the thirties.

women workers were organized, (eight hundred thousand out of five million), whereas organization among men was approaching two-fifths.

At the end of the thirties, after the most thorough survey made of the movement (at least since the pioneer work of the Webbs), to which officials of nearly all the main unions had contributed, G. D. H. Cole gave this considered judgement:

At the present moment British trade unionism is in serious danger of missing its chance. As I write, a boom has been in full swing; but very little attempt has been made to take advantage of it. Now,

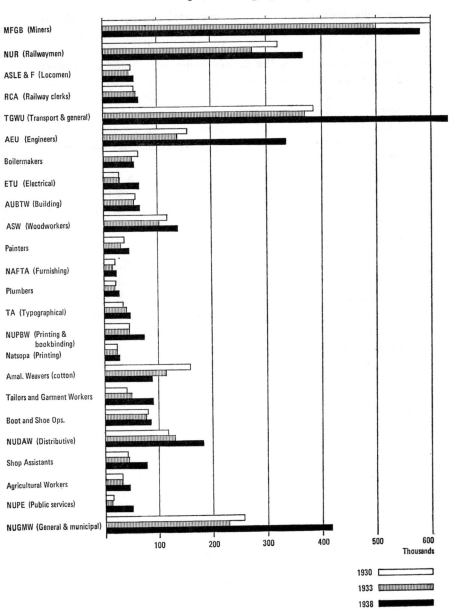

Fig. 6 Changes in membership of large trade unions.

assuredly, is the time both for the organized workers to win advances by militant action and for the movement to bring effectively within its ranks the mass of unorganized workers in the rapidly-developing industries and services. But the old leaders only found in the recent boom a new excuse for inaction. Every sign of Trade Union militancy can now be attributed to the machinations of a handful of Communists, who have somehow found the art of being in a hundred places at once, and in whom it is regarded as a crime to induce non-unionists to join a Trade Union, or to suggest to the workers that they had better act promptly, while profits are high, instead of staying quiet until the precarious chance passes away. In 1934 the Trades Union Congress made a great affair of celebrating the centenary of the Tolpuddle Martyrs. If George Loveless and his friends got into trouble with the police today, they would probably be told that they were a pack of Communist agitators, who deserved all they got.[19]

But the events turned out differently. The recession being felt in 1938–9 never developed into slump: it was overtaken by the outbreak of war. In the acute labour shortage which followed, the unions were able to build strong organization on the foundations maintained with so much difficulty and sacrifice during the nineteen thirties.

9

Wages – Real
and Unreal

How far did the trade union actions of the nineteen-thirties described in the last chapters succeed in maintaining and advancing
real wages and living standards? In general they were not able to
prevent real wages in the older industries, already depressed in
1929, from being further cut in the thirties. The General Council
of the TUC in 1931 boldly declared that 'Wage Reductions Mean
Industrial War' and promised that against a policy of widespread
wage reduction 'we would throw the whole of our resources and
power'. In practice, however, as we have seen, these brave words
were not followed up with action, and each section of the workers
faced with wage reductions had to struggle alone, sometimes (as in
the case of the cotton workers' dispute) with limited financial
support from the TUC.

Trade union leaders were generally unwilling to push resistance
to the point of national strike action. Funds and membership had
fallen; and in any case the dominant leadership in most unions
saw no hope but acquiescence in the rationalization and cutting-
down to size of the basic industries by the employers, supported
by the banks and the government. Only in the cotton industry was
there large-scale and officially-backed strike action to resist the
demand for wage reductions. Nevertheless there was considerable
resistance to wage cuts, industry by industry and job by job, and
as soon as prices began to increase again in 1934–5, pressure for
wage rises. The trade union movement over industry as a whole,
by its refusal to accept that 'the wages of all workers must come
down', did succeed in roughly maintaining real wage standards in
the early part of the decade and increasing them in the later years,
though by far less than the rise in productivity.

In retrospect it seems as if the General Strike of 1926, while it ended in defeat for the unions and the miners, nevertheless had a delayed influence over the thirties which was not all in the employers' favour. The employers as well as the TUC were nervous of another upheaval on the 1926 scale. If the union leaders were disinclined and ill-equipped for all-out resistance, the employers were also afraid to push cuts too far, impressed by the stubborn defensive strength of the workers. Except where the unions were crippled by long-term depression (as in mining and cotton), the cuts made by private employers were generally smaller than the government had made in the pay of civil servants, teachers and men in the forces: and some of the more strongly-organized sectors were not touched at all.

Real wages were, however, very low by comparison with the standards of the nineteen sixties. From 1930 to 1970 prices rose by roughly 4 times (396 per cent).[1] The skilled man's wage-rate at the beginning of the thirties was £3 to £3 10s – equivalent to £12 to £14 in 1970. The labourer's rate was around £2 2s (equivalent to £8 8s in 1970) except in agriculture where it was around £1 11s (equivalent to £6 4s in 1970). Labourers' rates in particular, by today's standards, were equivalent to dire poverty. The average engineering male earnings of 70s or so in 1935 would be worth £14 in 1970. The miner's figure of 9s 3d a shift would correspond to some 37s a shift at 1966 prices; or £8 13s for the average number of shifts then worked in a week.

Again, the impact of the crisis on different industries and sections was very uneven. From 1928 to 1933 time rates of wages for a full-time week were cut by 14 per cent in cotton textiles, by 20 per cent in wool, by 8 per cent in shipbuilding, by 12 per cent in building. On the other hand, printing compositors' rates remained unchanged, and skilled men in engineering, though affected by cuts in piecework percentages and in extra payments for overtime and shift work, maintained their time rates. By the peak of the boom, in 1937, skilled engineers' rates had been increased to 10 per cent above the 1928 level, whereas mining, cotton, wool, railways and building were still well below it.

Many unions in the later nineteen thirties set about reducing

Time rates of wages in selected industries

(December)	1929	1931	1933	1937	1938
Agricultural labourers (male)	31/8	31/4	30/6½	33/7½	34/7
Engineering:					
fitters and turners	58/9	59/1	59/1	67/2	67/2
labourers	41/11	42/1	42/1	49/10	50/4
Boot and shoe:					
men	56/0	54/0	54/0	56/0	58/0
women	34/0	33/0	33/0	37/0	38/0
Baking (table hands)	64/1	62/1	61/7	62/7	63/4
Furniture:					
Cabinet makers	73/2	70/10	68/1	72/9	73/7
Print:					
hand compositors (book and jobbing)	73/10	73/10	73/10	73/10	73/10
Building:					
bricklayers	72/4	69/1	65/5	71/1	73/1
labourers	54/1	51/10	49/2	53/3	55/1
Electrical installation:					
wiremen	74/5	74/5	69/5	75/4	76/11
Railways:					
engine drivers	70/2	69/5	69/5	72/0	72/0
goods porters	45/10	42/10	42/10	47/0	47/0
Tramway drivers:	60/6	60/6	58/10	65/8	65/10
conductors	57/4	57/4	55/10	62/6	62/8
Shipping:					
able seamen (monthly)	180/0	180/0	162/0	180/0	192/6
Dock labour (daily min. rates, average of 10 large ports)	12/3	12/3	11/6	13/4	13/4
Local Authorities' non-trading services:					
labourers	52/5	51/9	50/10	54/4	55/8

(Source: Statistical Abstract for the United Kingdom.)

differentials by securing flat-rate increases on minimum rates from employers for workers of different grades of skill. Earnings, however, still tended to increase more for the skilled than for the semi-skilled, and it does not seem that differentials in the pay-packet narrowed much, if at all, over the period.

Manual and non-manual wage rates

In the crisis years, salaries were cut appreciably less than earnings of manual workers, except for those salaries directly under the control of the government, which were quite sharply reduced. Civil Servants suffered an average cut of 6 per cent, Post Office engineering supervisory and technical staff of 8 per cent and teachers (by far the most severely treated) of no less than 11 per cent, as much as the workers in the most depressed industries. In manufacturing, on the other hand, the cut in salaries reached only 5 per cent, and in distribution only 1 per cent. Compared with the position in the mid-twenties, teachers had lost ground very heavily, unlike professional groups in private industry.

	Male salaried workers *weekly earnings**	*Index* *(1929 = 100)*
1929	£4 0 10	100
1930	£4 0 7	99·7
1931	£3 19 5	98·2
1932	£3 18 0	96·5
1933	£3 18 0	96·5
1934	£3 18 7	97·2
1935	£3 19 5	98·2
1936	£4 0 2	99·2
1937	£4 0 10	100
1938	£4 1 7	100·9

* Earnings in October (corrected to a weekly basis) of administrative, technical, professional, clerical and analogous grades in industry, transport, national and local government service, national health service, teaching, banking and insurance. (Source: London and Cambridge Economic Service.)

By 1935 manual earnings had more or less regained the 1928 level, and in 1935-8 there was a rise of 8 per cent. Most salaries in private industry and commerce remained relatively stable, but rose little beyond pre-depression levels until the war.[2]

Wages and Prices: a corrected view

British statistics of wages and cost of living at this time were quite inadequate, and this has meant that at the time and ever since the measurement of real wages has been badly distorted.

The only reasonably complete and reliable figures in the thirties were those of agreed time rates of wages for a full week.[3] These took no account of other aspects of wage agreements, such as standards for minimum piecework earnings in engineering, or extra payments for overtime, nightshift and weekend duties, cuts in which seriously affected the standards of engineers and railwaymen in the slump. Non-union firms might pay much less than the agreed rates. Neither, of course, did wage-rate figures attempt to allow for the effects of short-time and overtime working on earnings, or for the great difference in piecework earnings between a time of boom, with steady employment and long runs on a particular article or component, and a time of slump when orders were irregular, and workers might spend much of their time underemployed though on the job. Earnings censuses, which were supposed to include the effect of these factors, were taken by the Ministry of Labour only in 1928, 1931, 1935 and 1938 (the results of the last being published only in part in 1940); and even for these years they were not on a strictly comparable basis, and were filled in optionally by the firms to whom they were issued, so that non-union firms, employing workers below trade union or even trade board rates, might well neglect to complete them at all. For the bottom slump years, 1932-4, there are no earnings figures on a comparable basis.

The official working class cost of living index was strongly criticized by the unions even at the time as seriously inaccurate. Not only was it based on an antiquated and unrepresentative list of individual commodities (including obsolete items like calico, black

worsted stockings and candles), which no longer formed (if they
ever had) the bulk of working class expenditure, it was also
grossly over-weighted for food, which was given a weight of 60
per cent, whereas the actual proportion of food to total working
class expenditure in 1937–8 was under 40 per cent*. Since food prices
fell much more than prices of manufactures, and expenditure on
fares and housing actually rose during the slump, the cost of living
index fell much more than the real reduction in living costs war-
ranted, automatically pulling down with it the wages of some two
million workers whose rates were governed by cost of living sliding scales. The rise of prices in the subsequent boom was similarly
exaggerated.

Since the cost of living index, despite its known inadequacy,
was then the only official consumer-price index available, it has
been generally used ever since in computing real wage movements
for these years.[4] This accounts for the widespread impression that
despite wage cuts, real wages reached a peak at the bottom of the
slump in 1932, and fell sharply in 1936, when trade improved,
money wage cuts were restored and trade union membership was
increasing. This apparent paradox (which tended to suggest the
uselessness or irrelevance of trade union action on money wages)
was taken as confirmation of J. M. Keynes' well-known theoretical
formulation (in *The General Theory of Employment, Interest and
Money*, 1937) that money wages and real wages generally moved in
opposite directions. Better statistical information, however, now
shows that for the nineteen thirties this is not the real story.

Since 1953, the alternative index of consumers' expenditure,
constructed by statisticians led by J. R. Stone at the Department of
Applied Economics in Cambridge, has allowed some check on the
old cost of living index. Although it is not entirely satisfactory as a
working class cost of living index (since it covers all consumer
expenditure, and includes luxuries and semi-luxuries bought only
by the middle class at that time), it is undoubtedly much closer to
the general movement of retail prices than the old index, and
indeed agrees pretty well with what would be shown by the old

* As the Ministry of Labour *Family Budget Enquiry* of 1937–8 subsequently
showed. This was not published, however, till the war.

index if the excessive weighting for food were corrected. It fell considerably less than the old index in the slump years. Real wage rates based on this index give a much more convincing picture. From this it appears that real wage rates per full-time week increased slowly with the fall in prices to 1932. From 1932 to 1934, the worst years of slump and cuts, there was no further rise in real wage rates. The rise was resumed in 1935 and was cut short by the end of the boom and the advent of war in 1939. This strongly suggests that, allowing for lower minimum piecework percentages and overtime rates, real wages even in well-organized firms were considerably lower in the slump years than in 1929 or in the subsequent boom. (See Table 8.)

Real *earnings*, organized and unorganized, undoubtedly fell much more than rates in slump and rose more as trade improved. Thus the years which brought disaster for the unemployed did not bring a bonus and an easy life for the employed workers. Short time and underemployment were common, alongside heavy overtime when employers were anxious to complete a hardwon order quickly without taking on more hands. And many employed workers, as a result of the means test, were forced to maintain unemployed members of their household out of their wages, so that they were in practice dragged down to the unemployed 'subsistence' level.

Variations by districts and industries

In any case heavy unemployment concentrated in the old industrial areas markedly pulled down the earnings of employed workers there. The Durham miner's income was closer to that of his unemployed neighbour than it was to that of the more prosperous Nottinghamshire miner.* In engineering in 1935, a marine engineer on the Clyde or Tyne earned 65s 4d a week and a textile

---

* In 1938 an unemployed miner with a wife and two children would get £1 13s a week on the dole. The Durham miner on average earned perhaps £2 a week for four shifts, and was lucky if he could get five shifts' work and earn £2 10s. The Nottinghamshire miner at the same date was earning £3 6s 5d for five shifts, or £3 19s 6d for six, with much less short time.

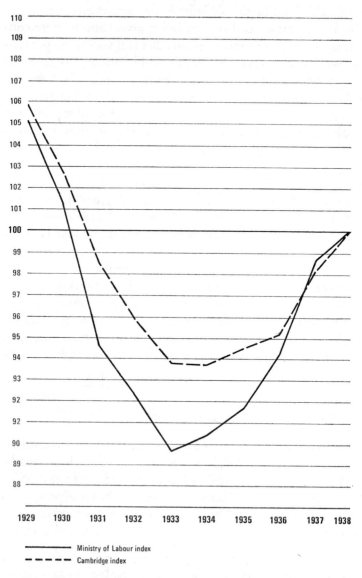

Ministry of Labour cost of Living Index (as published in the 1930s) compared with later Cambridge Index (1938 = 100)

Fig. 7 Cost of living indices.

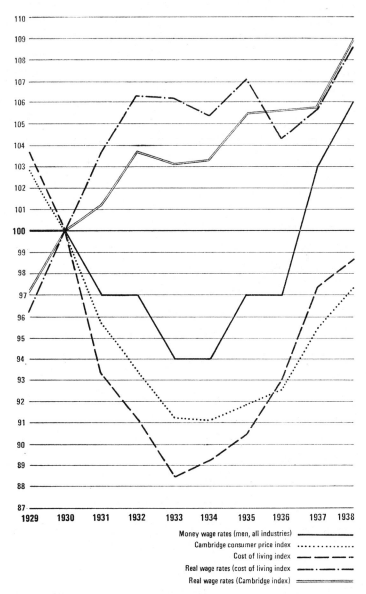

Fig. 8 Wage rates, prices and real wage rates.

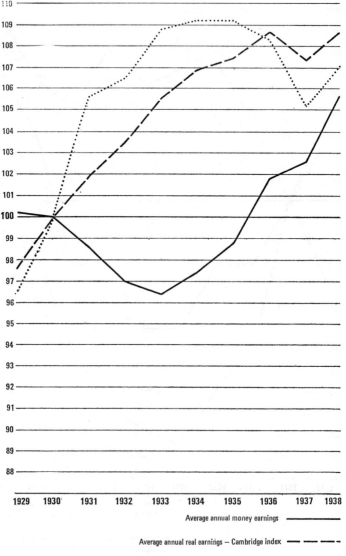

Fig. 9 Average annual real earnings.

engineer 55s 9d, whereas the average for men in the motor and cycle industry, centred in the Midlands and London, was as high as 78s 5d. In shipbuilding, although plain time rates were nominally within a few pence of the skilled engineering rate, earnings for men were only 62s a week, as against 74s 10d in aircraft engineering.

The highest paid group of men, printers on newspapers and periodicals, averaging 110s 9d a week, were above many 'middle class' salaried workers in earnings; they earned twice as much as the miners at the same period. In 1926 the political strike of *Daily Mail* printers against setting an anti-miner leading article had triggered off the nine days' General Strike. Perhaps the newspaper proprietors were prudent in allowing a relatively small number directly employed on their presses to maintain money wage standards at a time when wages were being cut in most other industries.

Wages and Productivity

The rise in productivity during the decade was achieved, as we have seen, not so much by new machinery and equipment (the rate of investment in manufacturing, mining and transport was indeed cut by over 40 per cent in 1929–33) but by sacking redundant workers and extracting more intensive labour from those who remained. The cost of time wasted through disorganization and interruption of work, or by poor material, or bad weather, was generally borne not by the employer but by the worker, for there was no effective minimum weekly wage to safeguard the standards of the worker underemployed or on short time (in many industries this was not established till the wartime Essential Work Order). In some cases, especially in the cotton and woollen industries, earnings of underemployed workers, who had nevertheless to stay in the factory for the full working hours, amounted to less than the benefit they would have received if they had been unemployed.[5]

Undoubtedly the campaign of speed-up and rationalization succeeded in increasing output per head without a corresponding rise in wages. The increase in output per head from 1929 to 1937 is put by modern research at 17 per cent for the whole of industry, and 21 per cent for manufacturing alone. However the calculations of real earnings are made, they rose far less than this. Even if we take real earnings per full time man-year worked in industry – ignoring the fact that the individual worker did not work a full man-year but lost earnings because of short time and temporary unemployment – real earnings rose only 9 per cent, or half as much as productivity. One might have expected the increases in productivity in the newer industries with modern plant, such as vehicles (35 per cent increase), chemicals (22 per cent) and tobacco (25 per cent); but the biggest increase of all was in the depressed textile industry (40 per cent) where there had been little new investment and 'more looms per weaver' represented speed-up in its simplest form of intensified work.[6]

Decrease in worker's share of output
Per Cent Increase in 1937
compared with 1929

All industries, output per head	+17
Manufacturing, output per head	+21
Average annual money earnings (per full-time man-year)	+2·4
Cost of living*	−6·1
Average annual real earnings (per full-time man-year)	+8·9

* Official cost of living index

(See A. Chapman and R. Knight, *Wages and Salaries in the United Kingdom, 1920–38;* and H. W. Richardson, *Economic Recovery in Britain, 1932–39*, p. 73.)

Earnings in 1924, 1931, 1935 (Industrial Groups)

	(Shillings per week) Men and Boys			*Women and Girls*		
	1924	*1931*	*1935*	*1924*	*1931*	*1935*
Textiles	51·0	48·0	49·2	28·6	26·9	27·5
Clothing	54·8	53·6	54·3	26·9	26·9	27·8
Food, drink, tobacco	58·0	57·5	56·6	27·9	28·0	26·6
Paper, printing	70·7	71·8	75·4	28·0	28·3	28·1
Gas, water, electricity	62·0	62·8	62·5	28·6	26·8	26·6
Coalmining	53·0	45·2	44·8	—	—	—
Metal manufacture	59·9	54·7	61·5	24·5	24·8	28·0
Engineering	51·1	50·4	55·0	26·3	26·8	28·0
Railway works	69·3	64·0	68·4	—	—	—
Vehicles	57·2	57·3	65·9	26·9	28·6	31·8
Ships	54·3	51·8	54·2	—	—	—
Metal Industries	53·3	52·8	55·5	24·6	24·7	26·0
Total Metals	56·4	53·8	58·8	25·2	25·6	26·9
Coke, cement	61·8	65·2	54·9	—	—	—
Bricks, pottery, glass	55·1	51·7	52·5	23·3	22·4	23·9
Chemicals	59·0	58·8	60·6	25·8	27·7	26·5
Total earth products	57·7	56·3	56·3	24·6	25·4	25·3
Building, contractors	59·9	58·2	56·2	—	—	—
Wood, furniture	54·8	52·0	53·8	26·3	27·4	28·1
Total Building etc.	59·0	57·2	55·9	26·3	27·4	28·1
Mining (other than coal)	51·0	51·3	51·7	—	—	—
Leather	54·6	52·7	53·7	25·7	25·4	25·4
Transport and storage	69·5	66·3	65·1	30·8	24·9	28·3
Local Government (non-professional)	51·6	52·7	52·7	27·8	26·2	28·0
Others	59·2	58·1	55·4	28·5	26·0	26·5
Total miscellaneous	63·5	61·6	60·4	28·0	26·0	26·8
Total: Actual earnings	57·6	55·7	56·9	27·5	26·9	27·3
full-time earnings	58·9	57·3	56·6	28·4	28·0	27·2
agriculture (men)	31·5	35·0	35·7	—	—	—

(Source: Bowley, *Wages and Income in the U.K. since 1860.*)

Average earnings in last pay-week of October 1938

	All	Men	Boys	Women	Girls
Iron, stone etc.					
mining and quarrying	56/8	60/0	30/2	—	—
Treatment of non-metal					
mine and quarry					
products	61/0	66/5	31/1	29/8	17/11
Brick, pottery and glass	47/8	63/2	27/8	27/10	14/10
Chemical, paint, oil etc.	55/0	69/3	29/5	32/8	18/2
Metal, engineering,					
shipbuilding	59/8	75/0	26/1	33/4	19/11
Textiles	37/10	57/3	24/0	31/9	19/8
Leather, fur etc.	46/9	64/1	25/4	34/11	17/6
Clothing	35/0	64/3	24/9	32/9	17/6
Food, drink, tobacco	47/0	65/3	28/1	32/11	19/0
Woodworking	51/10	66/3	23/4	33/8	17/5
Paper, printing etc.	57/7	84/3	24/8	34/1	17/1
Building, contracting	61/2	66/0	25/8	—	—
Other manufacturing	46/6	69/1	26/8	31/9	18/5
Transport and Storage	65/6	70/0	27/1	34/11	—
Public utilities	59/8	63/1	27/7	27/8	21/5
Govt. indust. ests	70/6	75/3	32/7	44/9	—
All above	53/3	69/0	26/1	32/6	18/6

(Source: *Ministry of Labour Gazette,* March 1941.)

Low Wages and Minimum Wage

Unskilled men in most industries, and skilled men as well in the most depressed industries, generally earned too little throughout the thirties to keep a family at a standard that would maintain full health.

The 'Human Needs of Labour' standard worked out by B. Seebohm Rowntree in 1936 for his survey of poverty in York[7] allowed about 53s a week in 1936 and about 56s in 1939 for a family of man, wife and three children; 31s for a single woman; and 41s 4d for an agricultural worker's family. In 1936 unskilled rates in most industries were well below 50s, and in *none* of those listed by the Ministry of Labour did they reach 56s; while agricultural labourers' rates averaged 32s 4d at the end of the year, 9s below the minimum standard.

Overtime and payment by results might, of course, raise the earnings above these levels; but short time was no less prevalent, especially in building (which had then no guaranteed wage for bad weather), and there were many trades, such as building, mining, and railways, where a large proportion of the lower-paid workers had no piecework or bonus earnings at all.

The minimum 'subsistence' rates in mining, the legalized piece-work lists in cotton, and the legal Trade Board minima in the worst organized industries were all far below Rowntree's stringent estimate of poverty. As for women workers, their *average* earnings, piecework and all, were well below the Rowntree minimum for a single woman in the majority of industries, including some, like cotton textiles and pottery, where they formed a large proportion of the skilled workers.

In 1935 it is estimated that some 47 per cent of adult male workers earned less than 55s a week, and 23 per cent less than 45s.[8] Very large numbers indeed therefore must have failed to reach the standard 'below which no worker should be forced to live'. The number of employed workers who earned less than the Rowntree minima was put by one statistician at 3 million men and 1·8 million women:[9] and this is probably an underestimate.

Class Structure
and Class Outlook

While the industrial workers were fighting their prolonged defensive battles, some significant shifts were taking place, not so much in the class structure of society as in the occupations, the habits and to some extent the outlook within each class.

British society continued to be made up overwhelmingly of manual wage-earners, who amounted to three-quarters of the working population. But there was, as we have seen, a considerable shift from heavy to light industry, and to some degree from highly skilled craftsmanship to semi-skilled work. The most marked change of all, however, was the shift from productive industry to service industry. Employment in the distributive trades rose continuously even during the worst years of the depression, and by the end of the decade distribution had taken on far more people than mining and shipbuilding had sacked between them, while those employed in the service trades – hairdressing, catering, hotels, garages and so on – rose by half a million during the decade.

It is often assumed that the years after 1931 saw a striking increase in the numbers of the 'middle class'. How striking it was depends very much on how the term 'middle class' is defined. If hairdressers and shop assistants are counted as wage earners rather than salary earners – which seems reasonable since they worked with their hands and were normally employed on a weekly basis, and their wages were usually no higher than those of manual workers – then the proportion of wage-earners in the occupied population fell only from 80 per cent in 1924 to 77·7 per cent in 1938, while in the same period the proportion of salaried employees rose only from 17·8 per cent to 20 per cent.[1] The drop in the proportion of wage-earners was thus not large. On the other hand, the shop assistant was doing a very different kind of job and in very different surroundings from the manual worker in productive industry, and up to a point his outlook and tastes and style of life were influenced by this – he tended to stop identifying himself with the 'cloth cap'.

The Salaried Class

Professional workers were increasing in numbers and relative importance during the thirties – though not nearly as rapidly as later during the nineteen forties and fifties. This was a necessary result of the rise of new science-based industries like chemicals, rayon, electrical equipment and aircraft as well as of large-scale administration. Professional workers were still, of course, a small proportion of the whole working population, but their absolute numbers increased by more than half from 1931 to 1951 (968,000 to 1,493,000). Much fewer of them however, were 'professional' in the older sense of a self-employed doctor or lawyer – the great majority were employees of industrial firms or local or government authorities.

There was a substantial increase generally in the salaried staff in industry – technicians, draughtsmen, supervisors, progress-chasers, and clerical workers, as well as professional engineers and scientists – in the period 1929–38. This was especially marked in the metal and metal-using industries; in fact, wherever mass production and scientific methods were important the proportion of salaried workers tended to increase, while the large-scale administrative and sales apparatus required by the big concerns involved more clerical workers.

However, the major increase in clerical and salaried staff was not in productive industry at all. The state apparatus was growing fast. There were three civil servants in 1938 for every two in 1929. And the insurance and banking system, developed in the palmy days when Britain was the workshop and banker of the world, took on another sixty-two thousand salaried staff – almost a fifth more – in the thirties when its leading position was threatened.

By 1938 almost a third of the employed population – whether wage or salary earning – was in 'non-producing' occupations – administering, financing, grooming people and cars, nursing, teaching, litigating and above all selling. Some of this increase in tertiary occupations meant a real improvement in the quality of life, adding to enjoyment and comfort and convenience. But much of the extra work done in distribution and service trades was pure waste from the point of view of the community as a whole. Goods were hard to sell primarily because so many families were too poor to buy what was needed, so an increasing effort had to be put into selling to those who did have money to spare. This meant a huge increase not only in advertising, but in door-to-door selling and free gift schemes, as well as more elaborate and expensive shops.

Much of the new advertising was directed towards the black-coated and clerical class, better paid than manual workers★ and more numerous than before, but also more insecure than before. For unemployment in the kinds of jobs hitherto considered 'safe' was now a danger to be reckoned with, particularly at the lower end of the scale. The 1931 Census had already recorded seventy thousand clerks as unemployed, and it was a deep and lasting shock to the middle-class sense of security when, during the slump, City of London stockbrokers, exporters and finance houses dismissed thousands from what had been traditionally regarded as 'safe' jobs. Many of the new 'blackcoats' had been recruited from the families of manual workers, and were afraid of nothing so much as that they or their children might be forced back again into the manual working class. It was from unemployed office workers that the ubiquitous door-to-door canvassers were primarily recruited; they had lost their regular jobs and were desperately trying, on a commission basis, to keep up their old status.

Even so, unemployment among blackcoated and professional workers was much less common than among manual workers.

★ It was uncommon to find blackcoated or salaried workers earning much less than skilled production workers in industry, as not infrequently happens today.

Their salaries, except for those of state teachers, were cut much less than wages during the slump, and the subsequent years showed growing improvement in their standard of life. They were the core of the new class of owner-occupiers; many were buying their first cars. The life-style of lower middle-class people was, indeed, much more sharply demarcated from that of the working class than it is today. They were housed on separate estates, were differently dressed and usually educated at different schools. And they were under greater social pressure to keep up appearances even on inadequate incomes. A particularly large proportion of their income was mortgaged in advance for fixed expenses such as housing, hire purchase and school fees. They therefore valued especially highly such privileges as monthly payment, permanent staff status and – in public concerns and banking – the prospect of a small pension. This made them doubly unwilling to question employers' attitudes or to risk victimization, and, with the exception of certain special groups such as teachers, trade unionists remained a small minority among them.

Taxation favoured the middle class not only much more than it does now but much more than it had done in the twenties. For while the burden of indirect taxes which fall more heavily on the poor was increased, income tax did not rise above 4s 6d to 5s in the pound, so that middle-class incomes between £250 and £1,000 a year enjoyed the lowest percentage burden of direct and indirect taxation combined.*

* The table below illustrates the changing burden of total taxation, including estimated shares of indirect taxation, on a family with three dependent children at different levels of income. It excludes local rates, which were even more regressive, and death duties and profits taxes, which fell more heavily on the rich. For smaller families the regressive effect was even greater.

Taxation as percentage of total income

Income of	£100	£200	£500	£1,000	£10,000
1913–14	5·4	4·0	4·4	5·2	8.0
1923–4	14·1	11·8	8·0	14·1	37·1
1930–1	11·0	9·6	4·5	9·7	35·8
1937–8	10·4	8·4	5·6	11·8	39·1

(Shirras and Rostas, *The Burden of British Taxation.* Quoted in C. L. Mowat, *Britain between the Wars.*)

All this was an important element in cementing support for the National government and the Conservative Party among the lower middle class. They had as yet little voice, however, in the higher councils of the Conservative Party or the state. The roll-call of Conservative and National government MPs continued to read like excerpts from Debrett and the Directory of Directors, with few grammar school products included. And the lower middle class did not, as a rule, rise to senior positions in the Civil and Diplomatic Service or the armed forces, which remained very much the preserve of the upper middle class.

Independent employers and farmers

In contrast to the salariat, which was expanding, the number of independent employers was probably falling. Employers and proprietors, including owners of very small one-man businesses, amounted in 1931 to only 6·7 per cent of the occupied population. During the twenties the effective control of industry was already becoming rapidly concentrated into fewer hands, as formerly independent firms were taken over by the large trusts, and the process continued in the thirties. Often a controlling interest was bought by a holding company while the firm continued to trade under its original name, so that the process went unobserved. And some of the smaller independent employers, whether selling out in time to a big concern or going bankrupt in a hopeless effort to compete, became managers, foremen or supervisors in a larger enterprise, thus joining the growing ranks of the salariat, while the control of policy in industry passed increasingly to the financial interests, usually in London. Although there were still a vast number of firms in 1935 (some fifty-three thousand), only one in twenty-five had a labour force of five hundred or more. On the other hand, large firms with over five hundred workers already provided more than half the total employment, and the two hundred largest firms and amalgamations employed one-third of all workers.[2]

The trend towards concentration was not a uniform one, however. It seems likely that in manufacturing – especially textiles and metal – in road transport and in farming, the proportion of small businesses declined. But the very small one-man business with little capital outlay – the self-employed plumber, taxi-driver or shopkeeper – did not decline in numbers to the same extent, partly because older craftsmen who had lost their jobs often tried to set up as independent workers, or used what savings they had to start a rudimentary shop in the front parlour. There was also a genuine increase of opportunity for small businessmen in garages, hairdressing and catering.

In the countryside the crisis led to lowered prices, and intensified the longstanding depression in farming. A good many farmers went bankrupt, unable to meet their rent and interest charges; there were anti-tithe demonstrations in the Eastern Counties. From 1932 onwards state marketing schemes and subsidies, together with tariffs and import quotas for foodstuffs, helped to raise farm prices even where they restricted production, and by the end of the decade the bigger farmers (who in practice got the bulk of the subsidies) were more prosperous than they had been in living memory. Throughout the thirties, however, the total acreage of cultivated land continued to fall, and so did the number of farm workers, even though there were more dairy cows and pigs, more sugar beet and more market gardening. The political loyalty of the farming community to the National government had been maintained – at a price paid by the consumer and taxpayer – without making Britain appreciably more able to feed itself in case of war or scarcity. It was not until the war years that it was found economically possible to plough up rough pastures and hillsides, and greatly to increase food production.

The Upper Classes

What was happening during this period to the upper middle classes and the well-to-do? It must be emphasized that they were a very small part of the total population. Contemporary statisticians were in the habit of dividing the twelve million families in Britain into four social grades, classified according to the chief earner or income receiver in each family. In this sense the social pyramid in 1937 looked like this:

Income of chief earner per week	Number of families	Per cent of families
Class A. Over £10	635,500	5·2
Class B. £4 to £10	2,580,000	21·3
Class C1. £2 10s to £4	4,581,000	37·8
Class C2. Under £2 10s	4,318,000	35·7

(Source: *The Home Market,* 1939*.)

Social class does not, however, depend primarily on the level of income, though this may strikingly reflect inequalities between classes. The basic determinant of social class under capitalism is the relationship to property, to *capital,* whether in land, stocks and shares or other investments, and whether inherited or newly accumulated. And property in the thirties was a great deal more unequally distributed than incomes. Of the twelve million families it was reckoned that eight million, even if they sold up everything they had, realized all their insurance and put all their savings on the table, would have had less than £100 – in other words, they had *no* capital.[3]

At the other end of the scale 5 per cent of the adult population owned 79 per cent of the wealth in private hands, and the richest 1 per cent owned 56 per cent.[4] This concentration of capital at the top had only changed a little in the previous twenty-five years (in 1911, 5 per cent owned 87 per cent of the wealth of which 1 per cent owned 69 per cent) in spite of the introduction of death duties.

* In terms of mid-sixties purchasing power, £2 10s was worth about £8 5s, and £4 (which 73·5 per cent were below) was worth about £13 4s. The *Family Expenditure Survey* of the Ministry of Labour in 1965 showed about 35 per cent below this level. Broadly speaking, Class C2 comprised the pensioners, the unemployed, most unskilled labourers and also many skilled working class such as some miners, cotton operatives, railwaymen, and so on. Class C1 comprised the great mass of skilled workers' families and many in less well paid distributive and clerical jobs. Class B included at the lower end the best paid or most highly skilled manual workers, most clerical workers and many in professional occupations.

Indeed such change as had taken place was caused largely by rich people distributing their capital among their relatives before they died, as a precaution against death duties.

The upper class (which included both the upper middle class and the aristocracy) could be distinguished from other classes by the fact that it was, by and large, the propertied class; it was here that ownership of capital was concentrated. Members of the upper classes who did not personally own capital for the most part belonged to families, or had relations, who had owned or did own capital; or they had the expectation that they might later inherit some; or they had connections which enabled them to marry into families which had some. This was the basic factor, but upon it had been built a whole style of life, a set of cultural habits which in turn assumed an importance of their own. So that although wealth was continually sought after, birth and 'breeding' were treated with, if anything, greater deference. Thus you could be the penniless younger son of a younger son, but if you came of 'good' family it could enable you to marry an heiress from among the newer rich, or get a top job in the Diplomatic Service if you were clever, or in the armed forces if you were not so clever. Conversely, families with great newly-acquired wealth could buy their way into upper-class circles, but would not necessarily be accepted there until they had acquired the veneer of upper-class behaviour, which could take a generation, and was usually managed by sending their sons to Eton or Harrow.

Although it was possible to be a member of the upper classes and yet be impecunious, by and large affluence could be equated with ownership of capital. In this sense the upper classes were much more distinct than they have been since the Second World War, when heavy taxation on unearned incomes, combined with payment of enormously high salaries to the top men running industry, has blurred the outlines of the property-owning class, making the high-salary earner often appear both more affluent and more influential than the big shareholder. In those days an unearned income was only subject to relatively light taxation; it was not necessary to arrange affairs so that one's income came in the form of expenses or other fringe benefits.

The aristocracy and their near relations (the 'cousinhood') remained very influential in social and political life. People who were in Society customarily kept two large houses going, one in town for the London 'season' and perhaps part of the winter, one in the country for other times in the year. Some also had a grouse-moor with a castle in Scotland. The stately homes were not in those days show places on view to the public at 5s a time, but were kept up at the owner's expense for his own use.

Not all the country houses belonged to old-established families, of course. Especially after the First World War, the makers of large business fortunes had added extra dignity to their wealth by a title ('for political and public services' including contributions to party funds) and by buying one or more country estates. Harold Macmillan has emphasized the extent to which social and political life revolved round the great private houses, particularly the great country houses (such as Cliveden, Hatfield and Blickling):

> We all lunched and dined a great deal together. Today this is much more difficult, and the restaurant or club has had to be substituted for the home. Or that abomination, the cocktail party, which allows of no real conversation, has necessarily become the substitute for the great evening assemblies ... In addition, the country houses – Hatfield, Cliveden and many others – were the almost weekly scene of gatherings of all kinds of people ... Indeed, there was nothing so agreeable as the country house party in a large English house. There were no rules except the necessity of appearing at dinner and a certain bias in favour of turning up at lunch. Otherwise, in a large company the groups organized themselves for golf, tennis, walking, talking, or quiet reading.[5]

And he recalls that the Duke of Devonshire's Christmas family party at Chatsworth commonly amounted, including servants, to a hundred and fifty people – each family of sons and daughters bringing their own maid, their own nurse and nursemaid, and many their own string of ponies and their own groom.

This pattern of social intercourse depended on the almost unlimited supply of low-paid domestic servants. The great houses all had great servant establishments, of course, but dependence on servants was not confined to the great houses or to the very rich;

the pattern repeated itself, albeit on a more modest scale, right throughout the upper middle class. You did not normally invite people to a meal at a restaurant, you invited them to lunch or dinner in your home, and the meal would be cooked and served by your domestic staff. You did not normally spend your holidays in hotels; you either owned or rented a house, and stayed there with a staff of servants to look after you while you invited other friends to stay. And if you were unattached, you could spend most of the summer getting yourself invited to stay at one house after another, owned or temporarily rented by your friends or relations.

Cheap domestic service was the foundation upon which this structure of social intercourse was based. The average young couple of the upper middle class would not consider marriage and setting up house without the minimum establishment of cook, housemaid and parlourmaid, and a nannie when the children came. Or if they did consider it because of straitened circumstances, they were objects of pity or of admiration for their 'courage' in the circles in which they moved.

Society seemed determined to ensure that the upper class married woman did nothing useful. Cooking, housework and babycare were largely taken out of her hands – indeed she commonly had less knowledge of housecraft than her grandmother had had, and much less than her daughter was one day to acquire. But equally she had no job or profession – had often not been educated or trained for one. There was a prejudice against married women working which was common to all classes. Women teachers and civil servants were compelled to retire on marriage (some indeed lived in sin for many years to avoid losing their jobs). So it was that the upper middle-class woman did neither professional nor household work. Instead of the 'two-job' problem there was the servant problem, which occupied the upper-class woman a great deal. There was no absolute shortage, but women complained that the girls available were 'independent', incompetent and wanted too much money. Meanwhile the numbers of domestic servants living in, which had dropped sharply during the First World War, rose steadily throughout the twenties and thirties, thanks to heavy unemployment in the industrial areas. They rose also in the hotels and catering trade. Nearly one quarter of all women in jobs were in private domestic service.

The crisis and the depression affected the standards of consumption and the way of life of the upper classes surprisingly little. True, profits fell in the slump years (by 30 per cent at the lowest point, in 1932), but since a higher proportion of profits was paid out in dividends, shareholders' incomes fell much less than this, while income from rent and fixed interest stocks remained more stable in spite of the fall in prices. Consumption was on the whole maintained, even if some of it had to be done by reducing investment or temporarily spending out of capital. Expansion of consumption was postponed somewhat – those with two cars already put off buying a third, perhaps, and so on down the line – but there was no visible sign of a turn to austerity.*

The London season was still in its full glory, including the ritual of the debutante's presentation at Court in white dress and ostrich feathers. A Society or County family with a marriageable daughter would still be expected to launch her with a 'coming-out' dance, to which other suitably chaperoned debutantes were invited, together with a list of eligible bachelors; this was preceded by dinner-parties given by the mothers of other 'debs', made up

* Figures in the British Association's *Britain in Recovery,* based on Colin Clark's estimates, suggest a fall of 9–11 per cent in consumption expenditure of those with incomes over £250, from 1929 to 1933 – which was almost certainly less than the fall in prices. 'On the whole we may, perhaps, conclude that consumption by the rich was comparatively well maintained during the depression and expanded during the recovery, although there are indications that this expansion was somewhat delayed' (G. D. A. Macdougall, *loc.cit*). Estimates of working-class consumption in this source are subject to the reservations noted in Chapter 6 on Wages, since they exclude short time and overtime, and rely on the cost of living index for prices.

Persons with incomes over £250

Indices (1929 = 100)

	1929	1930	1931	1932	1933	1934	1935
Spendable income (after tax)	100	86	74	69	79	84	92
Consumption expenditure	100	98	91	91	89	90	99

from the list of chosen guests. Each such dance cost several hundred pounds, apart from the cost of the dinner-parties, and the average deb went to at least three a week throughout the season, which lasted from May to July. The object of the season, so far as debs were concerned, was undoubtedly marriage, and girls still unengaged at the end of two or three seasons were sometimes given a trip to British India to find an eligible husband there. For the overseas Empire, if harder to control than it had been, still provided with the Army and the Civil Service 'a vast system of out-relief for the younger sons of the upper classes'.

Parallel with all this went the more sophisticated gatherings for the older members of Society, which was of course divided into every kind of clique and set – for instance, the Prince of Wales's set, and numerous political and diplomatic sets, as well as hunting and shooting sets. Day after day they met one another at lunch parties, dinner parties and evening gatherings in the great houses of Mayfair and Belgravia.

This was the setting for those violent contrasts between luxury and destitution which pervade the memoirs and literature of the period, and which to so many, on left and right alike, seemed to threaten revolution. Thus Tom Jones[6] records without comment in his diary in 1936 that he dined at Sir Abe Bailey's with thirty or forty others with a 'table loaded with gold plate. Waiters six feet high', and shortly after writes to Sir Harold Wernher, chairman of Electrolux and owner of the great house of Luton Hoo, about the girls who were being taken into domestic service from the distressed areas:

What we have found in some of the more remote mining villages is this: Girls of 17–20 who have never slept alone in a room, who have never known what it is to have ordinary bedclothes, and some who are unfamiliar with knives and forks – all of which seems incredible today. You can imagine the bewilderment of one of these young girls when transferred to a strange house in London.

And Harold Macmillan has recalled that 'very often the transition from a few days at Stockton among my poor unemployed, to the various degrees of comfort and wealth which we all either commanded or enjoyed left me with a growing sense of the great

Changes in Occupational Class
(Percentages)

	1921	1931	1951
Professional	4·53	4·60	6·63
Employers and managers	10·46	10·36	10·50
Clerical	6·72	6·97	10·68
Foremen and manual	78·29	78·07	72·19

(From tables based on census figures in *Occupation and Pay in Great Britain*, 1906–60, by G. Routh.)

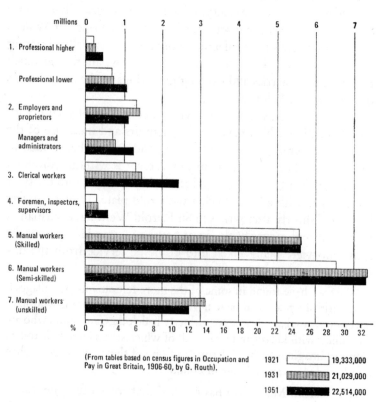

(From tables based on census figures in Occupation and
Pay in Great Britain, 1906-60, by G. Routh).

1921	19,333,000
1931	21,029,000
1951	22,514,000

Fig. 10 Numbers in each occupational class.

gulf'.[7] Shame and anger at such contrasts was felt at moments even by the most privileged and comfortably off, not only in the worst slump years but right through the thirties. It was one of the factors in the radical movement among the middle class so strikingly shown in the formation of the Left Book Club, whose writers, speakers and organizers came largely from comfortable professional backgrounds. Not a few, indeed, were rebels from the governing class itself, who rejected easy careers in a system they believed to be both immoral and doomed.

Others, however, reacted with stronger determination to have and to hold their great possessions. This led to a tolerance and even sympathy for fascism which may now seem hard to credit. Thus Harold Nicolson notes in 1938 a chance meeting at his club with 'three young peers who state that they would prefer to see Hitler in London than a Socialist administration'.[8] And Lord Halifax, member of the government in 1937, visited Germany at Goering's invitation and told Hitler that although there were things in the Nazi system that offended British opinion, 'I was not blind to what he had done for Germany and to the achievement from his point of view of keeping Communism out of his country'.[9]

11

Babies and the Birthrate

In 1933, the birthrate which had been falling steadily touched its lowest point in any peace-time year before or since. Thus the year of highest unemployment was also the year of fewest babies. Some people at the time saw a connection between the two – particularly as in the following year, when the depression lifted, there was also a slight shift upwards in the birthrate once more.

Yet the thesis that the falling birthrate was linked with the depression did not seem to be altogether borne out by the facts. It appeared, for instance, that the trend towards small families was much more definite in the relatively prosperous south of England than it was in the areas of heaviest unemployment in the North or Wales. And though all social classes seemed to be having fewer children, the tendency was most marked among those least directly affected by unemployment – the professional and salaried middle class.

Furthermore, it could be shown that though the birthrate always tended to fluctuate marginally with the trade cycle, the tendency towards ever smaller families had been a continuous process going on for the past sixty years, though it seemed to have accelerated since the First World War. The trend had nothing to do with the age of marriage, which had not changed much in the previous three decades. For women, the mean age of marriage in the early thirties was twenty-five and a half.

It was clear, however, that a new climate of opinion had grown up around the whole question of the role of women. The First World War and its aftermath had seen a revolution in ideas and attitudes in many walks of life. Among them were all the issues surrounding women's rights, from votes to birth control, which had been struggling up since the turn of the century, bursting into full daylight by the twenties.

For many of the young women of the thirties the ideological battle seemed largely over, much of it settled. The idea that you must have as many babies as God gave you was as much out of date as tight-laced stays or flannel petticoats. Those from working-class families had seen for themselves the drudgery involved in rearing a large family on an inadequate income, the additional skimping caused by every new mouth to feed. They had seen women of their parents' generation worn out with too many pregnancies, had heard them going on and on about their dropped wombs and varicose veins.

The younger generation were going to be different. They wanted a breathing space between pregnancies as doctors now suggested they ought. They wanted cosy little families where the children would be given a chance.

The instinct was particularly strong among young lower middle-class couples, many of whom had rather precariously become owner-occupiers along with a heavy mortgage and furniture on hire purchase. Giving their children a chance meant not only clothing them and feeding them, but paying for their education if they were to get beyond the elementary stage. And there was nothing to counter-balance the expense – no family allowances, for instance. Even the process of having the baby was a major expense with heavy doctors' or midwives' bills. And if a child fell ill there was no free doctor. So it was that the middle class had begun to set a fashion for small families in the twenties, and before the decade was out the working class was following suit. They would have said – and *did* say when they were asked – that they 'could not afford' to have more children.[1] Many of them were less poor than their parents had been. But in their view their parents hadn't really been able to afford children, they had had them without being able to afford them, and look at the results! Little by little the large family began to be looked on as a cause for pity rather than pride, except perhaps among the Irish Catholics, whose religion forbade them to interfere with nature.

The trend was helped by, but not wholly dependent on, the

growing availability of and knowledge about contraceptives. Until late in the thirties, however, these were in much more common use among the middle class than the working class, who relied less on the use of birth control appliances than on other methods of family limitation. As the wives put it, their husbands were 'being careful'.[2] And there were still great areas of ignorance about birth control, so that working women's organizations such as Coop Guilds and Labour Women's Sections were in many areas busy crusading to bring knowledge of it to the younger women as one of the means towards female emancipation. In the end, women who got married in the thirties were to have on average fewer babies than either their predecessors or their successors.

The fall in the birth rate caused alarm among sociologists and ultimately in governing circles. For one thing, intelligence-testing (still in its infancy) was held to have revealed that the children of the lower social classes were on average less intelligent than the children of the higher social classes. Since the poor were still having larger families than, for instance, the professional classes – the poorest and most backward having the largest families of all – it was argued by some experts that this must result in a lowering of the national intelligence over a generation. The theory was hotly contested by other experts, but meanwhile became rather submerged by the even more alarming discovery that not enough babies of any class were being born to ensure that the nation reproduced itself. The experts were pointing out that if the trend continued the number of deaths per year would soon exceed the number of births and the population would then begin to fall. At forty-six million for the UK in 1931 it was predicted that it would fall below forty million by 1961 and within a hundred years would have dwindled to about five million. Within each decade the proportion of old people would rise and the proportion of young would fall. Thus the menace of under-population replaced earlier Malthusian theories of the menace of over-population. Discussion was not confined to the experts; it found its way into newspapers and radio programmes and one of the leading experts, Dr Enid Charles wrote a book for the lay public entitled *The Twilight of Parenthood* (1934) which had considerable impact.

At the top, characteristically, it was the threat to the future of the Empire that was posed by a fall in the home birthrate which appeared to be causing the most alarm. Announcing a marginal increase in the income tax relief for children* in 1935, Neville Chamberlain, then Chancellor of the Exchequer, observed:

> I must say that I look upon the continued diminution of the birthrate in this country with considerable apprehension . . . the time may not be far distant . . . when . . . the countries of the British Empire will be crying out for more citizens of the right breed, and when we in this country shall not be able to supply the demand.[3]

And the first full-scale debate on the question in the Commons in February 1937 took place around a resolution which spoke of the 'danger to the maintenance of the British Empire' as well as to the 'economic well-being of the nation'.[4]

In spite of all the alarm officially expressed, increases in tax relief which applied only to a small minority were almost the only thing done to encourage couples to have more children. Miss Eleanor Rathbone, MP, Mrs Eva Hubback and their band of supporters organized around the Children's Minimum Council carried on a persistent campaign for family allowances – a campaign which was not, however, supported by the labour movement, which was sharply divided on the issue, the TUC having decided against family allowances on the grounds that they would encourage employers to pay wages only adequate for a single man. Certainly in the economic climate of the time anything like family allowances seemed Utopian. Yet only a few years later, after the war had broken out, a large number of official measures designed to prove that society valued children were suddenly in being or in the pipe-line. They included family allowances, free milk for expectant and nursing mothers, free milk in schools, free secondary education, and free medical service.

The thirties may well stand out as the decade in which most was said about babies and least was done. Perhaps, as in some other

---

* It raised the allowance for the second and subsequent child from £40 to £50. Since tax was 4s 6d in the pound the value of this concession was £2 5s a year for taxpayers on the standard rate, then numbering not more than three million people.

spheres, those in charge saw their way forward in terms of reverting backwards; the solution was for women to return to the child-bearing habits of the Victorian era, and throughout the public discussion there was often to be detected an implied reproach that they did not do so. Yet paradoxically the young couples of the day seemed to be exercising those very virtues enjoined upon them in the Victorian era – prudence and restraint.

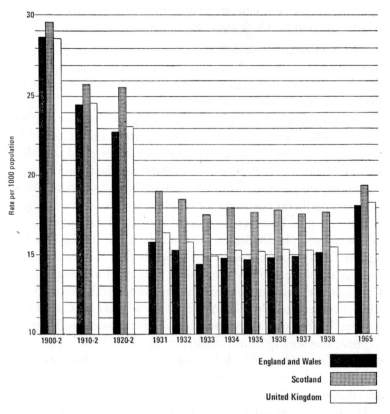

Fig. 11 Births per thousand of the population.

Educational Pyramid

Parents who wanted their children to get on in life knew that the kind of education they received could make or mar their chances in the future. In both the lower middle class and the working class were to be found plenty of parents who wanted their children to better themselves, who longed to see their sons established more securely than they were. Miners dreamed of rearing sons who would not be obliged to go down the pit. A scholarship to the local secondary school could lead to a different kind of job altogether – perhaps even to teaching. Precariously placed people in black-coated employment knew that if their sons were to obtain secure and stable jobs with prospects of promotion they must be given a secondary education, even if it meant paying fees. Established middle-class people knew that their sons must go to a fee-paying school where they would mix with their own kind. Education for them was not seen just as a way of obtaining qualifications, but equally as a method of ensuring the right social background and making the right friends in preparation for adult life. The newly rich who still felt uneasy when they mixed in high society knew that their sons could escape such uneasiness if they sent them to Eton.

Society was still stratified into layers divided by rigid class barriers. The education system helped to perpetuate the stratification, but it also offered to a few a way of jumping over the barriers and moving up one. At all levels education was considered to be much more important for boys than for girls, whose main chance of bettering themselves was by making a good marriage.

The quality of the education received depended on the ability to pay fees. Even within the state system fees had to be paid for a secondary school education except for children who won scholarships.

Children from families at the top of the social pyramid were educated outside the state system in independent fee-paying schools of one kind or another, the most influential of which were the great public boarding schools for boys, headed by Eton, Harrow and Winchester, which took boys from the age of about thirteen up to eighteen. Leading up to them were the preparatory boarding schools for boys aged about eight to twelve. The public schools were stepping stones to Oxford or Cambridge University, or to Sandhurst if an army career was chosen. For the Navy, the usual road was Osborne prep. school followed by Dartmouth Royal Naval College. The public schools were regarded as training grounds for 'leaders of the nation'. Most generals, admirals, bishops, ambassadors, Conservative politicians, top civil servants, big industrialists and bankers had a public school background. 'When the call came for me to form a government', said Stanley Baldwin in a Harrow speech-day address which the left-wing never allowed anyone to forget, 'one of my first thoughts was that it should be a government of which Harrow should not be ashamed. I remembered how in previous governments there had been four, or perhaps five, Harrovians, and I determined to have six.' The annual fees at Eton and Harrow were over £240 a year – a good deal more than the average industrial wage of the period – and competition to get into such schools was less keen than it later became.

Apart from the well-known public schools, which offered quite exceptional educational facilities, there was in the private sector a considerable number of lesser fee-paying day and boarding schools in which the education varied from the intensive to the incompetent. Some of them were not very reputable. Then there was a cluster of pioneer schools experimenting in new methods of education, which were favoured by liberal or left-wing intellectual parents. Mostly founded in the twenties, they included Dartington Hall, A. S. Neill's school, Bertrand Russell's school and so on. The education theories which were being explored by these experimental schools derived from new discoveries in psychology, which had begun after the First World War to influence and change attitudes over the whole field of human relations, and in particular attitudes to the upbringing of children. The pioneer schools believed in free expression rather than regimentation, and the cultivation of the natural curiosity and interest of the child in the world around it, rather than the stereotyped methods of instruction from above which made learning a bore.

Of all children, however, 95 per cent were educated through the state system. Within this system the state-aided or maintained secondary schools (in later decades all known as grammar schools) formed an élite. They provided an intensive course for children aged about eleven to eighteen. Not more than 14 per cent of eleven-year-olds got to secondary school, and of these only half (7 per cent of the age group) went there free having won a free place in a scholarship exam at the age of ten or eleven. The other secondary school pupils were fee paying and came largely from lower middle class or 'blackcoated' sections. The free place at a secondary school was virtually the only opportunity of serious schooling leading to a qualification offered to the children of manual workers. But competition for free places was less keen than the competition over the eleven-plus in the fifties. For one thing, professional parents could get their child a place by payment of a small fee; for another, many manual workers wanted their children to leave school and start earning as soon as possible. Moreover, some had reservations about letting their child go to a school where there would be extra expense – for instance for a uniform – and where he might be made to feel inferior among the children of parents better off than his own.

The state secondary school curriculum was strongly biased towards arts, and towards classics in particular; more pupils learnt Latin than learnt physics. Though French was taken by almost all, few studied a second modern language. The more imaginative and project-centred type of education already officially favoured for the junior schools was not as yet approved by the authorities for the secondary stage, where concentration on the traditional subject disciplines was held to be essential. The core of a good grammar school education was supposed to be the English subjects (including religious knowledge). The officially recommended aim of English teaching in the earlier years was to teach clear simple expression, and accurate grammar and spelling. 'Power of invention, facility, attempts at style, ornament, these are for the moment irrelevant.' The pupil who survived some years of training in compositions 'restricted in length, concrete in subject and, in general, objective in treatment' could be allowed to attempt 'more ambitious forms of expression'[1] – an almost exact reversal of the modern view that practice in free personal and imaginative expression at first leads to successful impersonal writing later. Indeed the demands of employers for well-trained office workers dominated secondary school thinking to a much greater degree than they do today, even though many dedicated teachers and enlightened schools contrived to give a much more imaginative and child-centred education.

The majority of secondary school leavers went into professional, commercial or clerical work in the Civil Service and local government. Roughly 4 per cent went into teacher training, and around 10 per cent to other types of higher education – usually secretarial or technical colleges. Though the state secondary schools reckoned to train a few pupils for university entrance, the numbers were small – only 5·8 per cent of secondary school leavers in England and Wales went on to university in 1932–3, a percentage which was to fall to 4·2 in 1936–7 as a result of the economies.

It was the fee-paying schools in the private sector, and above all the boys' public schools, which provided the main gateway into the universities. The body of full-time university students was small – only fifty thousand by the end of the decade.* Of these, about one-fifth had come up the hard way from a state elementary school to a free place at a secondary school. They were the highfliers whom nothing could stop, but they represented no more than one in two hundred of former elementary school children. At university they found themselves swamped by students from public and independent schools whose families paid for their tuition and upkeep. Even the scholarships which were awarded by some of the older foundations tended to be won by boys from

* Less than one-third of the number in the mid-sixties.

public schools – many indeed were confined to pupils of particular public schools.

The universities were largely independent of government funds – in 1938-9, for instance, they received only 36 per cent of their cost from the Treasury.* They got the bulk of their income from students' fees and from endowments by wealthy benefactors (notable benefactors of the period being Boots at Nottingham and Nuffield at Oxford, as well as the American Carnegie Foundation). They were overwhelmingly dominated by the arts faculties (which had twice as many senior staff as the science faculties), and especially by the classics departments which attracted a high proportion of the ablest students, partly because a classics degree was supposed to be the best recommendation for the Higher Civil Service.

The Base of the Pyramid

For the great mass of ordinary children who started their schooling at five years old or sometimes earlier in a state elementary school, the educational ladder was too steep to get into a secondary school, let alone go further. Elementary schools were of two kinds – either council or 'voluntary', which latter term usually meant either Church of England or Roman Catholic. The voluntary schools, though their current expenditure was paid for out of rates and taxes like that of the council schools, were often older and provided if anything rather worse conditions than the others.

A five-year-old starting at an elementary school in the country might find himself alongside children much older than himself in the same single classroom. If he started in a town he would often be one of a class of fifty or more five-year-olds. The official standard aimed at not more than fifty in a class for children under eleven. This standard was not universally achieved – in 1932 there were still nearly eight thousand classes with over fifty children.

Such conditions made almost impossible the application of the new educational ideas of the period. Two official reports on

* As against some 75 per cent in the mid-sixties.

teaching of younger children[2] had called for the widest use of activity methods and teaching based on 'projects' and centres of interest involving several subjects, placing stress on activity and experience rather than on knowledge to be acquired and facts to be stored. And there was some brave pioneer work going on, such as that of Marion Richardson which was giving art education a new importance in the teaching of young children. But the over-crowded and impoverished state of the schools meant that the new theories could make only slow headway.

At the age of ten or eleven elementary school pupils could, as we have seen, sit for a scholarship examination which enabled some to qualify for a 'free place' at a secondary school. At the same time some others whose parents were more fortunately placed moved on to secondary school as paying pupils. But 90 per cent of elementary school children stayed on within the elementary school system until they left school altogether at the age of fourteen.

In 1926 a government report, the Hadow Report, had advocated the division of the elementary school system into primary schools for children up to eleven and 'Modern' schools for those over that age who did not get into secondary schools. The 'Modern' schools, it was thought, should have a more practical bias than the secondary schools, but should be equal to the latter in status, staffing and equipment. Reorganization had then begun, and by 1931 about 28 per cent of the older elementary school children had been transfered to 'senior' schools as they were called (Hadow's term 'Modern' never came into use). But in practice the senior schools offered standards which were much inferior to those of the secondary schools.

The most crucial question of all was that of the school-leaving age. Hadow had advocated raising it from fourteen to fifteen. The previous Labour government had introduced a Bill for this purpose in 1930, but the Bill had been partially wrecked in the Commons over the issue of the Church Schools, and was finally thrown out by the House of Lords in February 1931.

This débâcle was followed in July 1931 by a cold blast from the May Committee, which stressed the fact that expenditure had trebled since 1913, and in particular that free places in secondary schools had doubled since the war:

> We fear that a tendency has developed to regard expenditure on education as good in itself without much consideration of the results that are being obtained from it and of the limits to which it can be carried without danger to other, no less vital, national interests.
>
> Since the standard of education, elementary and secondary, that is being given to the child of poor parents is already in very many cases superior to that which the middle-class parent is providing for his own child, we feel it is time to pause in this policy of expansion, to consolidate the ground gained, to endeavour to reduce the cost of holding it, and to reorganize the existing machine before making a fresh general advance.[3]

The prevailing view in the governing class was, indeed, that education beyond the elementary stage was unnecessary for the average working-class child, provided the gifted few could be given a chance. For the rest it was a luxury which the poor could do without, but for which the middle class would naturally be prepared to pay. But the May Committee statement also reflected the resentment and mistrust which the expansion of state services in the twenties had created in the minds of the more conservative lower middle class – those, for instance, who read the *Daily Mail*. Now the process was to be halted – even put into reverse for a few years.

The Economy Years

The cut in government expenditure on education announced in the emergency budget in September 1931 was a massive one – from a financial point of view it came second only to the cuts in unemployment pay. There was firstly a reduction of 15 per cent in teachers' salaries, which was subsequently modified, as we have seen, to 10 per cent. Secondly there was a reorganization of the educational grants to local authorities so that the Exchequer should bear a smaller proportion of the total costs – the increased burden on the rates as a result was a severe discouragement to any local authority disposed to offer resistance to the economy drive.

Almost at once after the 1931 crisis, newly qualified teachers, who had been officially encouraged to enter training colleges in expectation of the raising of the school-leaving age, began to find it difficult to obtain posts. By December 1932 there were one thousand one hundred newly qualified teachers unemployed, and some unemployment among teachers was to persist throughout the subsequent years.

All over the country school-building schemes were deferred – indeed total capital expenditure in England and Wales sank from £9·2 million in 1930–1 to £2·7 million in 1933–4. About one-third of elementary school children were in school buildings which were less than twenty-five years old, and the best of these, which incorporated the new ideas and standards of the period, seemed full of light and sunshine with large windows, cheerful decorations, reasonable sanitation, and adequate water supply. Some were even equipped with dining halls and gymnasia, and with large rooms for practical work and sufficient class spaces to allow for flexible grouping of children. They were in marked contrast to the older schools where the majority of the children were taught.

Many of the council schools were grim Victorian fortresses dating from the nineties, while the church schools might have been built at any time from 1830 onwards. In the crowded urban areas classrooms had been formed out of the partitioned segments of great rooms intended for the mass instruction of a hundred or more children at a time. They were ill-lit, badly ventilated, with sanitary accommodation which was barbarous. There were no gymnasia or facilities for practical work. Among other things the building cuts meant prolonging the life of some really unhealthy schools – 1,500 elementary schools were still on a 'black list' which had been compiled in 1924.

The most significant of the educational economies was the abolition of 'free places' in the secondary schools in favour of 'special places'. The secondary schools – some council-owned and some voluntary – had been entitled to be partly maintained by grants from the Board of Education and the local authority pro-vided they made available a minimum of 25 per cent 'free places' for children drawn from elementary schools who had qualified in the competitive examinations at ten or eleven. Many of them allocated far more free places than the statutory 25 per cent, and some councils had developed 100 per cent free secondary schools. For instance, Durham County Council had twenty free schools, Manchester had eight, and there were twenty-eight such schools in Wales. The fees paid in the other schools, which varied from three guineas to thirty guineas a year, on average covered not more than about one-third of the cost of educating the child.

In the autumn of 1932 the Board of Education took action. In a circular which stated that 'the system of admitting pupils free to secondary schools without any regard to the capacity of parents to pay is needlessly wasteful of public funds', it was announced that what had previously been 'free places' must be turned into 'special places' for which parents must pay fees – they would only be wholly or partially exempted from fees if they could show need under scales approved by the Board. Meanwhile fees charged to paying pupils were to be raised, so that those who could afford to would pay more.

This circular aroused far more passion than any of the other economies. Within a few weeks of its issue the Board received one thousand six hundred resolutions from meetings of protest. But the government remained adamant.

The effect of the new rules was perhaps not quite what had been foreseen, for they hit hardest the lower middle-class parents whose fees went up. For manual workers the results were curiously marginal. Of those admitted to secondary school, the proportion of non-fee-paying pupils fell from 48·7 per cent in 1932 to 44·4 per cent in 1934. The fact that the proportion fell no more than this reflects the unwillingness of many of the local education committees to operate the new rules rigorously. Accordingly they fixed their income exemption limits high, so that most working-class families came well beneath them and qualified for exemption from fees.

More significant than its actual effects was the philosophy behind the move. This was no mere temporary economy measure; this was something that put the clock back, and those authorities who had been looking forward to a gradual expansion of free secondary education, available to all who could benefit from it, saw the whole process beginning to go into reverse. They had to wait until 1944 to see free secondary education for all accepted as a principle.

1936 and the School Leaving Age

In July 1935 the teachers' pay cut was finally restored. The recession was officially over and with it, officially, the financial emergency. The Conservative Party went into the 1935 election promising social reform. Back in office they produced a new Education Bill to raise the school-leaving age from fourteen to fifteen. But the Bill was very different from the one which had been thrown out by the House of Lords just five years previously, for it permitted children to be exempted from staying on at school after the age of fourteen if they could secure 'beneficial' employment. Unlike the 1930 Bill, the new one contained no arrangement for maintenance allowances for children staying on at school after fourteen.

The Bill caused dismay in the educational world, where it was thought that the great majority of fourteen-year-olds would obtain exemption. It was well-known that many of the poorer families looked forward to the moment when a fourteen-year-old could leave school and start earning, for though general unemployment was still around the two million mark, youngsters often had much less difficulty than their fathers in getting work. In the absence of any family allowances most local authorities already found themselves obliged to provide maintenance allowances on a means test basis for the winners of special places in secondary schools, to enable them to stay on after the statutory age of fourteen.

A compulsory raising of the school-leaving age without maintenance allowances would under the circumstances have aroused much opposition. Unwilling to face the expense of maintenance allowances, the government decided to provide for exemptions.

Expense was the overriding consideration. But there was also pressure from certain groups of employers who did not want to be deprived of cheap juvenile labour. Annesley Somerville, MP, himself a former assistant master at Eton, voiced the opinion of farmers in his constituency when he said:

> Education is not merely book learning. Education is the result of every influence that is brought to bear upon the child. It is better to have a boy on the land learning farm work, having a number of land influences bearing on him, getting a love of the land – all making him more likely to stay on the land, as we want boys in the country to do. In many cases it is very much better that the boy should be working on the land than be in school.[4]

The Duchess of Atholl, Conservative MP for Kinross and Perth, shocked and embarrassed some government supporters when she maintained repeatedly that exemptions were necessary because certain employers in the Yorkshire textile industry needed 'small hands' to work their machines:

> I do say that in regard to certain processes which require small fingers, there ought to be kept open a loophole provided it is certain that the children will work under beneficial conditions. Otherwise, we shall be placing a very serious handicap on one of our most important export industries.[5]

The Duchess was no political lightweight; she had been chairman of the Juvenile Advisory Committee to the Board of Education for the previous ten years.

The Bill became an Act, but its operation was to be delayed for three and a half years on the grounds that the extra school buildings and teachers which would be needed could not be ready earlier. So the chickens hatched during the recession came home to roost.

Thereafter school building once more took an upward turn. But when the war broke out there were still 753 schools remaining on the old original black list. Of the older children 50 per cent were still in unreorganized all-age schools. The number of classes with over fifty children had fallen to 2,000 but nearly two million children were in classes of over forty.

No one was ever to know how the exemptions for beneficial

employment would have worked in practice, for the date on which the act became operative was the day of the invasion of Poland by Germany, 1 September 1939. Two days later Britain was at war, and the schools in London and other target areas had all been evacuated. The operation of the Act was suspended and children went on leaving school at fourteen for the duration of the war.

The Fourteen- to Eighteen-year-olds

The majority of fourteen-year-olds went straight to work on leaving school, having done with education. Serious-minded parents would persuade their children to attend evening classes. This was not easy for youngsters with little leisure – a five-and-a-half-day week was the universal minimum at work.

Even at the height of the slump there was in most districts a demand for juvenile labour, in particular a demand for workers under sixteen. Employers took children on for a few years at low juvenile rates and got rid of them when the juvenile rate no longer applied. After this they would be looking for jobs at adult wages, having failed to acquire any particular skill or training in the intervening years.

Parents made great efforts to get their children into 'safe' jobs where this would not happen – the railways, the post office, gas and electricity. Skilled craftsmen tried to get apprenticeships for their sons but often found that the path which they had trodden themselves was now closed. For the growing mechanization in industry of so many processes formerly done by hand was giving rise to an increasing demand for youth labour on unskilled, purely repetitive work. The distributive trades on the other hand were involved in a remarkable expansion and it was here that over a quarter of young boys and girls found jobs.

Most school leavers were children barely on the threshold of adolescence. In stature and physical maturity they resembled the twelve- or thirteen-year-olds of the sixties. They were still growing, and much of their intellectual development lay ahead.

Abruptly thrust into a demanding adult industrial world, working long hours, subject perhaps to speed-up, they needed to be tough and self-reliant to hold their own. These qualities they rapidly developed. But in other respects their horizons were limited, their lives rather bare, their opportunities for enjoyment meagre. The sort of discussion about teenagers' problems, teenagers' needs, teenagers' demands and tastes which has been such a feature of the post-war decades was quite unknown. Unknown also was the concentration of advertising and selling techniques on teenagers as a group; inevitably so, since the money they earned was small and often virtually absorbed by the demands of the family budget. So there were no special teenage fashions in clothes or cosmetics, no teenage magazines to speak of, few teenage activities or entertainments laid on. It was not the custom to interview teenagers on the radio or to solicit their opinions and explore their attitudes to their work or to their parents. Indeed the word 'teenager' didn't exist.

The worlds of culture, entertainment, sport and recreation revolved round the eighteen- to twenty-five-year-olds. That those days was the best time of your life when, provided you weren't unemployed, you had money to spend but as yet no family responsibilities. Consumer advertising was also directed towards these age groups.

The school leavers were on the way to this envied state but hadn't yet arrived. They were the category most in demand by employers but they were also the most neglected by the rest of the world, and the least noticed. Soon they were going to be in front of the world's footlights – at Alamein and Arnhem. Just now they were like unseen players watching their elders from the wings.

13

Homes, Landlords and Building Societies

At the time when the 1931 National government took office there was a very severe housing shortage. The census had just revealed that though there were 11½ million families in Great Britain there were only 10½ million dwellings, which meant that a great many families were sharing a house.

The numerical shortage seemed even worse because room space was very unequally distributed. In England and Wales about 3·2 million people (8·5 per cent of the population) had ample space with more than two rooms per head. At the other end of the scale 4·5 million people (12 per cent of the population) were crowded together with two or more persons to a room. In Scotland the overcrowding was much worse – 35 per cent of the population lived *more* than two persons to a room.

Probably less than one house in five was owner-occupied. The private landlords, ranging from comparatively humble individuals to great property companies, dominated the scene. Between seven and eight million families rented their houses, or their bits of houses, or their rooms from a private landlord. Council house building had begun in a big way during the twenties, but as yet council tenants numbered only about seven hundred thousand altogether.

Most people lived in old houses. These included the spacious and dignified houses of Mayfair and Belgravia, which had hardly begun to be taken over for commercial uses, and the large country houses. On the next and more modest rung came a host of pre-1914 houses occupied by middle-class people. These included some very good expensive houses modernized according to the highest standards of the day. Many more, however, had not been modernized. They were mostly of Victorian origin, and since they had originally been designed from attic to basement on the assumption that there would be plenty of maids, the standard of comfort in them depended on the size of domestic staff which the family could afford. The houses might be reasonably spacious and soundly built, but they were draughty and the open fires required endless coal-carrying in order to achieve a rather inadequate standard of warmth in winter. Running water in bedrooms was unusual, and the customary washstand with jug and basin required a maid to carry the hot water up and the slops down. The bathrooms were, by later standards, barbaric, and stoking the boiler in the basement to supply hot water was heavy work. There was often not enough hot water to go round.

Middle-class people who wanted a change from this sort of environment had certain choices open to them. In London and some other cities, new flats to let, ranging from the luxurious to the smart but cramped, were beginning to be available. Much more numerous were the new houses which had been built for sale in the twenties. There were already a million of these. For the most part much smaller than the pre-war houses, they were to an increasing extent designed for the lower middle-class housewife who did not have resident servants, though she might have a daily help, and who wanted something labour-saving. They were usually two-storey houses without basements and with few stairs. They were compact, with modern plumbing and tiled bathrooms, well-equipped kitchens with small independent boilers, gas and electric water heaters at the sink, up-to-date cookers. Many were semi-detached villas, sprawling out on the fringes of towns, creating new suburbs which were soon to be outflanked by still newer suburbs. A large proportion had been built by speculative builders and were being bought through building societies. The more expensive of them cost around £2,000, but smaller and cheaper ones costing as little as £600 were rapidly becoming available in 1931. At that price they were largely confined to the lower middle class; only the exceptionally highly paid worker at £5 a week or more could contemplate buying such a house on mortgage, particularly since it normally required an initial down payment of £125 or more.

For most working-class families the only hope of a new house was a council house. The new council houses built since the war offered standards which were considered revolutionary for working people. They had bathrooms, which the majority of pre-war working-class houses lacked. The normal three-bedroom two-storey house had a 760 sq. ft. floor space. This meant that one of the bedrooms was only 65 sq. ft. Less than twenty years later this standard was criticized as being too small, and indeed since the furniture of families who moved in was often of the massive type designed for much larger rooms, people found themselves very cramped. Normally there was a coal cooking range in the only living-room, so that the whole family lived and ate in it. The small scullery at the back would have a sink and draining board and a copper for washing clothes. The copper would also be used for heating water for the bath, which would be on the ground floor. By 1931 gas and electric cookers had begun to be installed in these sculleries.

Superior as the standards offered by such houses were, many had an overwhelming drawback as we have seen in Chapter 5. They were built on the outskirts of towns, not only far from the workplaces of the breadwinners, but also far from shops, pubs and other amenities. So while the family income was depleted by money spent on fares, the men-folk spent long hours travelling, and the women-folk suffered from a terrible isolation. They longed for, and sometimes drifted back to, the cheaper and more matey surroundings from which they had come.

The vast majority of working-class families of course did not live like this at all. They either rented small single family houses which had been built for working-class people by private enterprise at any time during the previous century, or they filtered up into large old houses that had seen better days. The best of the working-class houses were sound, bnt they were cramped, dark and most had no bathrooms. They were built in long dreary rows, with small back yards. Many of them were still gas-lit.

The worst houses were damp insanitary slums. The typical

London slum was a two-storey four-bedroomed terrace-type house with a lean-to wash-house. The fabric of the house would be porous, the roof leaking, the wall plaster perished, the ceiling sagging. A defective water closet would be in the yard, so would the only tap. Another common type was the large house, consisting perhaps of three storeys and a basement, built originally for a single family, but now taken over by at least one family to a floor and sometimes one family to a room. There would be one water-closet for the whole house, one tap in the yard, and decay would be far advanced.

Some towns in the north had even more intense problems. Leeds had scores of thousands of 'back-to-back' houses built at seventy or eighty to the acre, damp, decayed, badly ventilated, dark, with one outside lavatory to every three or four houses. Birmingham too, had 40,000 'back-to-backs'. Liverpool had probably the worst slums in England; here there were people living in cellars and courts whose building had been prohibited in 1854. In Liverpool 20,000 people were living more than three to a room. In Glasgow, where the slums were far worse than the worst in England, nearly 200,000 were living more than three to a room.

Bedbug infestation was a major horror of slum life, and indeed not only in slums but in many other quite well-built houses. The bedbug lived on human blood, but it lodged not only in bedding, but in furniture, in cracks in walls and ceilings and behind the wallpaper. Self-respecting people did not talk about it much, possibly because it was frequently suggested that the best defence against the bug was cleanliness, and to have bugs could be taken as a reflection on housekeeping standards. The truth was that once it had entered the fabric of the house no amount of scrubbing and scouring could dislodge it, and no quantity of floor polish could disguise its smell. Local sanitary inspectors fought a losing battle keeping it in check with fumigation. When the tide finally turned after the Second World War and the bedbug was on the way out, it was not primarily scrubbing and scouring that did it, but the discovery of DDT and other new insecticides. In the early thirties all this was still far ahead.

This, then, was the situation when the National government

was elected in 1931 – an acute shortage of working-class houses with some shocking slum conditions; much less of a shortage of middle-class houses thanks to the volume of speculative building since the war. Local authorities, however, had some big programmes in the pipe-line for building subsidized houses for general needs under the 1924 Wheatley Act, and were beginning to plan programmes for slum clearance under the 1930 Greenwood Act.

The Private Building Boom

At the end of 1932 the government dropped a bombshell in the form of a Bill to abolish all subsidies for council building in England and Wales except those for slum clearance under the Greenwood Act. In other words, all municipal housing designed to relieve the *numerical shortage* of working-class houses was to be stopped. The Scottish subsidies were not to be abolished but to be drastically reduced.

Sir Hilton Young, Minister of Health, who introduced the Bill on 15 December 1932, did not argue that the shortage of working-class houses was over; he argued that the way to overcome the shortage was to abolish the subsidies. The demand for larger houses was almost saturated, he said, and private enterprise was thus seeking a new outlet. Prices had fallen and so had interest rates – why then had private enterprise not provided the smaller houses so badly needed? The answer was that private enterprise could not compete with subsidized municipal housing. 'If you wish to provide the supply of houses that we need, the most obvious course is the withdrawal of the subsidy.'

He told the House that he had been in close consultation in the preparation of the Bill with the National Federation of House-builders:

They say, to summarize their statements, that on the withdrawal of subsidies houses will, in their opinion, be built in very large numbers to supply the whole of the demand shown by the waiting lists of the local authorities, and that this building will continue until there is a margin of vacant houses comparable to that which existed before the war. I submit that it is impossible to neglect the weight of testimony of that sort, coming from the fountain, as it were, of knowledge on the subject.[1]

These smaller houses would, it was hoped, be houses to let, not for sale. For it was admitted that only a minority of the best paid workers could contemplate buying a house however low prices fell.

So the decks were cleared for what was to become the biggest private building boom in British history. The output of privately built houses went up to 293,000 in 1934–5, and continued at a high annual rate right up to the outbreak of war. There was one thing wrong with the calculation however – the great majority of the houses were built for sale, and of those that were built to let, most of them in the late thirties, the majority were at rents that only middle-class people could afford.

Small houses for sale, bought with a building society mortgage, dominated the building boom. The building society movement, which had always had official blessing, was publicized and elevated into a sort of crusade for good against evil. The Prince of Wales appeared at an international building societies' congress in London in June 1933, and eminent persons spoke of the contribution that the movement could make to political stability at a time of great unemployment and unrest. Thus the *Daily Telegraph* in a leading article entitled 'Building Societies: Their Record of Social Service' observed:

Before the war it was unusual for the middle-class man to be the owner of his home. Today the number of householders whose good fortune it is to be in so enviable a position grows consistently and rapidly. It would be difficult to exaggerate the influence of this silent revolution on the habits and outlook of the population. Viscount Cecil says truly that the ownership of property cultivates prudence. Clearly it encourages thrift, fosters the sense of security and self-dependence, and sensibly deepens citizens' consciousness of having a 'stake in the country', and the influence is surely one which, spreading from the individual to the community and linking up all classes, must contribute appreciably to national stability.[2]

The speculative builders who depended on the building societies to finance their sales were riding on the crest of a wave which spread out over the countryside engulfing rich farming land and ancient villages, creating new problems to confront future generations. True, the 1932 Town Planning Act gave a nominal power to local authorities to control the location of the new houses and the layout of new estates. In practice, the compensation that had to be paid to any landowner who was refused permission to build as he liked was heavy enough to deter local authorities from using their powers effectively. All over everywhere little brick houses were erupting like pimples, chaotically thrown up, often without adequate transport, without shops, pubs or any of the amenities that make life worth living. Nearly always far from the offices or workplaces of the new occupiers, they sprawled out along the approach roads to every big town. The Restriction of Ribbon Development Act of 1935 did little to curb the flow, and anyhow did it too late. The problem of long journeys to work, born in the twenties, began to grow into a monster.

A third of the houses produced in 1931 cost less than £600 each – by 1939 nearly half the houses built cost less than this. Houses began to be offered at £500 and even £400. Building societies financed most of the sales; they lent the new owner-occupiers the money at 5½ per cent repayable over twenty years. By 1934 the prevailing mortgage rate had fallen to 4½ per cent.

Initially the building societies were advancing 75 per cent of the purchase price. This meant that on a £500 house a cash deposit of £125 was still required. With a struggle many middle-class and salaried people could manage this, but it was far beyond the means of industrial workers, and indeed most clerical workers. The builders were, however, striving to attract customers further down the social scale, since the market for middle-class houses was drying up, and to this end arrangements were increasingly developed between the building societies and the builders for the latter to provide collateral security. Under these arrangements the builder himself guaranteed part of the purchase price and deposited some of it in cash in a 'builder's pool' from which the society could recoup itself in the event of loss. In return for this guarantee, the building society was able to advance not 75 per cent but up to 95 per cent of the purchase price to the prospective owner-occupier, so that a £500 house could be bought for only £25 deposit. These builders' pool arrangements enabled not only clerical workers but better paid industrial workers (i.e. those earning £4 a week or more) to begin buying their own houses in quite considerable numbers, since a £480 house involved only £24 downpayment, plus 13s 6d a week mortgage repayment over twenty years. To this figure, rates had to be added of course, and repairs.

These builders' pool arrangements were an added financial strain for the builders, and probably helped to encourage the jerry-building about which complaints were increasing. The builders were already cutting corners in order to build an ever-cheaper house; if in order to find customers they were obliged to guarantee 20 per cent of the purchase price and deposit some of this in cash, there was an incentive to cut them even closer. And anyhow there were plenty of rogues among the builders and little control over what they were up to. So a year or two after moving in, the new occupiers, already under a financial strain from mortgage payments they could barely afford, might find themselves facing heavy repairs bills for serious structural defects.

It was this sort of situation that led to the celebrated Borders Case. Mrs Elsy Borders was sued by the Bradford Third Equitable Building Society who claimed possession of her house at West Wickham, Kent, on the grounds that she was more than three months in arrears with her mortgage payments – the mortgage being for a sum of £693. Mrs Borders' defence was that the Building Society had 'wilfully and fraudulently' misled her into believing that the house was built in compliance with the local authority's byelaws, of good materials and in an efficient manner. Instead of which the walls of the house were extremely damp; the roof leaked; the floor boards were warped and shrunk and the windows would not open; the woodwork was infested with a small beetle; the glass in the front door had collapsed and had had to be boarded up; the electric wires were misplaced, so that shocks could be received if a hand was put on the floor; there were serious cracks in the walls, and the plaster round the doors and windows continually fell out. She argued that the Building Society had infringed its rules by lending money on a totally insufficient security; she therefore counter-claimed for the return of £121 paid already by her in instalments, for £500 for the repair of the property and for £200 for loss and damage caused by the condition of the house. It was revealed at the hearing that the Society had in fact only advanced £650, the remainder being the builder's collateral security. The builder, Morell (Builders), was by this time in liquidation.

The case opened in the Chancery Division before Mr Justice Bennett on 13 January 1938. It made headline news because Mrs Borders conducted her own case. Youngish, wearing spectacles, and seemingly the very prototype of an ordinary suburban housewife, with her taxi-driver husband beside her, she confronted the Building Society's team of barristers, solicitors and clerks headed by a King's Counsel, cross-examined the society's witnesses in a manner which revealed a most remarkable grasp of the technical and legal issues involved, declared she could bring evidence from occupiers all round London who had similarly been 'wilfully misled by building societies and their agents', and some days later ended a six-hour speech by asking for an injunction to restrain the Society from using the assets of its members or conducting business until the defects in its houses had been remedied.

The case got bogged down in technicalities, and was held over until the autumn. When it was resumed on 13 October, Mrs Borders, who by this time was widely referred to as 'the modern Portia', again gave battle for a fortnight, winding up with an eight-hour speech. Mr Justice Bennett in the end dismissed both the Society's claim and Mrs Borders' counter-claim on a side issue – the validity of the mortgage deed which the Society alleged Mrs Borders had signed and which was not the same as the one she *had* signed. The judgement, however (2 February 1939) left all the major issues unresolved. Mrs Borders then went to the Court of Appeal, this time helped by some well-known barristers, and at the Court of Appeal she won most of her case; the Court found that 'in this matter the Society's business was conducted fraudulently'.[3] The Society then appealed to the House of Lords, which exonerated it on 11 May 1941.

Long before all this the case had had its repercussions. Some three thousand owner-occupiers involved with various societies went on 'mortgage strike' until their repairs were done. Some got redress, others lost out. On 21 February 1939, Ellen Wilkinson, Labour MP for Jarrow, tried to bring in a Bill which would give purchasers the right to withhold mortgage payments in cases where the local authority certified that the house had not been properly built. But she was forestalled. The government was hurriedly preparing its own legislation, for the Borders Case had put in doubt the legality of the whole system of the 'builders' pool', in which most of the big building societies were heavily involved. So the government's Bill, which became an Act in 1939, legalized the builders' pool arrangements retrospectively. It put the societies out of danger, but did almost nothing to protect the house purchaser.

No adequate investigation into the extent of jerry-building in the thirties was ever carried out. No doubt houses as bad as the Borders' house were a small minority, but there was enough shoddy building to affect the reputation of the speculative builder, while the building societies, regarded as worthy pillars of society at the start of the thirties, appeared in a rather more dubious light at the end of the decade.

The builders' pool arrangements did mean that for the first time a good many wage earners were able to start buying houses. For the great majority of industrial workers, however, owner-occupation even at its cheapest was never a financial possibility. Which meant that about two-thirds of the families in the country were out of the running.

The Slum Clearance Campaign

While private enterprise was being given its head, local authorities were told that they must confine their activities to slum clearance and rehousing of slum dwellers. Since this involved demolition simultaneously with new building, it meant that a municipal contribution towards overcoming the numerical shortage of houses was ruled out. For thousands and thousands of families the chance of a new council house appeared to have vanished with the Wheatley Act. Only if they were 'fortunate' enough to live in a slum so appallingly bad that it had been scheduled for immediate demolition would they get a look in.

As though to justify the course that had been taken, the establishment launched a sort of propaganda campaign suggesting that the battle against the slums was a great new adventure. The services of the Prince of Wales were mobilized and he made a series of powerful speeches about the slums:

I personally inspected many such places, and I have been appalled that such conditions can exist in a civilized country such as ours. Every generation has a dominating social task, and so let our age, our generation, be remembered as the one in which we swept away this blot that disgraces our national life.[4]

Simultaneously the Church issued a national appeal; the BBC and the newspapers made special investigations and published horrifying revelations, and many social surveys were undertaken by voluntary organizations.

But despite all the brave words it soon became clear that the anti-slum campaign was in practice going very slowly. In 1931–2 the output of council houses in England and Wales had been over 70,000. By 1934–5 output had fallen to about 41,000. For various reasons this was inevitable. Slum clearance and rehousing of slum dwellers is a much more difficult job than building for general needs. It involved at that time cumbrous legal processes, with the slum landlord using every legal loophole to fight a bitter rearguard action. So it was that the anti-slum campaign took several years to get going.

Throughout this campaign some local authorities merely secured the demolition of the old houses, and offered the displaced slum dwellers accommodation on new cottage estates somewhere else – probably on the outskirts of towns in dormitory estates with all their disadvantages. But some authorities began to take the more difficult way out, that of rehousing the tenants in houses and flats on or near the site on which they had formerly lived. To an increasing extent in the big towns, and particularly in London, the creation of cottage estates on the outskirts began to give place to the building of blocks of flats at the centre.

For the most part the blocks built at this time were severely utilitarian in character. Often five storeys high, they were usually served by concrete staircases with outside balcony access making one side both dark and noisy. The bleak paved yards were not often relieved by trees or grass. The rooms were small – a flat of three bedrooms, living-room, kitchen and bathroom had a floor space of about 658 sq. ft. The equipment was fairly rudimentary – hot water had to be pumped to the bath from a copper installed in the kitchen.

Built as though to last a hundred years, some of these blocks seemed to emphasize that they were rough places for rough people. But not all of them. Some Labour-controlled authorities had a different idea; there were councillors who believed passionately that only the best was good enough for the working class, and were always striving to get their beliefs to materialize in spite of all the financial difficulties. Some authorities were in advance of their time. Leeds pioneered some experimental features in its great estate of flats at Quarry Hill – it installed automatic passenger lifts in face of all the prophets of doom and all the arguments that if you gave lifts to slum-dwellers they would be abused. The lifts at Leeds were a complete success, after which people all over the place began to demand that *their* new flats should have lifts. And some did, but lifts in council flats only became common after the war.

In spite of the fact that the government cut the subsidies once more, the anti-slum campaign really did get going in the end. By March 1939, out of 472,000 slums scheduled for closure, in England and Wales, 272,000 had been dealt with. Yet as later generations were to discover, the process of getting rid of the slums had hardly begun.

Meanwhile in the eight years up to 1939, 2½ million new houses were built in Great Britain – 70 per cent of them by private enterprise. The boom had been sufficient to overcome the numerical shortage on paper. For it was probable that by 1939 the total housing stock of about 12½ million exceeded the total number of families. But the new houses had gone overwhelmingly to the better-off third of the population. It is probable that the houses vacated by them had eased the situation for the less well-off who thereby had more elbow room. There must indeed have been some filtering up into houses thus vacated, and it seems likely that the larger quantity of roomspace resulted in a reduction in over-crowding (though there was no 1941 census to prove it one way or another).

Landlords and Tenants

Both council tenants and owner-occupiers were still a small minority. The great millions rented their homes from a private landlord.

The landlords formed a heterogeneous group. There were great well-heeled property companies owning thousands of dwellings, particularly in London. There were smaller private companies, some of a more dubious and 'fly-by-night' kind. There were charitable trusts which owned tenements built to house 'artisans' in the days of Queen Victoria. There were individual landlords ranging from important people owning hundreds of houses to unimportant people owning a handful of houses. There was the much publicized widow who might own two houses, living in one and getting an income off the other.

The landlord system was structurally confused. There was the simple case of a dwelling rented direct from its owner. There was the complicated case of a dwelling part-occupied by a sub-tenant, who paid rent to the main tenant, who in turn paid rent to a leaseholder, who in turn paid rent to a ground landlord.

In the endless monotonous working-class streets of the big towns, it was quite common for tenants to be ignorant of who their landlord was. All they knew was the agent who managed the letting and collected the rent. The real owner was a faceless man without identity.

Some landlords, particularly the owners of better-class property kept their houses in good repair, expected only a normal return on their investment, and had a relationship with their tenants which was quite amicable. At the other extreme were landlords who had neglected their property, had for years regarded it as a sort of milch-cow from which all possible money must be extracted while the going was good, did no repairs unless and until the sanitary inspectors were on their trail, and even then would wriggle out of it, until at last their crumbling, decaying, damp, bug-ridden properties were only fit for demolition.

In between these two extremes of 'good' and 'bad' landlord was every possible variation. Those who lived in the less decayed areas got the impression that the really bad landlord was in a minority. Others who lived in the poorest areas found the 'good' landlord an uncommon phenomenon.

At the time when the National government took office in 1931 a large proportion of the privately rented houses were controlled under the Rent Acts. These Acts owed their origin to the industrial unrest which had developed during the First World War when landlords, particularly on the Clyde, had taken advantage of the housing shortage to raise rents to scarcity levels. The rents in 1915 had been frozen at their August 1914 level, and the tenents had been given security of tenure. After the war the houses had remained controlled but in view of the sharp rise in the cost of repairs, the landlord had been permitted to raise the rent by 40 per cent, the tenant being entitled to withhold the 40 per cent if the repairs were not done. Since then, however, repair costs had fallen sharply.

In the early thirties, the owners were agitating for the abolition of rent control and freedom from the restraints which the Rent Acts imposed upon them. It was constantly stated that they had been singled out and deprived of their liberty and freedom to bargain. Also that the Rent Acts deprived them of the chance of improving their property, and deterred investors from providing new working-class houses to rent. The last argument could not really be said to hold water, since no post-war houses were subject to the Rent Acts. Meanwhile representatives of tenants' organizations were always pointing out that the position of the investor in existing house-property, even where still controlled, was not at all unfavourable. Unlike the business investor who had been hit by the depression, the landlord of an old working-class house could be sure of letting it owing to the scarcity, and the fall in prices meant that in real terms he was probably getting more in rent from a controlled house than he did when it was let on a free market prior to 1914.

Meanwhile, not all pre-war houses were controlled. Since 1923 any house which became vacant had automatically become decontrolled, which meant that after obtaining vacant possession a landlord could charge what rent he could get to an incoming tenant, and could evict him whenever he liked. The continuing housing shortage meant that a landlord could obtain rents 25 per cent or more higher than those permitted for a controlled house. Thus by the early thirties rents varied very much according to whether the house was still controlled or had become decontrolled. In London working-class streets you could get identical houses, one let at a controlled rent of perhaps 15s a week, the other at a decontrolled rent of 20s or more. In the provinces a house with a controlled rent of 9s might be next door to a decontrolled house let at 11s 3d. And so on.

The first action taken by the National government in this field came in 1933 in the form of one more Rent Act which decontrolled rather more than half a million of the larger or most expensive houses. Thus the landlords saw a small step taken towards the freedom they so desired.

But for middle-range houses (known as class B houses) and the lowest range (known as class C) control was continued for another five years. Moreover, special steps were taken in relation to class C houses which were estimated to number some 5,700,000 and included nearly all slums and near-slums. Such houses had hitherto been decontrolled if the tenant moved out. Though houses already decontrolled in this way were to remain so, there was to be no further decontrol of class C houses. Which meant that if such a house became vacant the landlord could not legally charge the incoming tenant more than the controlled rent.

The government made clear that continuance of control was repugnant to it, and was to be regarded as a temporary measure justified only so long as the abnormal housing shortage continued. And all proposals for 'mediating' between landlord and tenant by means of rent tribunals were resisted. 'We cannot by this Bill do anything to make a final peace in the age-old contention between landlord and tenant', observed Sir Hilton Young, the Minister of Health. 'There is that conflict of interest which always exists between buyer and seller, between the one who supplies and the other who demands. That conflict of interest has existed since time began, and will, I imagine, exist until time ends'.[5]

Conflict there certainly was, and it was to grow as the years passed. Under the new Act, landlords were required within three months to register any class C house which had become decontrolled through vacant possession between 1923 and 1933; if not registered the house was held to be still controlled and would remain so no matter how many tenants moved in or out. There was immediately a great deal of illegal registration by landlords. Indeed some landlords automatically registered all their class C properties as decontrolled whether they were so or not. From then on one of the most complicated tasks facing tenants' associations, and unofficial rent advice bureaux, was tracing the past history of a tenancy in order to prove that the house although registered as decontrolled was really controlled by law.

While some landlords, including many of the bigger ones, were busy registering everything as decontrolled, there were others, many of them small ones, who were oblivious to the necessity and failed to register at all. This could however be remedied, since a late registration could be made on application to the court. Applications for late registration went on for years.

Illegal overcharging for controlled houses was widespread. And the right of the controlled tenants to withhold the 40 per cent increase in the rent if the repairs were not done was not nearly as effective as it appeared on paper. For the 40 per cent could not be withheld without a certificate from the local sanitary inspector and local authorities varied very much in their attitude to this work. Some tried to make full use of their power, others, it was constantly alleged, were not so helpful, and complaint was merely the signal for a lot of bullying and unpleasantness from the landlord.

It was in this situation that tenants' associations began to spread in many areas. If, as a result of assiduous research, a landlord could be found to have been overcharging for a controlled house, the tenant could by law withhold the rent until the excess paid during the previous six months had been recovered. The Glasgow Labour Party Association, which dealt with thousands of tenants' cases, had actually found it necessary to issue printed forms for the use of tenants reclaiming amounts illegally collected by a landlord in the past. In the East End of London, tenants' defence leagues began to be established – tentatively at first. An initial leaflet issued early in 1937 in Poplar inviting membership of a 'League of Tenants to help Tenants' stressed that the names of members would not be disclosed to anyone but would be kept confidential to the secretary. Eighteen months later the Poplar League, with Dr Somerville Hastings as its president and the Reverend G. Shaw as its chairman, was publicly announcing a membership of eight hundred. It had secured reductions in rents for its members of £1,395, repayment of £717 for overcharged rent, and numerous repairs. In the neighbouring borough of Stepney, events moved further and faster. Here a powerful tenants' league was by 1938 claiming that in a period of nine months it had reduced rent rolls by £18,000 a year and obtained nearly £10,000 in repayments.

While much could be done to enforce the law for the controlled tenant, decontrolled tenants, whose grievances were often much greater, seemed to have no redress. In slum areas they were often paying twice as much as their neighbours and were frightened to ask the landlord to do repairs in case they were evicted. Even in the less decayed areas there were stories of unpleasant rackets. It was alleged that in Birmingham landlords were encouraging tenants to do their own repairs and put in small improvements.

Having got the house improved, the landlord would evict the tenant.

If the tenant of a decontrolled house got into arrears of rent, the landlord still possessed the ancient power to levy 'distress' for rent, which meant that without leave of the court he could enter the house, seize sufficient goods to cover the arrears and sell them in order to recover the debt. The Ridley Committee, which had been set up by the government to examine the working of the Rent Acts once more, and which reported in 1937, described 'the harshness of this procedure, which can change a minor misfortune, such for instance as a week's sickness of the breadwinner, into a major calamity making it almost impossible for the tenant and his family to recover their previous position'.

Since class B houses were still subject to decontrol on vacant possession, tricking controlled tenants of such property into moving, and intimidating them so as to secure vacant possession, was common in some parts of London.[6] And as the five-year time limit for the end of all control drew near, there was considerable activity by property companies buying up working-class controlled property in anticipation of all-out decontrol.

Long before the five-year time limit was up, however, it had become clear that the shortage of class C houses was almost as acute as ever, and that the general surplus of working-class houses which, in the government's view, would make all-out decontrol possible had simply not materialized. Accordingly early in 1938 the government produced one more Rent Act which freed from control a small slice of about 450,000 houses in the upper half of class B. The rest remained controlled, and moreover 'creeping decontrol' for the remainder of class B was abolished.

In the summer of 1938 the grievances of decontrolled tenants in the East End of London began to erupt in a series of rent strikes. It was perhaps inevitable that the 'conflict' between landlord and tenant which Sir Hilton Young had recognized should manifest itself in its most acute form in the East End. On the one hand, all the characteristics of slum landlordism were present in their most oppressive and corrupt form, with get-rich-quick owners using every device to extract every possible penny from decaying and insanitary property, and to evade the law when it came to repairs. On the other hand, the East End was one of the few places in England where the Communist Party had a decisive following, which had been built up partly as a result of anti-fascist activities in the years before. Here, therefore, the overriding Communist aim of developing mass action against the class enemy was not just a theoretical perspective for the future. Conditions were ripe for it to become a reality.

The rent strike movement began in a block of three hundred and forty-six dilapidated flats at Quinn Square, Bethnal Green. The block was owned by a property company. The flats had no separate water supply, one tap being normally shared between four families, and one lavatory between two. Only ninety of the flats were still classed as controlled; the rent for a four-roomed de-controlled flat sharing tap and lavatory was as high as £1 0s 8d, compared with 11s 7d for a similar controlled flat. The movement started as a result of the attempted eviction of a woman who turned out on investigation to be occupying a controlled flat for which the company had been illegally overcharging for years. With this experience, the tenants of Quinn Square formed a tenants' association, and drew up and put before the company a new proposed scale of maximum rents for the whole block. The company refused and all the tenants went on rent strike. For two days an embarrassed rent collector followed by a horde of shouting children called at the flats and got nothing, after which he stopped coming. Meanwhile women were picketing the company's office, and parading the borough with posters asking for support. After a fortnight, the company suddenly gave in and signed a 'collective agreement' with the tenants' association.

The affair had immediate repercussions in Stepney. Here the Tenants' Defence League was a huge affair with thousands of members. Father Groser, a well-known Anglo-Catholic priest, was its president; its secretary was a Communist known as 'Tubby' Rosen. It had tenants' committees actively engaged in helping controlled tenants enforce the law. The Quinn Square affair seemed to set the borough alight. In street after street in rapid succession rent strikes took place. It was a planned operation, and in the main it succeeded. One after another landlords agreed to come to terms and signed 'collective agreements'. An exception was the landlord of Langdale Mansions and Brady Mansions, who decided to have a showdown. The properties were two big blocks comprising three hundred and twenty flats. The landlord was a company known as C. and G. Estates Ltd. This strike went on for twenty-one weeks. Some of the most active tenants were given notice to quit, but no attention was paid to this. Some were then served with court summonses, and a few weeks later court orders were served on them. The tenants replied by barricading both blocks with barbed wire. Then on 27 June 1939, while the men were at work, bailiffs arrived. Supported by foot and mounted police, they forced their way in with crowbars and hammers. While the police drew their truncheons and fought the crowd, mainly women, five families were forcibly evicted and their furniture thrown into the street. The news spread, men left work and ran home, thousands of people gathered round the flats. By evening the five evicted families were back in their flats and crowds were marching to the police station, where further baton charges and disturbances took place. By next day most of the press had vivid photographs, and many carried accounts of the tenants' grievances. The landlords issued a statement to the press:

The struggle in the East End is no longer a private matter between a particular landlord and his individual tenants. It is a struggle between mob law versus the law and order of this country. The question arises whether an organized mob can defeat the orders of our law courts by physically preventing their enforcement. If the answer is in the affirmative none of us in this country is safe with our possessions and rights.[7]

In spite of these emphatic words, the landlords were constrained to negotiate, and after two days during which the parties were brought together at the house of the Bishop of Stepney, an agreement was signed reducing the rents of all decontrolled tenants by amounts varying from 2s to 8s a week, while the company agreed to spend £2,500 on repairs to both blocks without delay, and a further £1,500 on repairs every succeeding year. After

H

this there were victory celebrations in Stepney every night for a week.

A New Pattern

All through the thirties there had been two schools of thought about the housing problem, neither of which in the end was translated into reality. That represented by the government, while welcoming the extension of home-ownership for the middle class, had hoped and believed that the private investor would supply the working class with houses to rent. The vast mass of the people had been housed that way in the nineteenth century; it seemed natural that the same thing should happen again. This hope never materialized. The existing landlords held on to their existing properties and made what money they could out of them, but they hardly extended their field at all, nor did many new would-be landlords come into being except as providers of purpose-built middle-class flats. As a decade the thirties was to set the stage for the slow eclipse of the private landlord which has continued ever since.

The opposite school of thought was the traditional one of the labour movement. Believing that private landlordism was responsible for all housing ills, including the slums, it held that the way forward was massive provision by public authorities of subsidized houses at rents the workers could afford. This road was blocked by the election of the 1931 government and the decision to confine local authority building to a minority role – replacing the worst slums and reducing the worst overcrowding.

What actually took place – an enormous growth in owner-occupation reaching right down as far as the better-paid manual workers – was something different from what anybody had planned or foreseen. It is probable that by 1939 there were three million owner-occupiers in the country – representing about one quarter of all families.

It was the beginning of a quite new stage – a stage ushered in at great social cost. The urban sprawl which accompanied it was to jeopardize the rational planning of our towns for generations to come. And the individual cost was also high in many cases, as people strove to meet mortgage payments they could barely afford and found they had been cheated by the jerry builders. But as a new way of living it set a pattern which was to stay and to spread.

Housing Output (numbers completed)

Year Ending March 31	England and Wales		Scotland	
	Local Authorities	Private Enterprise	Local Authorities	Private Enterprise
1931	55,874	127,933	8,122	4,571
1932	70,061	130,751	8,952	4,766
1933	55,991	144,505	12,165	6,596
1934	55,840	210,782	16,503	10,760
1935	41,593	287,513	15,733	6,096
1936	52,357	272,503	18,129	7,326
1937	71,740	274,313	15,683	8,167
1938	77,970	259,632	14,077	7,977
1939	101,744	230,616	19,909	6,604

Totals for Great Britain

1931	196,500
1932	214,530
1933	219,257
1934	293,885
1935	350,935
1936	350,315
1937	369,903
1938	359,656
1939	358,873

14
Eating and Not Eating

How hungry, comparatively, were the 'hungry thirties'? Recently there has been a tendency by historians to dismiss the phrase as the sentimental exaggeration of intellectuals of the period learning about poverty for the first time. The thirties, we are now told, was a period of steadily rising standards of living, despite the depression – a period when the working class ate better and had far more money left over for luxuries and comforts then ever before. People on average were spending more on cinemas and furniture and tobacco. Obviously, it is argued, they must have had enough to eat.

It is not easy to sum up exactly how much standards changed over the period, because average consumption covered such wide differences between prosperous and depressed areas, and between the well-to-do and the poor – differences much wider than they are today. What can be said categorically is that there was a great deal of malnutrition and semi-starvation in the thirties of a kind that is scarcely ever seen in Britain now; and that there was probably more such malnutrition than during the Second World War when food supplies, though scarcer, were more equally distributed. At the same time the press reported food being burned or thrown into the sea, farm production restricted by State action, and tariffs imposed on imported food. This seemingly lunatic situation led to a growing unofficial demand for measures to feed children and pregnant and nursing mothers, while doctors and scientists made detailed investigations into minimum diets and the extent of malnutrition, on a scale never known before.

This did not mean that the standard of nutrition for the country as a whole was worse than it had been in the twenties or before the

First World War. Indeed, the average consumption per head of such 'protective' foods as eggs, butter, fresh fruit and vegetables was certainly higher. But consumption of these more expensive foods was distributed most unequally between classes. At the same time new biological discoveries (in particular work on vitamins and their effects) exploded the old notion that a sufficient diet was one with enough calories to satisfy hunger and supply energy, and showed that thousands of the unemployed and lower-paid were still getting avoidably ill for lack of the fresh and more expensive foods, containing protective vitamins and essential mineral salts, which were now realized to be not luxuries but necessities for health.

Certainly a greater variety was available in the shops for those who could afford it. Whereas at the end of the First World War, canned food meant corned beef or salmon, soup and perhaps Californian fruit, now almost every kind of food came in tins. Baked beans, canned peas and canned fruit became an important means of varying the diet in working-class homes, if not improving nutritional values. At the same time new refrigeration methods made it possible to eat fresh fruit all the year round, as cheap apples, oranges and pears were brought in from the southern hemisphere; while 'chilled' New Zealand lamb and Argentine beef tasted better than pre-war frozen meat, and ice-cream sales rocketed. And the already high consumption of chocolate and confectionery continued to rise throughout the thirties.

Another change in the thirties with the rise of big food trusts like Unilever's, Marsh and Baxter, United Dairies and Tate and Lyle, was the growth of pre-packaged, branded and processed foods. The small shopkeeper no longer blended his own teas or weighed out sugar, butter and salt. He became, in effect, a distributor for the combines; milkmen and bakers too had to sell at fixed prices. All kinds of branded convenience foods appeared, backed by high-powered advertising – custard powder, jellies, blancmange powders, Quick Quaker porridge, new types of breakfast cereals and hot bedtime drinks – all especially attractive to the working housewife without servants. Instead of competing through lower prices, shopkeepers rivalled one another with smarter shop-fronts, delivery services, and in middle-class areas, telephone orders.[1] But all this did not help to solve the problems of the poor.

How Much Malnutrition?

For the unemployed and for the low-paid workers, especially in agriculture, the regular diet still consisted literally of bread, margarine and tea, with a main meal of potatoes and a little stewed meat and gravy to give a flavour. Jam and dripping helped to get the bread down. In these groups, even households with young children or mothers expecting babies seldom bought fresh milk; they used only condensed.* The lucky ones might get a few vegetables from garden or allotment. Fruit was a luxury seldom eaten.[2] Many of the unemployed and old-age pensioners habitually went to bed early not only to save gas and light, but so as not to feel hungry. All this was not mainly, as was sometimes suggested in the press, because the working-class housewife was ignorant and bought the wrong foods, but because she was too poor to afford the right ones.

The government and official circles were at first generally reassuring about the effects of rising unemployment on nutrition and health. Thus Sir George Newman, chief medical officer of the Board of Education wrote in his report for 1931: 'The depressed state of industry and the need for national economy does not appear to have exerted, as yet, any measurable ill-effect upon the child population.' And Sir E. Hilton Young, Minister of Health, told the House of Commons in July 1933 that 'there is at present no available medical evidence of any general increase in physical impairment, sickness or mortality as a result of the economic depression or unemployment'.

Many expert observers, however, thought that the absence of 'measurable ill-effects' was due rather to the superficial nature of school medical examinations and the lack of established medical standards for measuring subnormal health and malnutrition. Thus

* Despite the propaganda for fresh milk, the sales of condensed went on rising during the twenties and thirties.

the *Medical Officer,* one of the organs of the medical officers of health, wrote editorially:

We must find out the clinical signs of malnutrition, for these we do not know. We know that at the present time a very large proportion of the population is imperfectly fed, but we cannot find the signs of it. We have districts where the amount spent on food is inadequate to cover the necessities, and we report the observed nutrition of the children – who should be the most sensitive members of the community – as 90 to 95 per cent good. We know that this is false, and those who quote those results as proof that all is going well, that the British people in times of difficulty thrive excellently on bread and margarine . . . and are quite happy in doing so, know that it is false also.[3]

So long as official estimates of malnutrition depended purely on impressions by school medical officers as to the 'general well-being' of the child, especially during a cursory examination without blood-tests or X-rays, the statistical results were more or less meaningless. There were wide variations between socially similar areas. Usually the doctor tended to take the general standard prevailing in his area as normal, so that 'normal' nutrition meant something quite different in Bournemouth and in South Wales. At Hebburn-on-Tyne the number of children classified as suffering from subnormal or bad nutrition more than doubled from 1934 to 1935, following the appointment of a new medical officer from a less distressed district. The composite national figure (10·5 per cent of school children with subnormal nutrition and 0·7 per cent with bad nutrition in 1936), being based on data containing such discrepancies, could have little scientific value, and reassurances based on it were equally valueless.*

But if malnutrition could not be assessed directly, there was plenty of indirect evidence that diseases associated with under-feeding and lack of protective foods were rife among the unemployed. Many medical officers of health, for example, reported increases in rickets among toddlers and schoolchildren, especially

* The Department of Social Science of Liverpool University carried out an enquiry into the reliability of school medical officers' gradings of nutrition, and found that not only did the doctors disagree widely in their assessments of children, but the *same* doctor assessed the *same* children quite differently at a second examination a week later.

from 1933 onwards. Even where the advance of medical science and treatment was reducing disease, as with tuberculosis, the death rate fell only half as much in the depressed areas as in the rest of the country. Since mothers in poor families often went short themselves in order to give the children the largest share of what food was going, it was not surprising that national maternal mortality rates actually rose. Dr Sharpe, MOH for Preston, in his 1932 *Report* wrote:

Possibly at no period during the last five years has work at the infant welfare centres been so difficult as during the latter part of 1932. It has become more and more evident that a high percentage of mothers has been attending in the hope of getting free milk, Ovaltine or other foods. One cannot help thinking that the means test was the responsible factor.

At the 1933 annual meeting of the Durham County Society for the Prevention and Cure of Consumption, Dr O'Hara said: 'Most of our children are suffering not so much from tuberculosis as from starvation. Seventy-five per cent of the cases admitted to the society's sanatorium were suffering from under-nourishment.' The School Medical Officer for Cumberland in his annual *Report* for 1933 said: 'There is evidence of a very definite increase, almost a dramatic increase, in the incidence of rickets amongst children of school age.'

Dr J. H. Rankin, MOH for the Gellygaer Urban District in South Wales, wrote in his 1933 *Report:*

The district has again had a continued epidemic of scarlet fever during the year, the majority of cases being of severe type, and complications were common. The general want of resistance to attack and severity of the symptoms were, in my opinion, due to general malnutrition among the children, the result of the present unfortunate economic situation in South Wales.

In Newcastle upon Tyne, the Corporation set up an independent medical inquiry under Dr Spence, the results of which were published in 1933. It showed that at least 36 per cent of a sample of children examined from the poor districts of the city were unhealthy or physically unfit, and appeared malnourished: some had active rickets. Comparisons with a sample of children of professional families showed that only 16 per cent of the professional families' children were at all anaemic, but 81 per cent of the poor city children were so. There was eight times as much pneumonia and ten times as much bronchitis among the poor children as among the well-off.

Similar results could be obtained wherever a local authority in a depressed industrial area took the trouble to collect them. Thus the energetic MOH for Stockton-on-Tees, Dr G. C. M'Gonigle, one of the first to campaign publicly on the malnutrition issue, found a standardized death-rate for 1931-4 of 29 per 1,000 people among unemployed households, compared with 21 per 1000, among employed households. The same survey showed a standardized death rate of 26 per 1,000 among the lowest income group (spending 3s a head on food) against a rate of 11½ per 1000 among the highest income group (spending over 6s a head). M'Gonigle showed, too, that when largely unemployed slum-dwellers from old districts of Stockton were rehoused on a new estate, where living conditions were better but higher rents and fares left less money for food, their death-rates and sickness rates considerably increased.[4]

Minimum Diets and Minimum Standards

Various investigators attempted to work out the lowest cost at which a family could buy sufficient nourishment to remain physically healthy, and then find out how many families could not afford even this minimum standard. Scientists and doctors disagreed among themselves about what the minimum figure should be, but generally speaking the more nutritional science advanced, the more costly the minimum requirements for health became. Even when a minimum was agreed upon the measurements based on it were bound to be somewhat artificial, since housewives could not be expected to work out their food bills to the last calorie and vitamin unit. It was very unlikely that any real family would spend every penny available on the most nourishing food regardless of taste, and real children, unlike minimum ones, often left bits on the side of the plate or demanded ice-cream rather than lentil soup. But as a rough measuring-rod the 'minimum' budgets had some value, if it was only to shock the comfortably-off.

The most widely-used minimum diet was that published by the British Medical Association in November 1933. It provided rather monotonous and tasteless menus, 50 per cent of it being made up of cereals and potatoes; nutritionally it was by no means ideal;* but even so it was clear at once that the majority of unemployed families were living at a level far below it. Later research, much of it not published until the war years, showed that virtually *all* families living solely on unemployment benefit or assistance were much too poor to afford the BMA diet.[5] The immediate reaction of the Ministry of Health was to challenge the BMA standard as too high; but although the ministry contrived to work out a fractionally cheaper diet, based on the cheaper prices for bulk purchase of food by institutions, the unemployed could not afford that either.

The various investigations into poverty gave different results according to the stage of economic recovery at which data were collected and the differing standards of minimum needs used; but all showed a great many families with incomes too low to provide them with a healthy diet. Thus in the Merseyside Survey of 1928–32 (based on Rowntree's earlier Human Needs minimum standard[6]) 30 per cent of working-class families were found to be living in poverty. In Bristol, a particularly prosperous city, in the boom year 1937, 10·7 per cent of working-class families were below the poverty line (a substantially lower one than Rowntree's) and 32 to 38 per cent below a 'more realistic' standard.† In Birmingham in 1939 a comparable survey on the new Kingstanding housing estate, at a time when employment and earnings in

---

* Indeed the League of Nations a little later published a minimum diet with much larger allowances for protective foods.

† The 'more realistic' standard used in Bristol and Birmingham estimated the balance available for food *after* paying voluntary insurances, hire purchase instalments, and a small allowance for wage earners' personal expenditure on beer, tobacco, newspapers etc.

Birmingham were higher than ever before, showed 14 per cent of families (31 per cent of the children) below a bare theoretical minimum, and 31 per cent (60 per cent of the children) below a 'more realistic' figure.[7]

Orr and his findings: Half the National below Optimum

The best-known of all the campaigners against malnutrition was Sir John Boyd Orr, director of the Rowett Institute in Aberdeen. In the late twenties he had carried out an experiment in Scotland and Belfast, which had shown conclusively the remarkable improvement in the health of children getting milk at school. Yet the average consumption of milk, he found, was probably no higher in the early thirties than it had been a hundred years before, and in rural areas possibly lower.[8]

The famous survey published in 1936 as *Food, Health and Income* was carried out by Orr in 1934–5 with the assistance of the staff of the Rowett Institute, and civil servants in the Department of Agriculture. Unlike earlier studies, which had attempted to assess *minimum* nutrition requirements, Orr's set out to consider how many people in Britain were *in fact* living on a diet completely adequate for health according to modern standards – an *optimum* diet. He came to the conclusion that such a diet was only reached at an income level above that of 50 per cent of the population, and that for 30 per cent of the population the actual diet was very seriously deficient.

For the purpose of his survey Orr classified the whole population roughly into six groups according to size of family income per head. Actual food budgets were then collected to show the amount spent on each kind of food at the different income levels. The results showed that while consumption of bread and potatoes was almost uniform throughout the different income groups, consumption of milk, eggs, fruit, vegetables, meat and fish rose sharply with income. Thus in the poorest group the average consumption of milk, including tinned milk, was equivalent to 1·8 pints per week; in the wealthiest group 5·8 pints. The poorest group consumed 1·5 eggs per head per week, the wealthiest 4·5.

The poorest spent 2·4d on fruit, the wealthiest 1s 8d – eight times as much.

Comparing the diets actually bought with the standard of nutrition required for perfect health,[9] Orr found that the average diet of the poorest group, estimated to include four and a half million people (10 per cent) was deficient in every constituent examined. Moreover, half this poorest group were children under fourteen, and between 20 and 25 per cent of the children in the country were in the lowest income group. The second group, comprising nine million people, had a diet adequate in carbohydrates, fat and protein, but deficient in all the vitamins and minerals considered. The third group, comprising another nine million, was deficient in several of the important vitamins and minerals. In practice an adequate diet was only approached where the income per head was 20s or more per week. This meant that the wage even of a skilled man was insufficient for a healthy diet if there were three children or more under working age, while the typical unskilled wage meant an inadequate diet if there were any dependent children at all. Further, Orr showed that relatively moderate increases in total national consumption of a number of the more expensive foods, such as milk, eggs, butter, fruit, vegetables and meat, varying from 12 to 25 per cent, would suffice to bring the poorer groups up to a satisfactory level of nutrition. There would be little difficulty in providing the food if the people were given the purchasing power to buy it.

Orr, however, was not merely a detached investigator, but a keen propagandist for a new policy. This activity, as he records in his autobiography *As I Recall,* was frowned upon officially:

Mr Kingsley Wood, the Minister of Health, asked me to come and see him. He wanted to know why I was making such a fuss about poverty when, with old age pensions and unemployment insurance, there was no poverty in the country. This extraordinary illusion was genuinely believed by Mr Wood, who held the out-of-date opinion that if people were not actually dying of starvation there could be no food deficiency. He knew nothing about the results of the research on vitamins and protein requirements, and had never visited the slums to see things for himself.

When Orr's survey was nearing publication, some of the civil servants who, on the minister's instructions, were helping to prepare it were ordered by a 'very senior civil servant' to withdraw. For this reason the report, despite the semi-official basis of its preparation, was finally issued as Orr's personal work. Fearing some last-minute censorship, he released the key facts in a lecture to the British Association meeting in 1935. But even after this a minister made a last-minute plea that the report should not be published:

I suggested that instead of trying to prevent its publication the government should take the line that owing to the great advance in the science of nutrition, they had promoted this enquiry, and that they recommended that it be studied by experts on the subject, with an assurance that it would be the policy of His Majesty's Government to take every means necessary to ensure that every British citizen had sufficient food for health. The minister agreed to this as a foreword for the publication, but his views were not accepted by the Cabinet. The establishment put up the strongest possible resistance to informing the public of what the position was regarding the under-nourishment among their fellow-citizens.[*][10]

* Although Orr's sample was admittedly small (some 1,200 budgets), later research has not invalidated his general findings. For example, an inquiry covering 5,000 urban families, carried out in 1936–7 and published by Sir William Crawford and H. Broadley in *The People's Food*, brought out the contrast between the well-to-do and the poor even more strikingly. They found that two-fifths of all families with annual incomes between £125 and £249 had a weekly food consumption below the BMA diet. Of the families whose incomes were below £125, no less than two-thirds had a deficient diet. Applying these figures to the whole country, this indicated that 35 per cent of the population, or about 16 million people, were living in homes where weekly food expenditure fell below the BMA diet level.

This same study showed that the well-off groups (the top 5 per cent of the population) consumed per head about twice as much fish, nearly three times as much dairy produce, twice as much vegetables and seven times as much fruit as the poorest group. At the same time, while their consumption of the more expensive protective foods was so much higher, they actually got more of the cheap 'fillers' – bread and cereals – as well.

Even more significant, perhaps, because involving larger numbers, was the contrast of the less-poor working-class group (60 per cent of the total) with the main middle class group (20 per cent). For all the more expensive types of food such as meat, fish, dairy produce and fruit, middle-class consumption was one and a half to two times higher – usually nearer double – than that of the better-off working class.

Rowntree's Complete Picture

By far the most complete study of poverty was carried out in 1936 in York, where Seebohm Rowntree, the veteran social investigator, surveyed the income and expenditure not of a sample but of *every* working-class family. In order to analyse his results he worked out a standard of 'human needs', which required for a family of man, wife and three children an income, after paying rent, of 43s 6d a week (53s including rent).* Unlike some of the other standards in use at the time, it made allowance for such conventional necessities as insurance, trade union subscriptions, wireless, a daily paper, and a small sum for personal

*Rowntree's Human Needs Standard, 1936 (Towns)
for Man, Wife, and Three Dependent Children*

	s	d
Food	20	6
Rent	9	6
Clothing	8	0
Fuel	4	4
Sundries: Household	1	8
Personal	9	0

sundries. Rowntree nevertheless wrote about his 'human needs' standard as a whole:

Let me repeat that standards adopted throughout this book err on the side of stringency rather than of extravagance ... Practically the whole income is absorbed in providing the absolute necessaries of physical health. After these and certain almost indispensable items are provided for, there remains scarcely anything – certainly not more than 3s 4d a week for 'all else'. Out of this must come all recreation, all

* Income included total earnings of children up to 15s, contributions for board and lodging by older children and lodgers, and value of vegetables from allotments, free school meals, half-price school milk, as well as insurance and assistance benefits.

luxuries, such as beer and tobacco, all travelling except that of the breadwinner to and from work, all savings for holidays – indeed almost every item of expenditure not absolutely required to maintain the family. No! my standard cannot be successfully attacked because it is too liberal. Rather is it open to criticism as being too low, and yet millions of our fellow citizens belong to families whose breadwinners earn less than my minimum figure.[11]

Rowntree's full results, not published till 1941, showed 31·1 per cent of the York working class (17·8 per cent of the population) living at an income level below his minimum standard. These included 28·2 per cent of all the children, and 43 per cent of the working-class children covered by the survey. Still more startling were his findings that of children under one year old in working-class families, over half (52·5 per cent) were below his poverty line, and 47 per cent would probably remain below it for five years or more, by which time permanent damage was likely to have been done to bone-structure, teeth and general health. Thus there is a striking degree of general agreement between Rowntree's findings and those of Orr, arrived at by a quite different method, and continually assailed by the establishment as exaggerated.

Poverty in York, 1936–7

Cause	Percentage of all families below Rowntree minimum
Inadequate wages in regular work	32·8
Unemployment	28·6
Old Age	14·7
Inadequate earnings of those working on own account or casually	9·5
Death of husband	7·8
Illness	4·1
Miscellaneous	2·5
	100·0

(Source: *Poverty and Progress*, 1941.)

Rowntree showed that virtually *all* families, of whatever size, living on unemployment benefit and assistance were far below his 'human needs' standard. Even a couple without children on full benefit fell short of it by one-eighth or so, and a family with three children by more than one-third. It is worth noting, too, that while much of the poverty found by the York investigators was due to unemployment, the major single cause was still low wages, and the most acute poverty was that of old people.

Agitation to Feed the Children

Meanwhile there were facts enough already available in the thirties to fuel the campaign for better feeding. The Committee Against Malnutrition, consisting of doctors and scientists, with F. Le Gros Clark as its leading spirit, had been formed to combat and expose the evil of under-nourishment, and the Children's Minimum Campaign Committee, under the leadership of the Independent MP Eleanor Rathbone, was campaigning for increased children's allowances for unemployed families. If the nutrition of the working class did not deteriorate sharply in the nineteen thirties it was largely because of the work done by such bodies, in alliance with the National Unemployed Workers Movement and the labour movement, to raise the level of assistance payments and to secure extra food for mothers and children.

Local authorities were already entitled to supply free school meals, under the Education Act of 1921,[12] 'to all children unable, by reason of lack of food, to take full advantage of the education provided for them'. The National government, however, made it a rule that children could only be provided with such meals when the doctor reported definite symptoms of malnutrition (which, as we have seen, was difficult to diagnose). Repeated efforts were made to get this rule removed, so that children from poor families could be provided with free meals *before* they reached the stage of actual physical damage by malnutrition, and some local authorities, such as Cambridge, announced that they intended to disregard it.

In the autumn of 1934, however, the government rebuked such authorities and issued instructions that the rule must be strictly adhered to. This led to strong protests. Dr Hugh Paul, School Medical Officer for Smethwick, Staffs, in his report issued in May 1935, was particularly outspoken, describing the government's attitude as 'brutal, inhuman and barbarous' and contrary to the letter of the 1921 Act. The government, he declared, was saying to the children: 'You must stop having free meals. You do not need them yet. When you have starved sufficiently to show signs of actual malnutrition, however slight, come back for meals. You may then have meals until malnutrition is cured, but only until then; after that you must have another trial period of starvation.'

A number of authorities continued to defy the interpretation laid down by the Board of Education; there were protests from the Association of Local Education Authorities, and deputations by the Children's Minimum Campaign and the National Unemployed Workers' Movement to the Board of Education. At last in the autumn of 1935 the board retreated with a bad grace, and issued new instructions explaining that there had been 'misunderstanding'. It still maintained in principle that 'the fact that the parent's income falls within a local authority's income scale does not by itself justify the provision of free meals'. But it conceded that *any* evidence (for example from teachers or attendance officers) that the child's education was suffering from lack of food could now be used, as well as evidence of physical deterioration; and children should in future only be removed from the feeding list 'where the authority are satisfied that provision of meals can be discontinued without risk of relapse'.

However, even after this only about 4 per cent of children got free school meals in 1938–9, and how many were fed depended not so much on the degree of poverty and unemployment as on the attitude and prosperity of the local authority.[13] Sir George Newman in 1925 had hopefully extolled school meals as something that would 'bring the elementary school a little nearer in character to the public boarding school'. But in practice it was not like that at all. Fewer than 10 per cent of the schools had canteens. For the rest of the children, halls had to be hired, often in the poorest part of the town, and were usually dark, ill-decorated, badly ventilated and without lavatories. Local medical officers reported that free dinners were looked on as a last resort, and many ill-nourished children of very poor parents did not attend the dinner-centre because of the Poor-Law stigma.*

Even in the countryside, where reorganization of schools made it too far for many children to walk home to dinner, the majority of schools had no canteens, and in 1936 the proportion of country children receiving school dinners (paid or unpaid) ranged from 10 per cent in the best counties to under 2 per cent in the worst, while in Wales only four counties served any dinners at all. Moreover the food was often monotonous, consisting at best of hash, stew and soup. Some authorities served potatoes, bread and gravy twice a week, or bread and butter, chips and tea; others gave cheese or salmon sandwiches and cocoa made with water. The Chief Medical Officer of the Board of Education commented: 'In some districts the poverty of the local authorities, like the poverty of the parents, prevents their supplying the more expensive protective foods.'

Many authorities dragged their feet because they argued that there was no demand – children preferred to take a bus home or to bring their own food (usually bread and marge). Charges ranged from 2d to 7d a head, and were admittedly above the means of the average farmworker. It was not until the war that subsidized meals for all children were instituted as a charge on national funds, and the alleged preference for bread and marge disappeared.[14]

* Alan Sillitoe in his Nottingham autobiographical novel *Key to the Door* describes how Brian and his family attend the dinner-centre every day, rain or shine, at 'the long hut beyond the recreation ground where at morning and mid-day meals were served to those whose fathers were on the dole... The bottom room of the house was merely part of the route, though on his way through, Brian wished they could eat breakfast there, but saw nothing on the table except a mug of tea to be drunk by his father.' But 'the breakfast, when it did come, was magnificent: three thick slices of bread and butter each, and a mug of milky cocoa. There was no breakfast to beat it, as far as Brian knew, except tomatoes and bacon, but that was a dinner '

The first milk-in-schools scheme

One of the most serious deficiencies in children's diet was the lack of fresh milk, although there was a glut of milk in the country. The price of 2s a gallon was too high for many consumers, and much of the surplus had to be sold at reduced prices (5d a gallon or so) for manufacture into condensed milk, cheese or even umbrella handles. Meanwhile the government through the Milk Marketing Board, compensated the farmers by a subsidy to maintain their prices – a situation reasonably described by *The Economist* as the 'economics of Bedlam'.

In October 1934, partly owing to public pressure, the government established the first subsidized scheme for cheap milk in schools. Children paid ½d a day for one-third of a pint of milk, and this both improved nutrition and helped to keep up the retail price (to 2s 3d a gallon in 1938). By 1939 twenty-six million gallons were being sold in schools, an addition of about 3 per cent to retail sales. The number of children taking milk gradually rose; but even so, by 1938 only about half were taking advantage of the scheme* and it was well known that among those not taking it were many from the poorest families. Although local authorities could provide free milk for ill-fed children under the same terms and rules as free meals, in practice free milk was only issued to about one child in thirteen. Teachers all over the country were testifying to the improvement in health and vigour of those who got school milk, and there was much discussion on how to persuade parents to let their children take part. The main obstacle was commonly said to be dislike of fresh milk by children who were quite unused to it; the poorer the family, the more it relied on tinned milk. Others argued that the main obstacle was the cost – even at ½d, many families did not feel able to afford it. Later

* *Percentage of pupils taking school milk*

	England and Wales	Scotland
1936	45·6	42·2
1937	49·2	45·7
1938	53·8	47·2

events were indeed to confirm this view. For when school milk began to be issued free during the war, the proportion participating rose immediately and dramatically to over 90 per cent and stayed there.

For mothers and children under five milk still cost the full retail price, except in a few areas where experiments with cheap or free milk to pregnant women and children showed striking improvements in health and maternal mortality.[15] Improvements in antenatal service without extra food showed negligible results.

The Total Picture

To sum up, certainly the *average* consumer, if there were such a person, did consume more in the thirties. The Great Depression caused a relatively small cut in *average* consumption (though it slowed down the rate of growth), mainly because the fall in the price of imported foodstuffs helped to keep up living standards in the worst years of the slump. For most foodstuffs, supplies available per head (and presumably consumption) increased somewhat while prices were falling, and stabilized after 1934 when prices began to rise again, partly because of tariffs and restriction schemes. There was a marked increase in the per head supply of milk (where half the extra 6 per cent went into the milk in schools scheme) and of butter (at the expense of margarine) and a smaller increase in green vegetables and eggs. There was not much change in the amount of meat eaten, and after 1934 fruit supplies were tending to fall. By 1938 food consumption per head was about one-twelfth higher than in 1929, most of the rise having taken place by 1934.[16]

It seems likely, however, from what evidence we have, that with the important exception of the milk-in-schools scheme, the increased consumption of protective foods went to the middle class and salaried workers, and to a less extent to the most skilled and steadily employed sections of the working class. More food was eaten in restaurants and hotels (notably the 'road-houses' patronized by motorists); but this was still overwhelmingly an upper-class and middle-class habit, since there were few factory canteens and most workers either took sandwiches or went home to dinner. An exception were the milk-bars which became popular with working-class youth during these years. While middle-income diets were improving, at the bottom of the scale, among the long-unemployed and in the most wage-depressed industries such as textiles, more people were probably under-nourished than in the late twenties.

Estimated Consumption of Certain Foods per Head per Week at Different Income Levels in the United Kingdom (1934)

	Group I	Group II	Group III	Group IV	Group V	Group VI
Proportion of Population	(10%)	(20%)	(20%)	(20%)	(20%)	(10%)
Income per Head per week	Up to 10s	10s to 15s	15s to 20s	20s to 30s	30s to 45s	Over 45s
Food expenditure per week	4s	6s	8s	10s	12s	14s
Meat (ozs.)	23·1	31·6	37·1	41·5	44·8	49·4
Bread and flour (ozs.) (in terms of flour)	66·0	68·0	68·0	67·0	65·0	60·0
Milk, fresh (pints)	1·1	2·1	2·6	3·1	4·2	5·5
condensed	0·7	0·6	0·55	0·5	0·4	0·3
Eggs (number)	1·5	2·1	2·6	3·2	3·6	4·5
Butter (ozs.)	3·0	6·5	7·5	8·5	9·5	11·0
Cheese (ozs.)	1·8	2·5	3·1	3·6	3·6	2·6
Margarine (ozs.)	4·5	3·5	2·5	2·0	1·6	1·3
Potatoes (ozs.)	53·0	56·0	57·0	57·0	57·0	54·0
Fish (ozs.)	2·7	5·5	8·2	10·4	12·2	13·5
Fruit (ozs.)	14·0	21·7	25·8	27·9	30·5	39·3
Vegetables (ozs.)	16·0	20·0	27·2	30·6	32·3	34·0

(Orr, *Food, Health and Income.*)

Over a longer historical period, the most valuable estimate is that of Seebohm Rowntree, who, after comparing the results of his 1936 survey in York with those of the similar one he undertook in 1899, concluded: 'We should probably not be very far wrong if we put the standard of living available to the workers in 1936 at about 30 per cent higher than it was in 1899.' It must be remembered, however, that unemployment in York at that date was well below the national average, and very far below that in the distressed industrial areas. The rise for the whole county may well have been less than 20 per cent.

1936–7 Inquiry: Sir William Crawford and H. Broadley,
The People's Food

Estimated weekly expenditure (pence per head).
Family budget data

	Class AA (1%)	A (4%)	B (20%)	C (60%)	D (15%)	All Classes (100%)
Bread and Cereals	18·4	19·6	18·1	14·6	13·1	15·3
Meat, poultry and eggs	69·6	61·5	47·4	29·4	20·3	33·3
Fish	15·0	12·2	8·8	4·0	2·9	5·2
Dairy products	36·5	33·3	28·0	17·9	12·1	19·9
Margarine and other fats	3·1	2·6	2·1	2·1	2·3	2·2
Vegetables	16·4	12·7	9·7	7·4	6·2	8·0
Fruit and nuts	19·3	17·0	12·9	5·5	2·5	7·1
Sugar	3·2	3·0	2·7	2·6	2·3	2·8
Tea, coffee and cocoa	13·2	10·6	8·2	6·5	5·4	6·9
Other foods	28·4	17·7	10·2	4·4	1·6	5·9

The Sick
and the Old

Since the turn of the century the health of the nation had been improving. The expectation of life of a new-born boy, for instance, had risen from forty-five in 1900 to fifty-nine in 1930–2. This improvement could be attributed to better housing and sanitation and to increasing medical skill. Great strides had been made in controlling infectious diseases. Nevertheless, between 3,000 and 4,000 people, mainly children, died each year of diphtheria; mass diphtheria immunization was still ahead. And 2,000 children died each year of whooping cough. The most dreaded killer was tuberculosis, which carried off between 30,000 and 40,000 people a year. And though this was nothing like the number dying of cancer and heart disease, the latter were both associated with old age – or at least advanced middle age; tuberculosis cut off the lives of young people between the ages of fifteen and twenty-five.

The most striking sign of improved health was the reduction in deaths of infants under one year. For the United Kingdom as a whole the infant mortality rate had fallen from 142 per thousand live births in 1900–2 to 68 in 1931. With minor fluctuations it continued falling, reaching 55 in 1938. Sir Arthur Macnalty, Chief Medical Officer to the Ministry of Health, expressed satisfaction at this fall in his annual *Report* for 1934: 'Nothing is more remarkable than the decrease in infantile mortality in the last thirty years, and, as was noted in 1933, no spectacular improvement can now be anticipated. The lower the rate the nearer one approaches the irreducible minimum which must always remain.' This observation was repeated in his subsequent annual reports. In retrospect he can be seen to have been wrong. In the ensuing thirty years the rate was to fall proportionately faster and further.

In contrast to the general trend the maternal death rate had shown no improvement for a quarter of a century, and even showed a tendency to rise, touching 5·04 per thousand live births in 1934. After the economic recovery this rate also began to decline and was down to 3·6 by 1938. Its decline was partly attributed to the use of sulphonamides in the treatment of puerperal fever.

Though the broad national trends towards improvement continued throughout the thirties, the mortality statistics revealed wide disparities between different regions. In the areas of poverty and high unemployment the risks of ill-health and premature death were far greater than for the rest of the country. Broadly speaking death rates were much higher in Scotland, the North of England and Wales than they were for most of the South of England. In 1935, for instance, when the infant death rate was only 42 per thousand live births in the Home Counties, it was 63 in Glamorgan, 76 in Durham, 77 in Scotland, 92 in Sunderland, 114 in Jarrow.

In 1936, when the maternal mortality rate per thousand live and still births had come down to 3·65 for England and Wales as a whole, it was 2·57 in the South East, but 5·17 in Wales and 4·36 in the North as a whole, including Durham, Northumberland, Cumberland, Westmorland, Yorkshire, Cheshire and Lancashire.

Deaths from tuberculosis showed the same disparity. For the years 1931–5 the tuberculosis death rate for women aged fifteen to thirty-five in Gateshead, South Shields and Merthyr was more than twice the rate in England and Wales as a whole.

These disparities persisted right up to the outbreak of war, and in some cases the gap got wider.[1]

Medical Services

While poor nutrition and bad environment were contributing towards ill-health, the financial arrangements for dealing with it when it came often acted as a deterrent to treatment. There was as yet no National Health Service. A limited state scheme had been grafted on to a much older system which had combined private enterprise general practitioners with working-class self-help, charity for the sick poor, and, as a last resort, the Poor Law.

For the middle class it was fee-paying all the way. The quality of the treatment depended to a large extent on the fee-paying capacity. The fees of general practitioners varied according to area and class of clientele. If specialist treatment or an operation was needed, there would be substantial surgeon's and anaesthetist's fees on top. It was customary to pay for nursing-home accommodation at ten guineas a week or more. In the private nursing-homes, the arrangements varied from luxurious and high-powered to sloppy and inefficient. The public wards in the big hospitals were reserved for working-class patients and were not usually available to single people with more than £4 a week, or married people with children with more than £6 a week. But the hospitals had begun to compete with the private nursing-homes, offering private wards to fee-paying patients. Here they got much more individual nursing care than patients in the public wards, and also avoided the martyrdom of rules and regulations – for instance, about visiting hours – which governed the public wards. The birth of a baby meant paying for a bed in a private maternity home or private hospital ward, or engaging a qualified maternity nurse who 'lived in' for the weeks before and after confinement. To some of the less affluent, medical fees were a continuous worry.

For manual workers the medical services were a confused mixture of compulsory insurance, voluntary insurance, free doctors, paid doctors, means testing and charity. All these elements and more besides could be combined in a single illness for one person.

A manual worker who fell ill was entitled to 15s a week health insurance benefit but nothing for his dependants. This was much less than he would have got if unemployed, so many families had other hand-to-mouth arrangements for voluntary insurance through trade unions, friendly societies and sick clubs. But if the illness went on for long they had to fall back on the ultimate horror

- public assistance. Inevitably the breadwinner tended to stay at work longer than he should have at the onset of illness, and tried to get back to work before he was well. This financial deterrent to treatment was most acute for tuberculosis sufferers, even though, for this unlike most other illnesses, treatment of all kinds was free. Early institutional treatment could have saved many lives, but since it meant that dependants would be left on the PAC, treatment was often put off until too late.

Health insurance, which was compulsory for all manual workers and for clerical workers earning less than £250 a year, conferred the right of a free service from a general practitioner, known as a 'panel' doctor. But the free service did not extend to wives and children – they had to pay. There was a jumble of schemes to cover this gap – doctors 'clubs', dispensaries, works contract arrangements – usually involving voluntary weekly payments. Inevitably most wives were not covered. Many of them would refuse to consult a doctor because of the expense so long as they could still stand on their feet – they dragged out the years suffering from chronic minor ailments feeling only half alive.

Health insurance did not extend to hospital treatment. Hospitals were of two kinds – the great voluntary hospitals, many of which had been originally founded by rich citizens to provide treatment for the 'sick poor', and public hospitals under the control of the local authorities, many of which had a poor-law origin. The voluntary hospitals were constantly appealing for funds. They ran great poster publicity campaigns ('*You* may need our help some day'), held flag-days, sought to involve titled people in fund-raising events with royalty present as the main attraction. But in practice, by the thirties, the income from voluntary funds nowhere near covered the outgoings. So working-class patients had two alternatives; either they paid what they were considered to be able to afford when they entered hospital, the amount depending on their circumstances after consultation with the almoner, or they paid 2d or 3d a week when they were well to a hospital contributory fund which gave them the right to free treatment in a voluntary hospital if and when needed. About half the total income of the voluntary hospitals was derived from patients' payments, either direct or through contributory schemes. The latter covered about ten million wage-earners by the late thirties.

The voluntary hospitals had the biggest proportion of beds for 'acute' cases, but the local authorities also had beds for such cases, as well as being responsible for tuberculosis, infectious diseases and the chronic sick. The bulk of the cost came out of rates and some from the government block grant, but in-patients and usually out-patients as well were assessed and required to pay what they could afford.

There were thus two very distinct standards – one for the middle class entirely fee-paying, one for the working class which however did not exclude fee-paying. This was very marked in the dental service. The middle class went regularly to a dentist, expected to have their teeth kept in order and paid substantial fees per visit. For the majority of the working class, bad teeth were one of the normal misfortunes of life. They never went to the dentist unless toothache became unbearable; they then expected to have the tooth pulled out, and indeed, by the time they reached the point of going to the dentist extraction was usually the only remedy. Even this, however, cost money, because although 'dental benefit' was available to some through the health insurance, it meant in most cases that only part of the cost was covered. Wives were not covered at all. A major calamity was to be forced to have so many teeth extracted that artificial teeth would be required.

For the birth of a baby the majority of working-class mothers relied on a local midwife. In the early thirties most midwives were 'independent practitioners' who relied on fees for their livelihood. The fee depended on the area or the financial status of the family – a fee of 30s was normal but in some areas midwives charged or received very much less. Many of them were nearly as poor as their patients. The official investigators who compiled the report on maternal mortality in Wales were clearly scandalized at what they had found – for instance, midwives whose hands were not clean, who knew nothing about modern ante-natal care, who had no appreciation of the importance of asepsis, whose only payment for services was a bag of coal, and whose main source of livelihood was something quite different like looking after a shop.[2] But taken as a breed, midwives were popular, and were held to be doing an efficient job under adverse circumstances. Less than one quarter of all births took place in hospitals or municipal maternity homes, and a good proportion of these were difficult or emergency cases rushed there after complications had set in.

The tendency for maternal mortality to rise in the early thirties resulted in the appointment of a departmental committee to examine the reasons involved. It found that at least half the deaths of mothers in child-birth were directly preventable, the four primary avoidable causes being lack of ante-natal care, errors of judgement or treatment by doctors or midwives, lack of reasonable facilities for medical care and negligence by the patient. This finding stimulated demand for improved maternity services, particularly from women's organizations, and some improvements were indeed made – including the foundation of a full-time salaried service of municipal midwives.

On the whole, however, the sick were inarticulate, putting up with all kinds of minor disabilities because of the expense or possible expense of treatment. It was not until the National Health Service was introduced after the war, when the demands on it so greatly exceeded all official estimates (particularly in the care of eyes and teeth) that the real extent of the deprivation was in retrospect made clear.

Old Age

Unlike the sick, the old were to become organized and articulate for the first time by the end of the thirties. For decades, the old had been objects of pity to others – in a sea of wretchedness, the aged poor were always the most wretched of all. Now at last the old were to speak up for themselves.

There had been various influences at work. The elderly of the thirties were the first literate generation; the universal compulsory schooling of the eighteen-seventies had been part of their childhood experience, so that all except the very oldest among them could read and write. They had lived their adult lives in a period of great trade union growth and had the habit of organization.

Above all, the new contributory pensions had given them a dignity and a unifying status – people had stopped talking about the 'aged poor' and talked instead about the 'old age pensioners'.

The contributory old age pension scheme gave to most manual workers 10s a week pension at the age of sixty-five, together with 10s for their dependent wives, and 10s for their widows. The scheme had not been long in existence at the beginning of the thirties.[3] The social investigators of the period still found it necessary to emphasize the great benefits that the scheme had brought to old people in comparison with earlier years. They also found it appropriate to explore other related topics such as the extent to which the pension scheme might have contributed to the weakening of the sense of family responsibility for the aged.[4] This had always been the main argument used by those who had doubts about the scheme.

The pension was not universally available, it was confined to those who had been insured under the National Health Insurance scheme which covered most manual workers but excluded a great many others. In fact, at the start of the scheme contributory pensioners numbered not more than 1·2 million people or 40 per cent only of the age group, and though the rate of entitlement was rising, it did not reach much more than 50 per cent by 1938.

The others – those who did not qualify, but could not support themselves – could after the age of seventy apply for a non-contributory old age pension, often known as the 'Lloyd George pension', established earlier. For this, however, you had to plead poverty, and it was only given after a means test. In 1931 the recipients of the Lloyd George pension numbered eight hundred and eighty thousand.

In spite of the widespread introduction of contributory pensions for the first time, the old people still suffered more acutely from poverty than anyone else. Seebohm Rowntree, for example, estimated that in York, 33 per cent of old-age pensioners were living below his own very stringent poverty line.[5]

Ten shillings was not of course enough to live on, nor indeed was 20s for a man and wife. Such sums were below anyone's minimum subsistence standards – the theory was that the pension was there to supplement the pensioner's own resources. Those who had no such resources could, as a last resort, apply to the local Public Assistance Committee for poor relief.

In practice most pensioners were partially supported by their families – the assumption that most of them had other resources was not borne out by the facts. Those pensioners who possibly could tried to go on working. Most were compulsorily retired at sixty-five if they had not already been part of the standing army of unemployed before that age, but it was estimated in 1937 that some three hundred and forty thousand pensioners (i.e. about 16 per cent of those drawing the contributory pension) were still working.[6] Their employers very often took advantage of them by reducing their wages, for there was no earnings rule – you still drew your pension, whatever your earnings. 'Many of these people qualifying for pensions when in employment have their wages reduced by the amount of pension received and they are left with no alternative but to submit to the reduction,' the National Federation of Old Age Pensions Associations complained later in their evidence to the Beveridge Committee.[7]

This was the main reason why the TUC and Labour Party linked their demands for higher pensions with the demand that it should be conditional on retirement. It was moreover widely believed that if a man of sixty-five could be given the choice of retiring on a reasonable pension or staying on at work, most men would choose to retire, and so help to reduce the standing army of unemployed. The idea which was to prevail for later generations that such retirement pensioners could be beset with boredom, or that it was better for a man's health and happiness to continue at work over the age of sixty-five, was remote from the thoughts of trade unionists in the thirties. The unemployment registers were teeming with elderly men who would never find work again; most of them had started work at twelve or even ten years of age and after a lifetime on long hours and low wages they longed for rest and security in their old age. Indeed, a pension age of sixty had been the movement's accepted policy right up as late as 1937.

As to other resources, few old-age pensioners were able to supplement their state pension with a pension from their former employer. Superannuation schemes were, of course, in existence for certain classes of public employees, such as civil servants, teachers, police, firemen and local government officers, and banks and insurance companies arranged pension schemes for their staffs. But a large proportion of these schemes applied only to people who were outside the state pension scheme in any case. In private industry the development of pension schemes was in its infancy.

The trade unions were indeed suspicious of occupational pension schemes, except where they had been parties to the agreement and had some certainty about the disposition of funds:

At the present time there are many promises of pensions handed out to them (J. M. Allen of the Shop Assistants' Union told the 1937 Labour Party Conference) but in a good many cases they are bogus schemes, as many of the old men know quite well. Money has been put aside for pensions out of profits, and the workers have been deluded into the view that when they reach sixty or sixty-five years of age they will have an adequate pension. What has happened very often is that the firm have struck a bad patch and fallen upon evil times, and have had to bring back into the trading account the money set aside for pensions, with the result that the workers of many years' service, when dismissed, have been dismissed without any pension whatever.

Very often people's homes got broken up, precious furniture and belongings accumulated over a life-time were sold, and the old people compelled to go and live with their families – those who could make room for them, at least. This created many human problems. 'Old grandfathers and grandmothers are afraid to eat too much food lest they should be taking the bread out of the mouths of their grandchildren', Ellis Smith MP told the House in November 1938.[8] And D. J. K. Quibell MP told of 'an old man bent and worn, who has worked in the steel industry all his life' and who had said: 'I only have 10s a week. I am living with my son, but his wife says she can no longer afford to keep me. I don't know what to do. I don't want to go to the workhouse, but there is nothing else to be done.'[9]

The 'workhouse' was the common name for what was officially

known as the 'institution' run by the Poor Law authorities, which took in old people who were too infirm to carry on. The last-but-one resort before the workhouse was to apply to the local Public Assistance Committee for outdoor relief. About one in ten pensioners got outdoor relief; the number rose gradually to about a quarter of a million when war broke out.

The local Public Assistance Committees were part of the local government apparatus, and the bulk of the relief which they distributed was met out of the rates. They operated differing scales. An old person living in York in 1936 with no resources but his pension, for instance, could get 5s from the Public Assistance Committee. Some Public Assistance Committees had no regular scales, but decided each case 'on its merits'.

An application for poor relief meant a visit from the Relieving Officer who asked a great many personal questions. In many areas the applicants would then have to appear before a relief sub-committee of the council and answer further questions. If he was granted relief he would line up once a week to draw the money. Some of it might be issued in kind, or in relief tickets which could be exchanged for specific items at local shops. Every fourteen weeks this procedure would be gone through again. The whole process seemed a humiliating one.

Many old-age pensioners refused to apply for relief even when entitled to it, dragging out their day half-starving on the pension alone. The most important deterrent to applying was the fact that the Public Assistance Committees operated a family means test, which was one step worse than the household means test applied to the unemployed. It meant that the PAC could and did try to recover any relief granted from sons and daughters, even if they were married with families of their own living far away. Rowntree came across a number of pensioners who said they would rather starve than force their children to support them by applying for relief to the PAC.

One greatly resented anomaly was that, although a man could draw the 10s pension at sixty-five, he could not draw the 10s pension for his dependent wife until she also had reached sixty-five. Since nearly all wives were younger than their husbands, most couples were unable to claim the joint pension when the husband first reached pension age and only got 10s between them.

In spite of a considerable volume of agitation from the labour and trade union movement for higher pensions, Conservative political leaders remained complacent about the scheme. It was described as a 'boon of inestimable value' in the 1935 Conservative Election address, and it was customary to stress that Britain was ahead of the rest of the world in this respect.* The Conservative leaders were moreover fortified by the opinion of many of their followers that the expansion of the social services had already gone too far. 'One must consider whether it is altogether an advantage for the working people of the country to have everything done for them from the cradle to the grave,' observed Lord Scone MP, on one occasion. 'The whole tendency of recent years ... has been to spoon feed the people of this country.'[10]

It was in 1938 that the old-age pensioners themselves began at last to organize. Old-age pensions associations were formed in Lancashire, London and elsewhere. In March 1939 some of the leaders of the movement, including J. C. Birtles of Manchester and the Reverend W. W. Paton, got together at a meeting in the YMCA in Tottenham Court Road. This was the forerunner of the influential National Federation of Old Age Pensions Associations which came finally into being in 1940. At the 1939 meeting it was decided to launch a national petition asking for the pension to be raised from 10s to £1. The movement grew rapidly. It was supported by some of the newspapers, and the *Daily Herald* ran a big campaign with a series of articles by Ritchie Calder on 'Life on 10s a Week'. By the time the petition was delivered to the House of Commons in July it had two million signatures.

The government used the widespread refusal of old people to apply for public assistance to suggest that the vast majority of pensioners were managing all right. Moreover, it was argued that though old people formed only 8 per cent of the population they

---

* For instance, R. S. Hudson, Parliamentary secretary to the Ministry of Health spoke to the House of 'our scheme of national insurance which, I believe, rightly, is at once the admiration and the envy of every other civilized country in the world'. (8 April 1937.)

I

would form a much larger proportion in later years, and any increase then would be an intolerable burden on the next generation.

It was not until a year later, when Britain was already at war, that some improvements were introduced. The pension age for women was lowered to sixty, thus removing for most couples the anomaly of husbands without wives' pensions. And pensioners who needed supplementation were removed from the Public Assistance Committees and given the right to apply for a supplementary pension from the Assistance Board, to be granted after a household means test (but not a family means test). Moreover, it could be drawn from the Post Office without the stigma of poor relief.

To the astonishment of those in charge, the number proving need and qualifying for the new supplementary pension reached over one and a quarter million, in place of the four hundred thousand officially expected. 'There has therefore been a remarkable discovery of secret need', observed a *Times* leader '. . . the surprise of the investigation is that for so many old people the level of existence should have been so low'.[11]

Funeral Insurance

If a family had no money to pay for a relative's funeral the local Public Assistance Committee arranged the burial. This was still commonly known as 'being buried on the Parish'. The shame and horror associated with being buried by the PAC was if anything more intense than the dread of being forced to live on the PAC. So families strove never to let death go unprovided for.

The normal working-class funeral was, by the thirties, a modest enough affair – yet its bare cost might be £13 or £15. Moreover, it was thought essential to have suitable clothes – a man needed to wear a dark suit if possible; women only felt correctly dressed if they were in black. For these reasons it was common for more than one relative to insure for the funeral expenses of the same person. And insurance against funeral expenses was often associated with other kinds of life assurance or endowments. It was customary for couples to take out policies not only on their own lives but on those of their children, and even parents, brothers and sisters.

There was no state funeral grant and four-fifths of the business was in the hands of fourteen insurance companies – of which the Prudential was much the biggest – and one-fifth in the hands of the friendly societies. Nearly 40 per cent of the premiums went in administrative expenses. They were collected on a door-to-door basis by a host of insurance agents who were as much part of the normal life of a working-class street as milkmen or postmen.

There was a good deal of lapsing because when people became unemployed they often found that they had to reduce their insurance, or cut it out. Even so a survey by the Unemployment Assistance Board showed that three-quarters of their applicants in 1938 were paying insurance premiums and of these three-quarters again were paying more than 1s a week. Even if people were obliged to lapse they nearly always started up again the moment they could afford it. And, if and when their resources increased, they would take out additional policies.

There was, in the thirties, a certain amount of criticism of the 'over-insurance' of the working class which was attributed to pressure by the ubiquitous insurance agents for new business on ignorant and gullible housewives. Pressure there certainly was, for the insurance agents worked on a commission basis. But the fact was that most people were anxious to insure to the greatest extent possible. It gave a sense of security to people whose lives often seemed dominated by frightening insecurity.

New Patterns
of Living

Clothing and Furniture

The women's fashions of the twenties, which had burst upon the world like a declaration that the age of female emancipation had arrived, disappeared suddenly at the beginning of the thirties. At the time they had seemed daring; in retrospect they seemed clumsy and curiously sexless. There was a swift and dramatic change back to deliberately feminine styles. Busts, which had been flattened and hidden, came into their own again. Waists, which had been concealed beneath rather sack-like garments tied in at the hips, went back to their normal place. Wide padded shoulders helped to make waists look small and neat. Knee-length skirts went out and the hemline fell to mid-calf – only ten inches from the ground in 1932. The masculine Eton crop and very short shingle faded away – now the aim was a girlish hairstyle flat on top, curling a little at sides and back. Cloche hats which had hidden the ears and come down to the eyes were abandoned in favour of little tip-tilted bowlers, berets and straws reminiscent of the nineties. Evening dresses went down to ankle length once more. Simultaneously their necklines fell also – the backless evening dress came in. The intention was romantic rather than startling, elegant rather than odd.

Some people suggested that the turn towards femininity in fashion was the result of a subconscious desire for security, for a retreat from the hazards of the new freedoms. But in fact the new fashions were in tune with the spirit of the romantic, escapist make-believe world which dominated the films and popular songs of the day. Moreover, they had a technical innovation to support them. The hour-glass figures of pre-war days had needed heavily boned and tight-laced stays, long since thrown off in the twenties. Now had come the invention of the 'two-way stretch' elastic suspender belt, which gave the appearance of a trim figure but did not hinder freedom of movement.

After the initial dramatic change there were only superficial modifications in style for the rest of the decade – an inch or two up or down in hemline, the suggestion of curls in front of the hair, an alteration in the tilt of a hat. The revolution, such as it was, in the ensuing years, was not in styles so much as in materials, and with them the beginnings of a mass market.

The difference between the clothes worn by rich and poor was still extremely marked; the age when these differences were to be blurred by the mass production of well-designed cheap clothes was still ahead. All the same, the process was beginning with the arrival of man-made fibres. There was as yet no nylon, but rayon was coming into its own in a big way as a substitute for silk – indeed it was commonly known as 'artificial silk'. Previously the rich had worn silk stockings and the poor had worn cotton ones – now, the new cheap artificial silk stockings (fully fashioned and with fancy 'clocks') were very little different in superficial appearance from best quality silk stockings. Crêpe-de-chine and satin women's underclothes still dominated the luxury trade, but the new rayon underwear, very glamorous in comparison with its wool and cotton predecessors, had now become cheaply available to millions of women. And the relatively inexpensive rayon dresses which were appearing seemed very attractive in comparison with what had gone before. Other man-made substitutes, however, were still ahead. Macintoshes were still made of rubber, knitted goods of real wool.

Chain stores like Marks and Spencers were expanding fast and opening up new branches in many areas, selling not only underclothes, but skirts and jumpers and cheap dresses of a much better design than before. Long runs and semi-self-service methods could mean good quality goods at relatively low prices.

Simultaneously there was a great expansion of cheap consumer goods other than clothes. More and more Woolworths were being opened where nothing cost more than 6d. A great variety of goods could be bought there, including crockery, glass, cutlery, cooking utensils, haberdashery, cosmetics, stationery, books, toys and ironmongery.

The small rooms and compact design of the new owner-occupied houses needed furniture which was simple, streamlined and compact. The furniture trade was slow to recognize this, however. The simpler and more economical designs were usually the more expensive, and tended to be confined to the quality market. The cheaper the line of furniture, the more grandiose. So that in spite of an instinctive revolt against Victorian clutter, many of the new houses seemed over-full of furniture.

The furniture shops offered large opulent-looking three-piece suites – sofa and two easy chairs – which were represented as a desirable status symbol for every front room, no matter how small. In practice they would be crammed into a room of about ten foot square, along with an inherited piano, a new wireless set, a cabinet with ornaments, and the rest. Dining-room suites, complete with table, side-board and chairs to match, came next in importance; for upstairs there were complete bedroom suites, including dressing table, chest of drawers and massive wardrobe. Smaller wardrobes were, however, beginning to become available – perhaps because of the difficulty of housing the old giant wardrobe in the average new house. Though working-class families still clung to patterned wallpapers, they were out of fashion with the more up-to-date owner-occupiers who went in for distempered walls – often cream, pale green or light grey.

Working-class families also went in for three-piece suites and inherited pianos in their front rooms. However, here the living pattern was marginally different. Very often the front room was reserved for Sundays and visitors; otherwise the family not only ate but passed its leisure hours in the kitchen in front of a coal fire, usually with background music coming continuously from the radio. By the end of the thirties three-quarters of the families in the kingdom had a radio.

The main method of buying furniture by both working-class and lower middle-class families was hire purchase. Buying on the 'never-never' was in process of a big expansion, though some essentials such as gas or electric cookers were more often hired. By 1938 it was estimated that 60 per cent of all furniture was being sold through hire purchase, and that five million families were involved.

Just as owner-occupation led to jerry building, hire purchase led to racketeering. The most widespread racket was known as the 'snatch-back', which arose because people so often fell behind with their hire purchase payments. Falling behind was inevitable at a period of such insecurity, but in fact high pressure door-to-door canvassing itself contributed to arrears in payments. For canvassers were trained to overcome reluctance and persuade housewives to sign up for things they could not really afford. And since many canvassers were paid on commission and were highly insecure themselves, there was an incentive to use all kinds of trickery to secure a sale.

When a customer got into arrears with payments, by no matter how small an amount, the law allowed the firm which was selling the goods to seize them and take them back, the customer would then not only lose the goods but forfeit all his previous payments. The 'snatch-back' was a regular occurrence in most working-class areas. A family which had bought a suite for £27 and had painfully over the months paid back £25 10s might be in difficulties with its final instalments, perhaps because of sickness. Some would be reasonable in such circumstances and give time to pay up. But there were many firms who would immediately remove all the furniture and the customer who had lost furniture and money would have no redress. Some of the firms even employed 'bruisers' or ex-boxers, strong-arm men who would intimidate and assault people if they tried to stop the goods being seized.

Certain firms made more money out of the 'snatch-back' than they could have done with normal sales, for it allowed them to resell goods several times over. J. R. Leslie, former general secretary of the Shop Assistants' Union and MP for Sedgefield, alleged in 1937 that seizures all over the country averaged about six hundred a day. He told the House of Commons that over five hundred wireless sets had been snatched back in one week in one city. 'One trader confided to another that he had taken a set back no fewer than seven times and had sold it for the eighth time at the original price, and he said that he had got his money back three times over.'[1]

In December 1937 the left-winger, Ellen Wilkinson MP, introduced a private members' bill to protect hire purchase customers, and got all-party support for her measure which became the first Hire Purchase Act in July 1938. The Act was a landmark in several ways. It was one of the few important measures of social reform inaugurated during the decade. And it signified the arrival of a new kind of consumer with a new pattern of living.

Motoring and Cycling

Still more far-reaching was the change in living patterns brought about by the motor car. By 1931 the motor age had already arrived. There were over 2,000,000 motor vehicles on the roads of which 1,000,000 were private cars, 600,000 were motor-cycles. There were nearly 350,000 commercial vans and lorries, and about 85,000 buses.

The vogue for motor-cycles had in fact reached its zenith; the adventurous young men with slicked-back hair and goggles who had scorched up the roads on motor-bikes in the twenties had now presumably graduated to the two-seater or small family car. The 'quality car' which had dominated the market in the twenties was now being overtaken so far as numbers were concerned by the small cheap car sold at prices within reach of the less affluent middle class. Thus in 1931 the world-famous Austin Seven was selling at £118; a Morris Minor two-seater at £100. That was the price when new; a second-hand car of sorts could be bought for much less.

Horse-drawn traffic was disappearing fast; yet though some new roads were being built, most were still more suitable for horse-drawn than for motor vehicles. They were badly surfaced, badly lit, narrow and full of sudden blind corners. All the same, motoring had compensations which were never to come again.

For you could still 'get away from it all'; unspoilt countryside and unbroken rural solitude seemed just a little way away; the first few who were taking holidays with a caravan on a trailer had no difficulty in finding empty fields to camp in and friendly farmers to supply milk.

The million-odd private cars on the road represented only one for every forty-four persons – not one family in ten possessed a private car. The majority relied on other means of getting about. In the towns there were plenty of trams which were, however, being steadily replaced by motor buses. For long distance, the railways dominated the picture. They were owned by the four mainline railway companies; a committee in the late twenties had advocated electrification, but only the Southern Railway had embarked on any sizeable electrification programme; the Great Western, the London Midland Scottish and the London North Eastern all stuck to steam. From the consumer's point of view this meant smelly and dirty railway stations particularly at the London termini – King's Cross, Euston, St Pancras and Paddington. On the other hand the state of the labour market meant a great many porters competing to carry luggage for small tips. Long-distance motor-coach travel was just beginning and was shortly to prove a strong competitor with the railways.

There were millions of pedal cyclists – no one knew how many but it was thought there were at least ten million, or ten times the number of private motorists. Cycling was the main means of getting to work. A brand-new Raleigh bicycle could be bought for under £5 in 1932, or on the instalment system at 9s 7d a month without a deposit. The Raleigh was the aristocrat; a Hercules cost less than £4 and there were even cheaper makes. And in any case a second-hand bike could be picked up for a few shillings.

Cycling indeed came into its own in the early thirties, not just as a way of getting about but as a recreation at weekends for the youth. Cycling clubs proliferated, organizing regular weekend cycling expeditions, and on all the main roads throughout the summer great groups of young cyclists could be seen; the girls often dressed like their boy friends in shirts, shorts and zip-up jackets. Most of them were in their twenties. They had their own sort of free-masonry, they patronized their own network of cafés and bed and breakfast places listed by the Cyclists' Touring Club and the National Cyclists' Union; impecunious and gay, they had their own conventions, fashions and crazes. And they were very determined about one thing – that the motorist should not be allowed to sweep them off the roads on to specially constructed cycle tracks running alongside. For the motorists and a lot of other people were urging that this should be done, and in some places it had been done. Most weekend cyclists however ignored the cycle tracks and kept to the main road, contending that the roads had been built for everyone. There were many young industrial workers among the weekend cyclists and many in office and sedentary jobs who yearned for fresh air and the open road. Those who could manage it went on cycling holidays; a week's holiday could be managed on £3 10s all-in at CTC accommodation – stopping at Youth Hostels it could even be managed for £2.

When the depression came expenditure on road-building was halved, and never returned to the level of the twenties. While the Germans were building four- to six-lane Autobahnen – great trunk roads which were essentially motorways (and built of course for military purposes) – the British trunk road was still a three-lane affair.

But the rising number of road accidents could not be ignored. By 1933 the number killed on the roads had topped 7,000 almost as many as the road deaths thirty years later, though with only one-sixth of the number of vehicles on the road, and the injured numbered 216,000. Two-thirds of the road casualties were pedestrians or pedal cyclists; old people and children formed a high proportion of the pedestrians killed. Road safety drill for children had hardly begun, while the elderly, who had passed their youth in the pre-motor age were not adapting themselves easily to the new hazard.

There was a tendency among motorists to blame pedestrians for the accidents. The *Motor,* a journal which represented the more aggressive school of motoring thought, observed tartly:

Nobody who drives a motor vehicle in the streets of London can fail to be astounded at the folly of which pedestrians are capable. Considering what traffic is today, the risks taken appal the man at the wheel of a motorcar who – it is no exaggeration to say – is constantly saving the lives of walkers.[2]

During the twenties there had been a general twenty-mile-an-hour speed limit, which had, however, been abolished in 1930 by Herbert Morrison (of all improbable people) on behalf of the Labour government on the grounds that it was largely disregarded and quite unenforceable. After that there was a free-for-all, with no speed limit anywhere except on a few special stretches of dangerous road.

Now the level of road accidents meant that something had to be done. In April 1934 the government took some far reaching steps in a new Road Traffic Bill which laid down a thirty-mile-an-hour speed limit in all built-up areas and provided for the first time for driving tests for all new drivers (until then anyone could get a driving licence just by paying for it, even if he had never driven in his life before). The Bill also enabled the Minister to establish pedestrian crossings and bring in other regulations.

The Bill provoked virulent opposition from some motoring circles. The *Motor* said it was a measure 'designed to apply still more shackles to the motorist' and constituted a 'surrender to the forces opposed to motoring'.[3] Sir Herbert Austin, head of the Austin car firm, said 'Much severe criticism will be levelled at the Government's proposed new Traffic Regulations by motorists and motor manufacturers all over the country, but as their numbers are small compared with other users of the road, naturally their interest will have to be sacrificed on the score of the political vote.'[4] And he added that the cause of road casualties would be found 'largely in the narrowness of so many of our roads, blind corners, treacherous road surfaces, misuse of the roads by cyclists, pedestrians and horsedrawn vehicles'.

Opposition to the Bill was voiced in the House of Commons where Lieutenant-Colonel Moore-Brabazon spoke as follows:

I consider this to be absolutely reactionary legislation ... It is no use getting alarmed over these figures ... It is true that 7,000 people are killed in motor accidents, but it is not always going on like that. People are getting used to the new conditions. The fact that the road is practically the great railway of the country instead of the playground of the young has to be realized. No doubt many of the older Members of the House will recollect the numbers of chickens we killed in the early days. We used to come back with the radiator stuffed with feathers. It was the same with dogs. Dogs get out of the way of motorcars nowadays and you never kill one. There is education even in the lower animals. These things will right themselves.[5]

The second reading was nevertheless carried without a division, though later when the Bill reached the Lords there was a lot more grumbling, with Earl Howe, a member of the committee of the Royal Automobile Club and chairman of the Road Federation, strongly opposing the thirty miles per hour speed limit.* But the Bill became law that summer.

Its first fruit was a regulation banning the sounding of motor horns in London after dark except in case of emergency. This prohibition had a marked effect. Driving 'on the hooter' had been normal practice, and the sudden prohibition not only cut down noise to a muffled rumble, but temporarily reduced many drivers to little more than walking pace.

By the late autumn, ten thousand pedestrian crossings were being established in London for the first time, and the pattern was spreading to other towns. The crossings were marked by orange globes set on black and white posts, which immediately became known as 'Belisha beacons', after the Minister of Transport, Leslie Hore Belisha. There was considerable criticism and indeed ridicule of these crossings at first; Hore Belisha had the last laugh when he was able to show later that pedestrian fatalities in London in 1935 were down by 24 per cent as compared with 1933.[6]

The year 1935 was indeed the first year for very many years to show a reduction in the aggregate of killed and injured, and from then on the figures never reached the 1934 level again until after the war broke out, but stayed more or less constant, although the

---

* There is, however, no record that either the RAC or the AA as such officially opposed the legislation.

number of vehicles on the road continued to rise. But expenditure on road building and road improvements continued to be starved – and indeed this was justified by some statesmen. 'If you make more roads you make more opportunities for accidents', observed Neville Chamberlain when Chancellor of the Exchequer in a debate on the Road Fund.[7]

By the end of the thirties the design of the private car had completely altered. The square box on wheels of the early thirties had been largely replaced by the streamlined model with sloping rear. So that by 1939 the 1931 model looked almost as archaic as your grandmother's hat. Private cars had nearly doubled their number during the decade and by the end of it represented about one for every twenty-four persons.

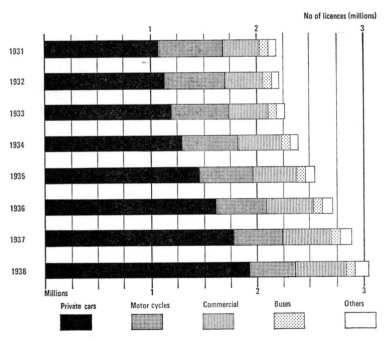

Fig. 12 Road vehicles in Great Britain.

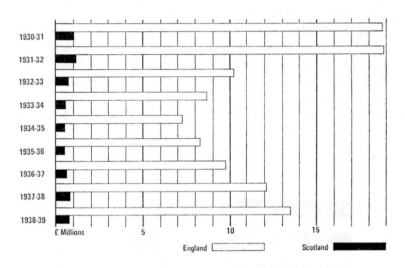

Fig. 13 Road-building expenditure.

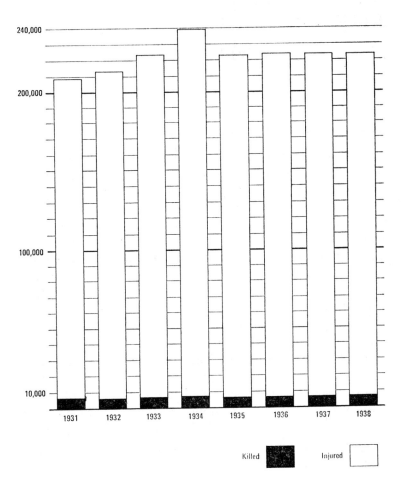

Fig. 14 Road accidents – Great Britain.

Leisure and the
Rise of the Mass Media

The thirties was the period when the mass media – press, radio, film, gramophone records – first began to assume their full modern shape and importance in people's lives. Big business dominated and exploited entertainment and leisure, and made more money out of people's spare time than ever before. While the number of workers directly employed in providing entertainment and sport increased from 65,000 in 1930 to 116,000 in 1937, it was also a period when intellectual interests, high-quality books and music came within the reach of millions for the first time.

Drinking as a way of spending leisure and spare cash declined in the slump, and never got back to the 1930 level. Less beer and less spirits were drunk per head than in the twenties, and much less than before the First World War. Although more was spent on liquor, nearly half the total expenditure went in taxation. Cigarette smoking, on the other hand, greatly increased, till it was estimated that eight out of ten men and four out of ten women were smokers. Cigarettes soothed the nerves, and compensated the poor for hungry and monotonous diets; and no one had yet heard of a connection with lung cancer.

People drank less partly because taxation made beer more expensive, partly because there were now so many other ways of relaxing after work besides going to the local. The wireless gave something to listen to at home, and for an evening out there were now the comfortable super-cinema, the dance-hall or the dogs. Newspapers and magazines were bigger, more attractively produced, and could be looked at, if not read, without effort.

Commercial sport, especially football, became a money-spinner.

Not only internationals and Cup-ties but League matches were normally packed. The sums paid to see the game were small, however, compared with those spent on the pools, started early in the thirties, which, along with the traditional forms of betting on horses, offered the workers, including the unemployed, the only chance (even if a one-in-a-million chance) of a radical change in their lives. By 1938 some ten million people a week were sending in their forecasts at about 3s an entry, and the promoters' turnover was about £40 million a year with £2 million or more as profit, some of which was reinvested to establish mail order stores and retail chain stores. Yet even by 1938 the turnover of the pools was only one-fifth of the money spent in betting on horses. Betting on the new sport of dog-racing, however, encouraged by the introduction of the tote in 1935, had risen to three-fifths of that on horses.[1]

There was much serious concern in the thirties, as there has been ever since, that the commercialization of leisure was making ordinary people more passive in their enjoyment, receiving entertainment and culture rather than making their own, listening to canned music instead of playing darts or singing round the piano in the pub, silently goggling at the pictures instead of cheering and booing in the music-hall or joining in the hymns at church. Such changes and their effects are inherently very difficult to measure. It does seem, however, that while the people who made active and constructive use of their leisure may always have been a minority, there was a boom in a great many hobbies of that minority – in cycling,[2] hiking,[3] darts clubs, evening classes, political discussion groups, youth clubs, amateur dramatics. The new housing estates provided their first bit of garden for millions of families, and for a large proportion this became an important new interest. Mr Middleton, who gave the BBC's gardening talks, was one of the earliest broadcasters to have a personal following of millions. Nor did the wireless, in home or pub, annihilate conversation to anything like the same degree as the telly has done since. Church attendance, on the other hand, certainly declined considerably, Rowntree in York in 1935 found it only about half as common as in 1901.

If one compares working-class life in the thirties, not with the early eighteenth-century village (about which opinions differ) but with working class life earlier in the twentieth century, it was on balance less monotonous and drab. On the other hand, never had it been made so easy for the factory or office worker to live a complete fantasy life in substitution or compensation for the hardships of the real world. Even the unemployed found pennies somehow for the cinema. Cheap Saturday morning shows for the children were crowded in the Distressed Areas as everywhere else. Cinema, rather than religion, was 'the heart of a heartless world, the opium of the people'.

The Press

The early thirties was a period of frenzied circulation warfare between the big newspaper groups – Rothermere, Beaverbrook, Odhams, Berry and Cadbury. With concentration of ownership and capital, newspapers got bigger and dependence on advertising revenue increased, so that circulation figures became a life-and-death question. The *Daily Herald,* which had struggled on, independent of both the press lords and the official Labour Party, got into financial difficulties and was taken over in 1929 by Odhams Press, in a deal which gave Odhams 51% of the shares and the TUC 49%, with a proviso that Odhams and the TUC would be equally represented on the board, and that the *Daily Herald* would always support Labour Party and TUC policy. The Communist *Daily Worker,* founded in 1930, took over from the old *Daily Herald* the role of organ of the extreme left; it consisted of four small pages and survived (contrary to expectations in Fleet Street) on a fund raised from month to month by its political supporters.

To retain the loyalty of readers, the mass-circulation papers offered huge prizes for crosswords and other competitions. Thousands of pounds a week were spent employing house-to-house canvassers. Free health and life insurance were another bait to catch regular readers, and the papers competed in the variety of risks covered. In 1932 the owners agreed to stop the insurance war and offer more or less equal policies, but other forms of competition continued – free gifts of all kinds, flannel trousers, cameras, tea-sets, encyclopedias, sets of Dickens and Shakespeare. The *Express* was first to reach the two million circulation mark, but announced that it had spent £30,000 a week getting there and that the new readers had been bought at 8s 3d a head. The *Herald* reached two million soon after.

Total sales rose less than might have been expected from so much sales-promotion in a period of economic recovery. National morning papers rose from 8,567,000 in 1930 to 9,903,000 in 1937; Sunday papers from 14,600,000 in 1930 to 15,700,000 in 1937. In the provincial press there was a tendency to decline in both numbers and readership, and over the decade as a whole the amount spent per head on reading-matter hardly increased. People were coming to rely more and more on the radio for the actual news. However, compared with other countries, newspaper readership in Britain was extraordinarily high. It is safe to say that in 1939 a morning paper was taken by the vast majority of families, an evening paper was read by half the families and there were very few homes without a Sunday paper, while perhaps a third took two or more. More readers, in fact, bought copies of fewer papers than ever before.

The style of popular newspapers was also changing. Headlines were larger, there was much more illustration (partly as a result of improved methods of reproducing photographs), and make-up was becoming more elaborate. In 1934, the hitherto Rothermere-owned *Daily Mirror,* with advice from the American advertising agency J. Walter Thomson, switched to the tabloid style, including telegraphic sentences, huge headlines, minimum letterpress and extensive strip cartoons.* Meanwhile the 'quality press', able to attract advertising because its upper-class readers had more to spend, continued with the traditional sober lay-outs (though *The Times* pioneered a new and beautiful type-face) for another thirty years.

---

* However the tabloids (*Mirror, Sketch*) had only 20 per cent of the popular daily readers in 1937, as against 35 per cent twenty years later, and 14 per cent of the Sundays, compared with 23 per cent twenty years later. (See Raymond Williams, *Communications*, Penguin Books.)

Compared with the later sixties, there was considerably more political variety in the press of the thirties. Although the Conservatives had a large majority in Parliament, two of the biggest national dailies, the *Herald* and the *News Chronicle,* were generally critical of government policy. The right-wing press, especially Rothermere's *Daily Mail,* was extreme in its views and often frankly pro-fascist, while Rothermere occasionally wrote pro-fascist pieces for the *Mirror* too. *The Times* and *Observer,* then owned by the Astor family, were the main bulwarks of respectable appeasement policy, against which Beaverbrook's empire-crusading *Express* periodically and unpredictably rebelled. The *Sunday Pictorial* was often radical, and *Reynolds' Newspaper* (owned by the Co-ops) gave the labour movement an independent Sunday voice. An increasingly influential weekly paper, especially among professional people, was the strongly anti-fascist *New Statesman.*

Woman, which offered readers and advertisers plenty of high-quality pictures much cheaper than the upper-class glossies, was launched in 1937, and had half-a-million readers by the end of the year. The vast multi-million circulations of women's magazines in the fifties would have been impossible before the war, however, according to *Woman's* original editor, because the widely uniform habits and tastes high sales required did not yet exist – and indeed living standards in the working class were too low for mass advertising on the scale developed later:

To be practical: no advice on personal hygiene could have included a casual reference to a daily bath. That would have been out of character. Similarly a 'phone in the house was out of character. So was a holiday abroad. The whole vocabulary of dietetics – calories, vitamins and proteins – was unknown.[4]

Picture Post, started in 1938 by Stefan Lorant, a refugee from Germany, raised pictorial journalism to a new topical intensity and had a strongly anti-fascist and socially-engaged angle. Such papers were made possible by the invention of the small Leica camera (which enabled news pictures to be taken unobtrusively) and the new techniques of cheap high-quality photogravure.

Radio

Radio, while enormously popular and influential, was restricted both in time and in the range of interests catered for. Under pressure from the newspapers, who feared its competition, the BBC gave no news bulletins before 6 o'clock in the evening, right up to the 1938 Munich crisis. Moreover until the late thirties it operated the 'Reith Sunday' – no programmes except the weather forecast until 12.30 a.m., when church and chapel were over, and after that programmes limited mainly to religious talks and serious music. The two networks, National and Regional, differed little in character; both offered more light music and fewer plays, features and outside broadcasts than today's programmes. There was no Light Programme and no Third, and those who wanted more dance-music were already tuning in to the commercial Radio Luxembourg. Sir John Reith, the awe-inspiring Director General, was convinced he had a divine mandate 'to carry into the greatest number of homes everything that was best in every department of human knowledge, endeavour and achievement';[5] but the best did not include unorthodox religious views or left-wing politics, and there was little attempt to give even an appearance of impartiality. Announcers' voices had to be strictly upper class standard English, without a trace of the regional accents heard today, and language was carefully disinfected. Thus at a time when American radio was already frankly commercialized, the BBC continued to offer traditional middle-class culture, self-improvement tempered by triviality, and establishment views. The possibilities of radio as a popular medium were, however, beginning to be explored – witness Tommy Handley's ITMA, which began its record-breaking ten year run in July 1939.[6]

Films

The coming of the talkies in 1929 opened a new age in the cinema. By 1937 twenty million people attended cinemas each week. It was estimated that 40 per cent of the people attended once a week and 25 per cent twice a week or more. In 1929 there had already been some 3,300 cinemas and two main controlling chains, Gaumont and British International. In 1933 Odeon was added, and by 1938 there were 4,967 cinemas in Britain. As well as the pictures – usually two main features plus a newsreel and a cartoon, on a programme changed twice weekly – the new greatly enlarged super-cinemas provided by the big groups offered plushier seats, richer decor, and colour-lit Mighty Wurlitzer organs rising magically from under-stage in the intervals.

In these years Hollywood dominated the British screen and provided the main consolation and escape for the sufferings of millions. Films set the popular fashion in hairstyles, clothes and Christian names, begetting generations of Marlenes, Shirleys and Garys. This was the age of the magical song-and-dance team, Fred Astaire and Ginger Rogers; of vast spectacular costume musicals; of the child actress to end all child actresses, Shirley Temple; as well as endless gangsters and Westerns. Hollywood in these years had become a centre for European artists and technicians, including refugees and many of the stars most beloved by British filmgoers – Garbo, Charles Boyer, Marlene Dietrich – had foreign accents and exotic names to make them even more glamorously remote from the world of the depression.*

Economically the American product had a vast advantage, because, with a home market four times that of Britain, a film could recoup its complete cost in the United States and then be exported at no more than the cost of distribution. The British market was especially vulnerable because there was no language barrier (as in France or Germany) and British working-class audiences could (and can) identify with a Mid-Western accent at least as easily as with southern suburban English. So British films

* A very few Hollywood films, especially in the later thirties, touched on the workers and the underpaid in New Deal America – notably *Mr Deeds Goes to Town* (with Gary Cooper, 1936), *Dead End*, about delinquents in New York slums (with Bogart, 1936), and *Grapes of Wrath* (with Henry Fonda, 1939). But the most penetrating social comment was in comedy – in Charlie Chaplin's *City Lights* and *Modern Times*.

remained unprofitable and negligible at a time when René Clair in France and Pabst in Germany were producing their early masterpieces.

Government protection was for a long time too ineffective and half-hearted to change this situation. The Cinematograph Films Act of 1927 had required renters and distributors to take a compulsory quota of British films (5 per cent at first, rising each year to reach 20 per cent by 1936). But the quota was so small that for years it paid distributors better to get very cheap films ('quota quickies') made and run off than to invest seriously in quality film production, and this earned British films a bad name. By the mid-thirties a few quality films were being made, notably by Hitchcock (thrillers such as *Blackmail, Sabotage, Thirty-Nine Steps*) and by the Hungarian Alexander Korda, who began with the sumptuous *Private Life of Henry VIII* with Charles Laughton, and followed up with a string of costume biographies (which, not being too obtrusively British, were all right for the US market). Gracie Fields, already a music-hall star, who expressed something of the humour, doggedness and cynicism of the workers in the old industrial areas, found a vastly enlarged public for her dialect songs and mimicry in screen farces like *This Week of Grace*. But all this together amounted to scarcely a wave in the flood of American films. Where government capital was made directly available, to the GPO documentary unit, British directors and technicians proved themselves as good as any in the world – notably in John Grierson's *Drifters, Night Mail* (poem by Auden, music by Britten), and other documentary classics, which, however, never received a mass showing.

American domination of the screen dream-world was thus one factor which indirectly helped to weaken respect for the old British ruling-caste values – titles, hereditary wealth, Oxford accents, public school manners – among the working class.

Theatre at a Low Ebb

In the West End theatre, Shaftesbury Avenue french-window drama still predominated. It portrayed Kensington or country-house life for the benefit of the largely suburban audience, or (more rarely) suburban life for an audience like the characters in the play (Somerset Maugham's *The Breadwinner* or Rodney Ackland's *For Services Rendered*). The West End successes of the early thirties were light romantic or comic plays like those of Dodie Smith (*Autumn Crocus*) and Esther McCracken (*Quiet Wedding*), society comedies such as Coward's *Private Lives,* and competent historical plays like *The Barretts of Wimpole Street* and *Richard of Bordeaux*. The outstanding spectacular musical was Noel Coward's historical pageant *Cavalcade,* with a cast of four hundred and the keynote line 'in spite of the troublous times we are living in, it is still a pretty exciting thing to be English'. 'Kitchen-sink' drama scarcely existed. Sex, if any, was straight – no Lesbians, no queers, no sado-masochists.

The home of Shakespeare in London was the Old Vic, then still an unsubsidized, unfashionable theatre where students and young people could easily afford seats. There were brilliant isolated West End productions of the classics, but except for Stratford-on-Avon there was neither National Theatre nor Royal Shakespeare Company to maintain any continuity north of Waterloo.

The majority of provincial cities no longer possessed a professional live theatre on any permanent basis,* though there were repertory companies on and off in Birmingham and Manchester, and experimental and financially viable small theatres in university towns. For most cities there were merely visits from touring companies before or after a West End run, though there was a lively and growing amateur drama.

The large-scale experimental theatre that grew up in Europe in the late twenties – the Berlin theatre of Piscator and Brecht and Kurt Weill, the Expressionist theatre of Kaiser and Toller – had no equivalent on the English commercial stage. Its influence was confined to small highbrow theatres like the Group in London, where the Brecht-influenced satirical plays of Auden and

* This reflected the growing centralization of top industrial management and finance, with its attendant personnel and incomes, in London and the South East, as well as the rise of the cinema.

Isherwood were produced, the Festival at Cambridge or the Maddermarket at Norwich.

Popular Reading

Books, in the early thirties, were usually borrowed rather than bought – from public libraries, or from Boots, Mudies or other 'twopenny libraries' occupying a few shelves in local shops. Hardback novels at 7s 6d or 10s 6d were prohibitive except as an occasional present; cheap editions came out later at 2s 6d to 5s, still a lot of money. Novels available in sixpenny unbound form were usually the expendable sort – Edgar Wallace or Zane Grey. Only visitors to the continent could buy cheaply, in Tauchnitz and other paperbacks, a great variety of good modern titles. The worker in search of self-education could try classics in the Everyman edition at 2s or 2s 6d, Watts Thinker's Library at a shilling, or Benn's pamphlets at sixpence – somewhat forbidding in format and style.

Two developments in book publishing radically and permanently altered the scene. These were the commencement of Penguin Books, as sixpenny paperbacks, in 1935, and the founding by Victor Gollancz of the Left Book Club (see next chapter). From the outset Penguin refused to distinguish between highbrow, middlebrow and lowbrow as separate reading publics, and founded its vast sales on appealing at many levels. The first Penguins were printed in editions of twenty thousand; within three years the minimum first printing was fifty thousand.

In 1937 Pelicans and Penguin Specials were started to satisfy and extend the taste for serious non-fiction books, covering science, politics, sociology and the arts. Especially important were the topical Specials, not reprints but books commissioned for the series, in which anti-fascist titles and criticism of official policy predominated. Penguins were apparently aiming mainly at the new radical market opened up by Gollancz the year before, and did not attempt in those days to balance each left-wing title with another from the right. Among political best-sellers were the Duchess of Atholl's *Searchlight on Spain*, Mowrer's *Germany Puts the Clock Back,* Tabouis' *Blackmail or War* and Gedye's *Europe and the Czechs.*

The most popular and effective form of escapist reading was the detective story and crime thriller. The number of new mystery-detective stories reviewed increased from a dozen in 1914 and a hundred or so in 1925 to over two hundred in 1939; and the technical quality steadily rose. More and more serious writers turned to the thriller form, not only to make money, but also as a way of holding a middle-class reader's attention through an exciting novel which might incidentally include comedy of manners, literary criticism or political analysis. Very few were at all like real-life crime as reported in the *News of the World.*

While the modern mass media were already taking shape, the flavour of mass culture, taken as a whole, was more often sugary and sentimental, less strikingly violent and sadistic than today's. The prevailing background in books, films and plays alike was middle class. Horror films were milder, sexy books less sophisticated and realistic. The horror-comic and the theatre of cruelty were yet to come; and the Saint was a gentleman compared with James Bond. Escapism was of a simpler and more obviously consoling kind – 'She Married her Boss' rather than 'I was a teenage drug-pusher for the FBI' – and traditional morality received at least token approval.* Neither in popular songs (most of them originally written for West End musical comedy), nor in novels, nor in films was there much reflection of the life, tastes and idiom of the British working class. That appeared only with the mass consumption market of the fifties and sixties.

* Some changes in 'popular' culture of the last thirty years – newspapers, magazines, songs and so on – have been interestingly considered by Richard Hoggart in *The Uses of Literacy,* based largely on personal recollections of this period.

The Radical Trend
in Culture

The years after 1931 undermined what remained of the long-standing sense of stability in British middle class and intellectual life. The once ordered society turned out to be disordered, immoral and dangerous. It was this, rather than any upsurge of romanticism, that led to the radicalization of many intellectuals, and a crisis in outlook reflected in every aspect of art and culture.

To begin with, economic security for much of the middle class itself had been seriously weakened. Small business was in difficulties, cuts in education and other social services meant unemployment among graduates, especially teachers, and there was a general lack of openings for talent. Orwell in *Down and Out in Paris and London* has left a vivid impression of the declassed intellectual of the period drifting from one unsuitable job to another. The numbers and size of student grants were reduced, so that the contemporary slogan 'Scholarships not Battleships' was apt enough. And at the same time mass unemployment was an outrage to all moral feelings. Teachers, doctors and architects found it impossible in the prevailing atmosphere of 'economy' to put into practice the scientific ideas and innovations learned from psychology, dietetics and engineering.

Moreover Hitlerism in Germany, with violent repression not only of the working class movement but of Jews, liberals, pacifists and academics, had a shattering impact, especially since the refugees included intellectuals and middle-class people whose presence, jobless and without permits to work, brought the horror alive to sheltered English families. Young men whose work took them overseas to the colonies, like Graham Greene, George Orwell and Joyce Cary, were made aware of growing resentment and revolt among the people of the once invulnerable Empire. And above all, as the intense economic depression began to ease, minds were overshadowed by the fear of imminent war.

It was in this atmosphere that powerful new intellectual influences began to modify science and the arts. In psychology the teachings of Freud and Jung, and others experimenting with similar ideas like Groddeck and Homer Lane, were becoming sufficiently widely popularized to form part of the idiom of artists and writers. In economics the failure of orthodox remedies to restore prosperity after 1931 gave a new impetus to the study of alternatives: the New Deal, Keynes, Douglas Social Credit and especially Marxism. John Strachey, who had left the Labour Party in disgust along with Mosley and then left Mosley as his fascism became obvious, restated a Marxist analysis in popular terms in *The Coming Struggle for Power,* which was widely read among younger intellectuals disillusioned by Labour's seeming failure.

Influential also were the new scientific and technical developments, which were felt to imply a wholly new aesthetic. In every field of intellectual life increasing numbers of people, especially young people, were not only seeking to make a sharp breach with traditional forms, but identifying the established rulers of society with restriction in art and science.

This radical trend was especially strongly expressed in the rise of the various student political and peace movements. Whereas in 1926 students had been conspicuous as strikebreakers, driving trams and buses, in the thirties they were more in evidence welcoming hunger marchers, demonstrating to the university authorities for improved scholarships and academic freedom, or taking part in processions against war and fascism. The changing mood was seen also in the Left Book Club.

True, university radicalism and revolutionary feeling, though strongly organized in a few centres such as Oxford, Cambridge and the London School of Economics, involved probably a smaller proportion of a much smaller student body than did corresponding movements in the sixties. Left-wing students saw themselves as joining in a struggle already being carried on by the working class, or finding a useful role in the wider peace movement, rather than as a separate estate with wholly distinct problems and attitudes,* or even a new revolutionary leadership. For the working class, especially the unemployed, were then clearly engaged in great battles. Specifically student issues seemed less urgent, partly perhaps because the majority of students still came from the upper and upper middle classes for whom the educational system had been designed, and were relatively comfortable in it. Anyway students felt their own conditions and prospects to be immeasurably better than those of working youth. But if legend has exaggerated the scale of student rebellion, it has scarcely overstated its seriousness or the consternation it caused the Establishment.

Science

The younger scientists were at once the most fundamentally hopeful and the most frustrated among intellectual workers. Far-reaching discoveries – for instance in nuclear physics by Rutherford and his school, Chadwick and Cockcroft, and in biochemistry by Gowland Hopkins – opened up vast new fields of research and, suggested ways of improving living standards and lightening toil undreamt of a generation before. But scientific research remained on a small scale, starved of funds by economies in education, its application hindered by the restrictions of monopolist cartels. A leading industrial engineer, Sir Alexander Gibb, told the British Association in 1937:

> The greater the success of research, the more immediate and drastic the effect on existing plant and equipment ... Many valuable inventions have been bought up by vested interests and suppressed in order to save the greater loss that their exploitation would involve to already operating plant. It is therefore not surprising that there is not always an enthusiasm for unrestricted research or a readiness to pursue it. But this is a shortsighted policy.

The scale and use of research, except for war purposes, was woefully

---

* At LSE in 1934 there was a large-scale challenge to the authority of the director, Sir William Beveridge, to discipline left-wing students; but generally student participation in university control did not become a central issue.

small. Total expenditure on scientific research from all sources in 1934 was estimated by Professor Julian Huxley at roughly £4 million a year. This was about one tenth of one per cent of the national income, whereas even at that date the USA was spending proportionately six times as much, and the far poorer Soviet Union proportionately eight times as much.[1]

Moreover, the working conditions and prospects for young scientists were severely limiting. Of the three thousand seven hundred graduating annually from British universities in science and technology, only some 4 per cent could expect whole-time research grants, and these mostly at mere subsistence level. A DSIR junior grant was £120 a year (reduced in 1931 from £140), or £200–250 at Oxford and Cambridge, and the young research worker was allowed to retain only one-third (or at Oxbridge one-sixth) of money earned by teaching. Generally scientists were paid less than people of a corresponding educational level in non-scientific subjects.

The idea that it was possible to plan and organize the advance of science, rather than relying purely on the brainwaves of individual genius, received a powerful stimulus from international discussions in 1931 in London on the history of science.* In the next year or two informal groupings of younger scientists and economists began intensively to discuss the social planning and application of science, prominent among them being J. D. Bernal, Patrick Blackett, Joseph Needham, Hyman Levy, Solly Zuckerman, J. B. S. Haldane, C. H. Waddington and C. P. Snow, along with economists such as Hugh Gaitskell and Roy Harrod. In contrast to the horrifying picture of a science-dominated future given in imaginative writings by Aldous Huxley (*Brave New World*) and E. M. Forster (*The Machine Stops*), the new science was popularized as a friend, not an enemy, by scientists who were also gifted writers – notably by Lancelot Hogben (*Mathematics for the Million, Science for the Citizen*), Julian Huxley (*Scientific Research and Social Needs*), J. B. S. Haldane (in regular science features for the *Daily*

---

* The Russian scientists' contribution to these discussions was published as *Science at the Crossroads*, an influential book although their attitude was strongly contested by the astronomer Professor Dingle and others.

Worker), Hyman Levy and John Boyd Orr. And at the end of the decade J. D. Bernal in *The Social Function of Science* (1939) documented in detail the frustration of science under capitalism and the social change needed for its growth.

Meanwhile scientists themselves were beginning to organize to improve their own conditions and to secure increased funds and better utilization for scientific discoveries. The Association of Scientific Workers, formed after the First World War, which had fallen into decay, was revived from relative insignificance to activity, especially among younger scientists, in the later thirties. Some eighty scientists, mainly from the Cavendish Laboratory, founded the Cambridge Scientists' Anti-War Group, which made a devastating exposure of the ineffective official Air Raid Precautions; this ironically led to some of the authors being given responsibility for improving ARP when war actually broke out.*

The Visual Arts

Rising modern painters, sculptors and architects, already at work in the twenties, in 1933 formed themselves into a group called Unit One to maintain 'a truly contemporary spirit' in art, by which they understood emphasis on design and form, on structure rather than spontaneous and unconscious creation, and on composition rather than representation. The group included the sculptors Henry Moore and Barbara Hepworth, painters Ben Nicholson, Paul Nash, Edward Wadsworth and Tristram Hillier, and the architects Wells Coates and Colin Lucas. Picasso and the Cubists were a strong influence. 'We are frequently invited to admire the "unconscious" beauties of the British School – so faithful to nature', wrote Paul Nash, announcing the group in a letter to *The Times* on 2 June 1933. 'Nature we need not deny, but Art, we are inclined to feel, should control.' While rejecting 'the discredited notion that art is in any sense a reproduction of nature', the leaders

* Indeed many of the young men most conscious of the frustration of science in peacetime got the money for large-scale experiment only in war – among them Bernal, Blackett and Zuckerman, who later became Chief Scientific Adviser on Defence.

nevertheless drew much from the study of natural forms, including pebbles and bones as well as living things and the human body.

Barbara Hepworth wrote: 'I do not want to make a stone horse that is trying to and cannot smell the air . . . How lovely is the horse's sensitive nose, the dog's moving ears and deep eyes: but to me these are not stone forms and the love of them and the emotion can only be expressed in more abstract terms.'

This kind of movement in art ('abstracting' if not abstract) was closely akin to architecture. 'In the field of scale and size architecture has the advantage', wrote Henry Moore, 'but sculpture, not being tied to a functional and utilitarian purpose, can attempt much more freely the exploration of the world of pure form.'[2] Scientists, as well as engineers and industrial designers, felt kinship with this new aesthetic.*

In sharp contrast to all this were the Surrealists, whose famous London exhibition in 1936 attracted twenty thousand people, and who derived their subjects from the unconscious and dream images and the discoveries of depth psychology. Herbert Read became a powerful exponent of their ideas, and Paul Nash and others painted surrealist works. Many of the French surrealists called themselves Communists, but it was a matter of dispute on the left whether an art so obscure and esoteric was truly revolutionary or an art of despair. Anthony Blunt, who with F. Klingender was the best-known of Marxist art critics, held that although surrealism was certainly subversive of bourgeois values, its revolutionary aspect was 'purely negative' because without hope. The New Realism as applied for example by the sculptor Peter Peri, which appeared to be far less revolutionary at sight, was, he thought, really more so, since more capable of appealing to the working class.[3] The influence of surrealist ideas on creative work was, in England, more important in poetry, where David Gascoyne, George Barker and later Dylan Thomas worked much from unconscious, irrational and dream material.

The Artists' International was founded in 1933 by 'artists who recognized the need to act as political men'. It included the directly

---

* Even artists who later turned to representational work were much influenced by the abstract movement at this time, e.g. John Piper and Graham Sutherland.

political satirists Fitton, Boswell and Holland, but also 'straight' realists of the so called Euston Road group like William Coldstream and Victor Pasmore, and for a time was also supported by some of the leading abstractionists, including Henry Moore and Paul Nash.* The attempt to discover and impose a single style or orthodoxy (Socialist Realism or the like) for progressive art did not yet exert its divisive and sterilizing influence on the creative workers of the left. 'Those whom art and politics have put asunder, an exhibition against war and fascism has joined together,' commented *Left Review* on the A.I. Exhibition of 1935.

It was a brilliant period also for left wing political cartoonists. Indeed, the circulation of Beaverbrook's right wing *Evening Standard* was largely sustained throughout the thirties by David Low's daily political cartoon – a tribute not only to Low's wit, but also to the popularity of anti-fascist and anti-Chamberlain jokes among the readers.

Architecture

The effects of a social rather than a purely aesthetic consciousness were especially marked in architecture and design. At a time when fundamental changes in building technique – such as steel-glass and steel-concrete construction – allowed completely new styles, architects like those in Unit One, and later in the MARS group, were beginning to develop in Britain the functional approach already strong in the twenties in France and Germany, whose pioneers were Le Corbusier and Gropius.† The aim was to analyse the human uses which a building – or a chair – was intended to serve, and then design directly to meet these needs by the most modern techniques, rather than accept the traditional forms of buildings or chairs as given.

---

* Like scientists, many artists who wanted their work to fulfil a direct social role ironically found their opportunity in the war against Hitler. Nash, Ardizzone, Bawden, Moore all did distinguished work as official war artists.

† The English translation of Le Corbusier's key book, *Towards a New Architecture*, appeared in 1931. Gropius, founder of the Bauhaus, and a powerful influence in all forms of design, came to London as a refugee when modern art was persecuted by Hitler.

K

At the same time, many of the younger architects and students were becoming acutely conscious of poverty and squalor, and keen to gear their work to meet the most urgent needs – for instance to provide shelter in quantity, rather than concentrate on one perfect building at a time. They hoped to design whole towns, as well as individual dwellings, in terms of convenience and comfort for the people living there, using new materials and prefabrication for speed and economy. As one influential group has since written:

We were not interested in architecture as a cultural object for the individual, nor as a status symbol for the official or commerical organization. The notion of the monument in architecture was anathema, and so was what we called the 'prima donna' architect. Equally suspect was the crystallization of architecture into a particular formal style.[4]

Unlike the sculptors, however, architects needed to be commissioned before they could attempt to put their ideas into practice; and the bulk of what was actually built bore little relation to their vision. A few modern-looking houses were commissioned by enlightened rich men, but the prevalent styles remained those caricatured by Osbert Lancaster as Banker's Georgian and Stockbroker's Tudor.[5] Public buildings were still 'stately piles', concealing their steel skeletons under masses of redundant Portland stone or brick.

Over much of the field, architects were not employed at all in designing the great new residential suburban belts. Here, in an assortment of styles ranging from mock Tudor to bogus 'modern', the builders shelled out houses like peas from a pod, generally as ribbon development along existing highways. Concepts of unified design or coherent architectural treatment for a group of buildings – let alone a group of streets or a neighbourhood – were largely disregarded. And the process whereby old squares and streets which had embraced just such concepts were ruined by the intrusion of incongruous new buildings, unrelated to their neighbours in size or shape, went on apace just as it had in the twenties and before.

Isolated opportunities were offered by one or two enlightened public bodies – for instance pithead baths for the Miners' Welfare Commission, Underground stations for the London Passenger Transport Board, the Penguin Pool at the London Zoo and the Elephant House at Whipsnade. A few blocks of luxury flats were erected using the new techniques, *and at the end of the decade, with the Finsbury and Peckham Health Centres, the Bexhill Pavilion and the new flats and nursery school at Ladbroke Grove by Maxwell Fry and Elizabeth Denby, the precedents were being created in local authority building for the schools, flats and public buildings that have changed the aspect of cities since the war. But the chance for large-scale planning came only in the fifties and sixties with the rebuilding of bombed areas like Coventry, the City of London and Poplar – and even then planning was limited by vested interests in land and property.

Literature and Revolt

The twenties had been a great period in English literary history, with James Joyce, D. H. Lawrence, E. M. Forster, Virginia Woolf and T. S. Eliot all publishing outstanding works. In the thirties Virginia Woolf was still writing *The Years* and *The Waves,* more difficult and less widely appealing than her earlier novels. But High Bloomsbury, with its emotional roots in the stability of Edwardian Cambridge, was no longer the dominating literary influence that it had been in the twenties. Its liberal distaste for direct social or political commitment by the artist, its apotheosis of personal relationships, began to seem inadequate to younger intellectuals, including the next generation of Bloomsbury itself (for instance Julian Bell and John Lehmann). Indeed E. M. Forster himself gave time and the weight of his great prestige to several of the anti-fascist movements of the time (notably the Council for Civil Liberties). Though always with regret that it should be necessary, he was prepared to give two cheers for democracy. 'There is no occasion to give three; only love, the beloved republic, deserves that.'[6]

* e.g. Lawn Road Flats in Hampstead, by Wells-Coates and Highpoint at Highgate, by Tecton.

T. S. Eliot had already passed from the horror of emptiness in *The Waste Land* and *The Hollow Men* into commitment to Anglo-Catholic religious orthodoxy as the only source of continuity in art, and the means to safeguard the values left to society against materialism and revolution. This was expressed poetically in *Ash Wednesday,* and more directly in the plays *Murder in the Cathedral* and *The Rock,* written for church performance. Eliot's *Criterion* quarterly took editorially an increasingly traditionalist and anti-democratic line, though remaining open to contributions from individuals on the left like the historian A. L. Morton: and it showed considerable sympathy with fascist, especially Italian fascist ideology (felt also in Eliot's poem *Triumphal March*).[7] When the Spanish Civil War broke out, Eliot was one of the few eminent writers in Britain (Edmund Blunden was another) who did not support the Republic.

A group of serious critics concerned among other things with the effect of the social environment on culture, the debasing influence of the mass media and the commercialization of literature, centred in Cambridge round Dr F. R. Leavis, editor of *Scrutiny* (founded 1932), and his wife Q. D. Leavis, who published in 1932 a searing attack on the middlebrow best-selling novel, *Fiction and the Reading Public.* The influence of Leavis and his co-workers (notably D. W. Harding) was especially important among young teachers, who began to encourage their pupils to examine the language of advertisements and journalism as critically as that of poetry. *Scrutiny,* compared with other critical journals, appealed less to the in-group of the traditional privileged intelligentsia, (whose Etonian coterie control of literary values it bitterly assailed) and more to the hard-pressed first-generation professional worker. Its contributors were more often agnostic than the *Criterion*'s, concerned with moral rather than religious interpretation, though equally suspicious of science, socialism and technical change. Itself sharply anti-Marxist, it was sometimes conducive to Marxism in its readers.

The serious novelists of the twenties, who explored so perceptively the experience of the uprooted individual, left surprisingly little record of the social upheavals of those years. The General

Strike was 'done' by Galsworthy and Wells at a very superficial level: the miners' lockouts not at all (for D. H. Lawrence's contacts and interests had moved away from the mining village). In the thirties, by contrast, a number of novelists began to set their characters and conflicts in a wider social and political context of crisis.

One example in popular fiction was J. B. Priestley, whose first best-seller *The Good Companions* (1929) had combined glimpses of the drab industrial scene with a cheery and frankly escapist way out of all the characters' difficulties. His later and sadder novel *Angel Pavement* (in which a financier lands in the Port of London to ruin the lives of the little people in a City office) took the economic crisis as a central theme, and in the documentary *English Journey,* his most moving book, a Yorkshireman's sense of outrage at poverty in the midst of plenty still comes through today. The doctor-hero of A. J. Cronin's *The Citadel,* the grandfather of today's Doctor Finlay, was typical of the kind of hero commonly found in the more popular realistic books – young, dedicated, fallible and basically good, like the miner heroes of the same writer's *The Stars Look Down* and Richard Llewellyn's *How Green Was My Valley.* A powerful novel about unemployment and the means test was *Love on the Dole,* by Walter Greenwood, a Lancashire man with first hand experience of what he described; this book was later successfully staged and filmed, though censorship held up the showing of the film till 1940 when unemployment had ceased to be a burning issue.[8] Winifred Holtby (*South Riding*), Phyllis Bentley and H. V. Hodson also wrote popular novels with depression themes.

Graham Greene, beginning as a near-thriller writer, in early books like *Gun for Sale* and *Confidential Agent* skilfully evoked the contemporary atmosphere of seedy menace. Small men in his stories were degraded and ruined by crimes in which big men, armaments manufacturers or fascist agents, used them as expendable tools. The strongly anti-fascist flavour and commitment of these early 'entertainments' passed with *Brighton Rock* into a more intense confrontation of Greene's own Catholic faith with a socialist or Marxist philosophy for which, in terms of the thirties world, he felt some sympathy and could find no complete refutation.* His sharply visual, economical style, much influenced by film, had lasting effects on the technique of the novel.

Evelyn Waugh, whose first best-seller *Decline and Fall* had appeared in 1928, registered contemporary obsessions and violence in another tone, in worldly irony and savage farce. Books like *Vile Bodies* and *A Handful of Dust* showed the kind of society depicted in the *Tatler* as smart, grotesque and doomed. This method of sophisticated and charming heartlessness reached its peak in *Scoop* (a satire on newspapers) and *Black Mischief* (with an Abyssinian-war-type background, in which the hero innocently ate the remains of his mistress in a tasty stew). It was only after taking sick humour as far as it would go in the thirties that Waugh developed his traditionalist high Tory manner of the forties and fifties.

George Orwell, like Greene, derived his sense of rottenness in the middle class world of his upbringing (he was at Eton and then in the Burma police) from service in the colonies, described in his novel *Burmese Days*. The metaphor of the white man's burden was ceasing to be fully convincing even to the white officers themselves.† Returning to England, Orwell reacted bitterly against the drabness and squalor of modern life, without idealization or much hope, but rather with savage contempt. In *Coming Up For Air* and other novels, and in the documentary on social conditions *Road to Wigan Pier,* he combined sympathy for the workers' sufferings with pungently expressed hostility to most socialists, especially socialist intellectuals, and a sharp sense of difference from the workers themselves, even of distaste. His experiences on the Republican side in the Spanish War, where he was associated with

---

* Like many other disappointed anti-fascists of this period, Greene in the forties and early fifties concentrated his interest on personal sin and damnation; he never became a mere cold-war gladiator. In the nineteen sixties, as he told P. Toynbee, he found it possible, with the decline of Stalinism, to resume something like his faith of the thirties, as witness books like *The Quiet American, Our Man in Havana* and *The Comedians.*

† A similar unease with a similar origin is expressed, perhaps with greater art, in Joyce Cary's early African novels, such as *Mr Johnson* (1939).

the Trotskyist POUM, later made him strongly anti-Communist, as he recorded in *Homage to Catalonia*.★

The remarkable Scottish trilogy of Lewis Grassic Gibbon (Leslie Mitchell), though published in the early thirties, was scarcely noticed by the critics till much later. *A Scots Quair* traced the life of a crofter's daughter and her son, spanning the hard life in the countryside and the black industrial town, where the boy became a tough and dedicated Communist; the mother returned to the land. The story was told in a vivid Scottish dialect that passed easily from poetic mysticism to bawdy satirical humour. These were among the very few novels of the period to deal imaginatively and intellectually with the contemporary socialist movement itself.

Auden and Others

Some of the younger writers with radical and left-wing sympathies brought their work together in the anthologies *New Signatures* (1932) and *New Country* (1933), edited by Michael Roberts, poet and schoolmaster. Among these new voices were W. H. Auden (whose first very obscure *Poems* had appeared in 1930), C. Day Lewis, Stephen Spender, Edward Upward, Louis MacNeice, Christopher Isherwood, and John Lehmann, who later founded and edited the quarterly *New Writing* (1936).

Though less of a close-knit group than is often assumed, these writers had a certain background and tone in common. All were educated at public schools and at Oxford or Cambridge. All belonged to the generation that grew up and graduated in the twenties, and not to that of the organized left-wing students of the thirties; and they felt and wrote very much as odd men out, lonely airmen or spies in a hostile world ruled by the Old Gang. A personal love-hate relationship with the values of their public schools (many were at some time schoolmasters) remained an important preoccupation in much of their work.

★ Ironically, his anti-Communist satires, *Animal Farm* and *1984*, written long after the thirties, were to become required O-level reading in the grammar schools twenty years later.

Nevertheless, they shared a belief – half-regretful, half-exultant – that the old order was doomed, that some kind of revolution ('death of the old gang') must come, and that the only hope lay with the oppressed workers (who as people remained more or less unknown). Their poetry took a new poetical view of the English landscape, not as backdrop, but observed from above or at a distance, 'as the hawk sees it or the helmeted airman', to disclose the pattern of social change. Moreover, their scenery included factories and power-stations, in which they saw not only menace but promise – ('Socialism plus electrification equals Communism,' Lenin had said). Hence theirs was sometimes termed 'pylon-poetry', with direct reference to Spender's *The Pylons*:

> But far above and far as sight endures,
> Like whips of anger
> With lightning's danger,
> There runs the quick perspective of the future.

This was a sharp contrast to the more traditional literary man's view of the industrial scene expressed around the same time by John Betjeman in *Slough*:

> Come, bombs, and blow to smithereens
> Those air-conditioned bright canteens,
> Tinned fruit, tinned meat, tinned milk, tinned beans,
> Tinned minds, tinned breath.

In the work of Auden, the most influential poet, the public school conflict was fused and cross-cut with the wider revolt against society. Imagery of prefect, schoolmaster and fag blended with grim suggestions of war and civil war in *The Orators* (1932).* The derelict landscape of industrial decay dominates his poetry of the early thirties, dwarfing what he ironically saw as the self-absorbed sensitivity of the intellectuals,

> Our metaphysical distress,
> Our kindness to ten persons.

When the newsreels every day showed

---

* Auden, like Roberts, Day Lewis, Upward and Warner, began as a schoolmaster, Isherwood was a private tutor, MacNeice a university lecturer.

> Ten thousand of the desperate marching by,
> five foot, six foot, seven foot high

it seemed like treason for the poet to heed

> the voice of love saying lightly, brightly,
> Be Lubbe, be Hitler, but be my good
> Daily, nightly.

Indignation at the human suffering of the depression was expressed in a less fantastic and startling form by Stephen Spender in poems like *Elementary Classroom in a Slum*.

> On their slag heap, these children
> Wear skins peeped through by bones and spectacles of steel
> With mended glass, like bottle bits on stones.

or by C. Day Lewis in *A Carol*:

> Oh hush thee, my baby,
> Thy cradle's in pawn,
> No blankets to cover thee
> Cold and forlorn,
> The stars in the bright sky
> Look down and are dumb
> At the heir of the ages
> Asleep in a slum.

Christopher Isherwood was especially influenced by his experience of depression Germany on the eve of the Nazi takeover (an experience shared in varying degrees by Spender, Lehmann, and Auden himself). The bankruptcy and the menace are delicately recorded in his stories *Mr Norris Changes Trains, Sally Bowles* and *Goodbye to Berlin*. In the three lively verse plays in which he collaborated with Auden – *The Dog beneath the Skin* (1935), *The Ascent of F6* (1936), *On the Frontier* (1938) – the influence of Brecht and of Berlin left wing political cabaret is strongly marked. All are witty satirical fantasies, which attempt to synthesize dramatically the Marxist and the Freudian diagnoses of man's sufferings. *The Ascent of F6* for example, is about a T. E. Lawrence kind of character – a mountaineer sent on a doomed climbing expedition to serve imperialist ambitions and vicariously gratify the frustrated 'little man' at home. At the tragic climax the veiled demon or dragon of the mountain, whose baleful influence has laid the country waste and is destroying the climbers, blends in the dying mountaineer's mind with the figure of his possessive mother.

Indeed, most of these poets knew more about the ideas of Freud and Groddeck than those of Marx or Lenin. When Auden wrote his poem *A Communist to Others*, it was as a conscious dramatic impersonation, not a statement of personal belief, and he seems always to have felt direct participation in politics to be an uncongenial chore and diversion from poetry. Others, such as Day Lewis and Upward, identified more closely for a time with Communism and apparently got rather more out of it.[9] Spender, according to his own later account,[10] was briefly involved in revolutionary politics out of a sense of duty and guilt, and inwardly much preferred the liberalism of Bloomsbury.

Gifted writers who placed their hopes on the working class, but were conscious of lacking first-hand contact with it, found the most satisfactory form for their prose writing not in realism but in a Kafkaesque kind of allegory – as in Rex Warner's *Wild Goose Chase* and Edward Upward's *Journey to the Border*. Realism was possible for them only in portraying the corruption of the old way of life – as in Arthur Calder-Marshall's skilful public school novel *Dead Centre*.

Isolation from the workers could be overcome, some writers thought, by objective, unemotional documentary.[11] In 1936 the sociologist Tom Harrison, the poet and Marxist Charles Madge, and the artist and film director Humphrey Jennings started 'Mass Observation', an organization which enlisted people to observe in detail the social habits of themselves and their neighbours. Some of its first observers were writers (for instance John Sommerfield and William Empson), and the technique was individual reporting rather than scientific sampling. *Britain 1936*, published by Penguin Books, publicized the idea; other reports covered pubs, attitudes to Armistice Day and the Coronation, by-elections and ARP. The potential usefulness of this kind of work for advertising and commerce was realized only after the thirties, when it came to be patronized by market research organizations.

The sense of isolation, so marked in the work of Auden and Spender, was hardly a problem for those writers and intellectuals who became directly and personally involved in left-wing politics and the labour movement. They were taken up with anti-fascist demonstrations, solidarity with the unemployed or aid for Spain, so much so that some of them stopped writing altogether. As for the young left wing intellectuals who grew to maturity in the thirties and confronted the crisis while still at school or university, they seemed, as Spender has said, almost like a different generation. They tended to see the Auden-Spender-Day Lewis set, not as leaders or elder statesmen, but rather as amateurs, gifted fellow-travellers but not quite serious, bogged down in what John Cornford called:

> The important words that come between
> The unhappy eye and the difficult scene.[12]

So this new generation were thrown down the stairs at Olympia; fought the toughs on Armistice Day; joined in all the routine jobs of the local working-class movement; knocked down the Cutteslowe wall dividing a council estate from snobbish Oxford; were arrested for distributing trade union propaganda outside factories; organized medical attention for hunger marchers. They would not have recognized themselves in Auden's drab lines:

> Today the expenditure of powers
> On the flat ephemeral pamphlet and the boring meeting.[13]

Many personal records of the period testify to the sense of purpose and commitment which enriched those otherwise bloody years for many participants.[14]

Left Review, founded in 1934, and edited by Montagu Slater, Amabel Williams-Ellis, Tom Wintringham and later Edgell Rickword, had a generally Marxist slant.* 'A writer's usefulness depends on his influence; that is to say, on the size and enthusiasm

---

* Through Edgell Rickword and Douglas Garman, *Left Review* had a connection with the nineteen twenties *Calendar of Modern Letters* and the earlier work of Leavis.

of his public,' it declared, and therefore sought a more straight-
forward and simple style than that of Eliot or the early Auden.
Closely in touch with left-wing European writers (traditionally
much less anti-political than English ones), its English contributors
included Ralph Bates, Ralph Fox, Jack Lindsay, Randall Swingler,
Hugh Macdiarmid, Storm Jameson and C. Day Lewis. It published
much documentary reportage and the satirical cartoons of James
Boswell, James Fitton and James Holland. Moreover it became the
focus during the Spanish Civil War for a very broad spectrum of
anti-fascist writers and artists, including Naomi Mitchison, Winifred Holtby, Charles Madge, John Lehmann, Amabel Williams-
Ellis, J. B. Priestley, Stephen Spender and G. B. Shaw. To many of
these, the traditional intellectuals' distinction between art and
propaganda seemed meaningless, and friendly arguments on this
point occupied a good deal of its space.

Those young poets who rejected direct political commitment
in their writing more often appeared in Geoffrey Grigson's little
magazine, *New Verse,* in which much of Auden's and MacNeice's
work was first published. Through John Lehmann's *New Writing,*
a hardback quarterly, many British readers made their first
acquaintance with notable writers of the European left such as
Ignazio Silone, André Chamson and Anna Seghers, as well as the
English *New Country* group.

Both *Left Review* and *New Writing,* between which there was a
good deal of collaboration, were particularly concerned to find
working class writers who could make literature out of their
direct experience of suffering and struggle. This proved difficult,
though some good reportage and documentary writers were
discovered – such as B. L. Coombes, a miner (author of *These
Poor Hands*), Lewis Jones, Rhondda unemployed leader (*Cwmardy*);
and a group of young Birmingham writers including Leslie Hal-
ward and Walter Allen. The conscious attempt to write in a way
that would directly influence readers towards political action
sometimes, of course, produced crude and even absurd results,
especially when the writer was addressing an imaginary and
remote working-class reader. There was some would-be super-
toughness:

> The people's flag is deepest red,
> Revolution means bloodshed.[15]

and some starry-eyed vagueness:

> Come then, companions. This is the spring of blood,
> heart's hey-day, movement of masses, beginning of good.[16]

This, however, was not (*pace* Julian Symons) the habitual level of either *Left Review* or *New Writing*. Poems like Edgell Rickward's *To the Wife of Any Non-Intervention Statesman,* MacNeice's *Birmingham,* Clifford Dyment's *Labour Exchange* are indeed more representative.[17]

One of the most successful attempts to reach a working-class audience was made when writers and amateur actors converted a church hall in St Pancras into the little Unity Theatre to provide a home for political amateur drama. Unity produced serious political plays like Clifford Odets' *Waiting for Lefty,* about a New York taxi strike; Stephen Spender's *Trial of a Judge,* centring on the conflict between justice and expediency in the mind of a judge in a fascist state, and *Plant in the Sun,* a strike play with Paul Robeson. But its main successes were in less formal productions, the *Living Newspaper,* (a kind of documentary) on the London bus strike, Montagu Slater's *Stay Down Miner,* and the post-Munich pantomime *Babes in the Wood* (1938) in which the wicked uncle resembled Neville Chamberlain, and Robin Hood saved the babes to the melody of *Affiliate with me.* In this production the Cliveden Set sang their support for the Munich agreement in four-part harmony to the tune of *Land of Hope and Glory,* and the Fairy Wish Fulfilment waved her tinsel wand, hoping with the sob-sisters of the press that all might yet turn out for the best.

The Left Book Club

The circulation of all the left-wing literary periodicals, however, – *Left Review, New Writing, Fact* and so on – remained relatively small. None of them touched anything like the public reached by the Left Book Club with directly political books.

The Left Book Club was founded in May 1936 by Victor

Gollancz, an extremely successful general and thriller publisher who had also for some time been issuing anti-fascist and socialist books by Cole, Laski, Strachey and others. He found, however, that reviewers were unwilling to give serious notices to this kind of work, and that anyway most potential readers could not afford the price of 12s 6d or 18s which was necessary if the edition was small. The club therefore offered a full-size book a month (jointly selected by Gollancz, John Strachey and Harold Laski) at a price of 2s 6d to subscribers who undertook to purchase the monthly choice for at least a six-month period. This tapped an unexpectedly large new market, monthly sales rising rapidly to a peak of fifty thousand – an unheard of figure for serious works of this type, which showed how widespread was the desire to understand the crisis from a socialist viewpoint. A few titles will indicate the width of interests covered. Professor Salvemini wrote on fascism, Edgar Snow reported from the Chinese guerrillas in *Red Star Over China* and R. P. Dutt wrote on *India Today*. The depression in America was studied by Leo Huberman in *Mans Worldly Goods*, in Britain by Hannington in *Problem of the Distressed Areas*, and by Ellen Wilkinson MP in *Town that was Murdered*. First-hand personal reportage came from prison (*Walls Have Mouths* by Wilfred Macartney), from the mines in *These Poor Hands* by B. L. Coombes, from slum schools by S. Segal in *Pennorth of Chips*, from the German underground movement by Jan Peterson in *Our Street*. C. R. Attlee contributed *The Labour Party in Perspective* and John Strachey *The Theory and Practice of Social-ism*. One of the most lasting achievements was A. L. Morton's *People's History of England*, a popular textbook written from a Marxist viewpoint. There were certainly a good many lapses, members failing to claim or pay for the books they had ordered; but these were balanced by a continual influx of new supporters to maintain total membership around the fifty thousand mark.

The appetite was greater than even the monthly choices could satisfy. Optional cheap editions of other Gollancz books and a special pocket educational series were added, covering all kinds of subjects from modern language and birth control to a pocket history of Greece and Rome and the Coles' factual analysis *Con-*

dition *of Britain. A Handbook of Marxism* brought the classical Marxist texts to a wider audience in Britain than ever before, and under a special agreement Lawrence and Wishart, the principal Communist publishers, supplied the club with cheap editions of their books.

Moreover the books were not only sold – they were read and discussed in the Left Book Club groups which sprang up almost spontaneously, five hundred within a year, and of which there were at the peak some twelve hundred in existence. Most of these groups had a wide mixture of members, socially and politically, and they tended to be strongest and most active in areas where the official political parties of the left were weak – notably in the outer suburbs of London and other cities, hitherto considered politically Conservative, as well as in smaller country towns and villages. Often they branched out into organizing meetings, Spanish or Russian film shows, Aid for Spain and so on. This activity was stimulated by a news-sheet, *Left News,* issued with the books, and from 1937 on by centrally-sponsored speakers touring the groups, (notably J. B. S. Haldane on Air Raid Precautions and others on Czechoslovakia and China), and by large mass rallies. The first of these, in January 1937, brought on Gollancz, Harry Pollitt, the Dean of Canterbury, Strachey, Sir Richard Acland, Lord Addison and Sir Charles Trevelyan and filled both the Albert and Queen's Halls.

The Left Book Club had the kind of energy and local initiative that later marked the early years of the Campaign for Nuclear Disarmament. The average age, however, was higher; there was less singing and more theoretical and political discussion; and the Club included more workers, partly because the range of issues was much wider and covered economics and social conditions as well as international politics. Members felt they were involved in something wider than immediate policies – they were contributing towards a more just and rational future.

By April 1937 the Labour Party was getting worried at the leftward challenge to its authority presented by the Left Book Club. Hugh Dalton approached Gollancz and was offered a place on the selection committee, but negotiations broke down because the Labour Party demanded three members to ensure 'equal representation of the official standpoint' against the left-wing three already there. In 1938 a Right Book Club was started by Foyle's Bookshop, and Transport House announced an official Socialist Book Club, but neither captured the audience.

The Left Book Club reached its zenith of membership and influence about the spring of 1938. It began to crumble as an organization with the German-Soviet Pact, the outbreak of war and the deep divisions this caused on the Left.* As a successful publishing venture it continued during the war (choices still selling upwards of twenty thousand in 1943) but it was no longer a crusade. Nevertheless, for a whole generation it had meant a unique and irreversible process of socialist education.

Spain and after

The Spanish Civil War brought to a focus all the hatred and fear of fascism among the intellectuals, and all the aspiration towards a new society. Indeed it probably gave rise to greater and more poignant English poetry than the Second World War, with its far vaster scale. As well as the poets who fought in Spain – Christopher Caudwell, Julian Bell, John Cornford, Tom Wintringham, David Martin and others – writers like Herbert Read, Stephen Spender, C. Day Lewis, J. Bronowski, A. L. Lloyd and Louis MacNeice wrote moving poems in tribute to the Republican fighters. Jack Lindsay produced *On Guard for Spain* for mass declamation at meetings; and Auden's long poem *Spain*, sold as a pamphlet to help medical aid, gave a vision of the whole of human civilization and history leading up to the moment of decision before Madrid:

> The stars are dead. The animals will not look.
> We are left alone with our day, and the time is short, and
> History to the defeated
> May say alas but cannot help or pardon.

* Thus Gollancz himself edited a collection of essays *The Betrayal of the Left*; the Left Book Club published *Barbarians at the Gate* by Leonard Woolf, a bitter attack on Soviet policy; G. D. H. Cole and Strachey took a similar view.

If some of these writers later turned away from political involvement for good, it was perhaps as much because of the agony of defeat as because their own side no longer seemed wholly without guilt. The poetry and documentary reporting – notably John Sommerfield's *Volunteer in Spain* and Esmond Romilly's *Boadilla* – remain as a permanent record of how writers felt then; even those who today regard their Spanish war poems as 'trash they are ashamed to have written'.[18]

There were, indeed, growing reservations and dissensions among the anti-fascist intellectuals from 1937 onwards, especially in relation to the Soviet Union. Reports of purges and treason trials in the Soviet Union, and the clash between the Spanish Republican Government and the POUM, suggested that the revolution was by no means the simple red-and-white affair it had seemed to those idealists for whom the Soviet Union had been a symbol of their own aspirations to a just society, rather than an actual underdeveloped and beleaguered country. The abstract artists were repelled by the conventional character of official Soviet art, and Gide's *Retour de L'URSS*, which indicated that the Soviet attitude to homosexuality was no more tolerant than the English, alienated some writers.[19] It became clear that freedom for intellectuals in the Soviet Union, rightly or wrongly, was strictly limited. Moreover, as the fascists gained ground in Europe, bitterness and mutual blame increased on the left, and all this was reflected in a tendency to retreat from politics. Auden and Isherwood left for the USA; and Louis MacNeice wrote ominously:

> Soon, my friend,
> We shall have no time for dances.[20]

With some writers and artists all this led to a permanent resumption of the traditional 'non-political' attitude of British intellectuals. With others it went a stage further, especially after the German-Soviet Pact of 1939, to retraction not only of their praise for the Soviet Union, but of their critical attitude to the capitalist system. Auden went through his poems for later editions deleting or altering the more political ones.[21] Spender, after many public recantations, eventually in the cold war period became editor of

Encounter, a magazine which he was not aware was financed by American intelligence.

These are well known cases; yet they are not entirely typical. The great majority of young people on the middle class and intellectual left in 1939 went neither to America nor to the Ministry of Information, but into war work or the armed forces. There their experience made itself felt, especially in the later war years (through ABCA and the Forces Parliaments), in radical discussions about the post-war world, and contributed to the refusal of the victorious armies in 1945 to vote for Churchill. Probably a majority of surviving intellectuals prominent 'on the left' in the thirties were still involved in some way with left rather than right in the fifties and sixties, as the lists of eminent protesters against nuclear weapons or British support for the war in Vietnam will show.

Fascists
and anti-fascists

In March 1933, Hitler came to power in Germany and within weeks British newspapers were reporting that all opposition parties had been dissolved and their leaders arrested; that trade union premises had been occupied and their funds confiscated; that brown-shirted Storm Troopers were beating up Social Democrats, Communists and Jews; that thousands had been thrown into concentration camps.

Hitler's support in Germany sprang from the hopelessness created by mass unemployment, the despair and insecurity of the ruined lower middle class, the splits and demoralization in the German working-class movement. Promising to make Germany great once more, glorifying militarism, preaching doctrines of racial purity, canalizing grievances into hatred of the Jews, Hitler had built up his following. In time the big German industrialists had begun to see in him their best guarantee against Communist revolution; they had financed him and helped him to power.

When Sir Oswald Mosley formed his British Union of Fascists in the autumn of 1932 it seemed that many of the ingredients which were shortly to bring Hitler to power existed also in Britain. Here also there was mass unemployment and a paralysing economic depression; here also the middle class were insecure and could be presumed to be searching for a 'saviour'; here also the labour movement had been demoralized by the recent failure of a Labour government and the defection of Ramsay MacDonald. Here also were people in high places who were prepared to lend Mosley their support.

Mosley was a wealthy man who had spent the previous thirteen years in the House of Commons, first as a Conservative, later as a member of the Labour Party in which he had enjoyed considerable popularity. 'Fascism today has become a world-wide movement, invading every country in the hour of crisis as the only alternative to destructive Communism,' he now wrote in his book *The Greater Britain*.[1] His policy included the abolition of parliamentary and local government democracy, the end of the 'party game' and substitution of the 'leadership' principle, the absorption of working-class organizations like the trade unions into a corporate state.

The British Union of Fascists attracted diverse elements including romantically-minded white collar workers and semi-literate toughs in search of excitement. Its leadership was predominantly middle class with a high proportion of ex-army officers. Within eighteen months of its formation it was claiming a membership of twenty thousand. Members were fitted out with black shirts, drilled and paraded and transported to meetings all over the country. A big building in the Kings Road, Chelsea was converted into a blackshirt barracks.

It was clear that the movement had ample funds. Lord Rothermere gave it his backing, which meant the backing of the *Daily Mail*, with its one and a half million circulation, as well as the *Evening News* and the *Sunday Dispatch*. 'Each week the *Sunday Dispatch* is presenting five £1 prizes to readers who send in postcards on "Why I like the Blackshirts"', it announced.[2] Every effort was made to enlist support among the best people. The *Tatler* published a full page photograph of Mosley with the caption 'We Stopped, and We Looked, and We Listened', paying tribute to Mosley's 'rare gift of political courage'.[3]

The motives of Mosley's rich backers were not hard to understand. It was a time of uncertainty in which the old values seemed to be crumbling, and with them, perhaps, the very foundations of the established order. The General Strike in 1926 had given a glimpse of the chasm which might one day open; the Invergordon mutiny another. Communists were increasing their following among the unemployed, while the universities appeared to be riddled with pacifism. But Mosley countered ideas of international working-class brotherhood with the slogan 'Britain First'; he answered pacifism with a sturdy pride in one's country; he offered to replace ineptitude and vacillation in high places with decision and authority. Yet he offered no threat to private property, but stressed that in his corporate state 'individual enterprise and the making of profit are not only permitted, but encouraged'.[4] Fascism, it was argued, had done much for Italy under Mussolini, where it had created a sense of unity between previously warring classes, had fostered ideals of service and obedience in place of the earlier unrest.

Thus it was that when Mosley staged a monster meeting at Olympia on 7 June 1934, quite a number of well known people were present. The hall held over ten thousand people and distribution of tickets was channelled through the BUF organization. But a few hundred left wing opponents managed to get in intending to show opposition – indeed it was rumoured that the Communist Party had forged some hundreds of tickets for the purpose. Simultaneously the Communist Party (which at that time numbered less than seven thousand members) called for a protest demonstration, and during the evening a few thousand people responded to this call and marched to the hall, outside which they were met by seven hundred and sixty foot and mounted police. There developed a good deal of shouting and booing, and the police retaliated by drawing batons, roughly riding into the crowd and keeping it 'on the move'.

But the police were not inside the hall, where the evening proceeded along a regular pattern. Sir Oswald Mosley stood on the platform and spoke with the aid of twenty-four amplifiers and a spotlight. Some interrupter would shout an objection, inaudible in the huge hall to all but those immediately around him. At once Sir Oswald would pause, the spotlight would be swung on to the interrupter, a posse of blackshirts would seize him, punch him, kick him, carry him struggling from the hall, beat him up in the corridor, perhaps throw him down the stairs, and finally eject him. Women interrupters were also ejected after much rough handling. After a bit, people who had come to listen began to protest at the treatment of interrupters near them; they too were bundled out and knocked about in the corridor. Sir Oswald appeared to be enjoying himself. 'As the interruption goes on', he said, 'the process of interrupting becomes increasingly painful, not for us but for the interrupters.'[5] The interrupters were indeed vastly outnumbered.

As the evening wore on, demonstrators outside became more and more involved in trying to help those thrown out to get to nearby first aid posts which had been set up by Mosley's opponents in anticipation of events. This was not easy, as the police persisted in their policy of moving on, chivvying and threatening those who stopped to pick up bruised and bleeding victims, the mounted police riding up on to the pavement and generally adding to the difficulties of rescue. The police were implored by those outside to go inside the hall and stop the violence, but they merely threatened those who begged them to do this with arrest, and indeed arrested some of them. After it was over some Blackshirts were followed from the hall by enraged anti-fascists and beaten up in revenge.

The next day there was a storm. Many eminent and respectable eye-witnesses were outraged at what they had seen. Among the most forcible were three Conservative MPs – Geoffrey Lloyd: 'I came to the conclusion that Mosley was a political maniac, and that all decent English people must combine to kill his movement'.[6] T. J. O'Connor: 'in the end we got up to go because we felt that we were being placed in the position either of being manhandled or of being cowardly cads for not interfering'.[7] W. J. Anstruther-Gray: 'I had not been in the meeting for more than a few minutes before all my sympathies were with the men who were being handled with such gross brutality'.[8] Other eye-witnesses who described what they had seen included Aldous Huxley, Naomi Mitchison, Vera Brittain, A. E. Coppard and a whole bevy of well known newspapermen.

After the experience at Olympia the directors of the White City, which had been booked for a BUF rally, cancelled the booking. Mosley's reply was to announce a rally in Hyde Park for 9 September. A newly formed Committee for Anti-Fascist Activities, headed by John Strachey, D. N. Pritt, Ellen Wilkinson, and others from the Labour left, then called for an anti-fascist march and counter-demonstration in Hyde Park on the same day. Leaflets were issued urging anti-fascists to 'drown Mosley in a sea of working-class activity' and the *Daily Worker* embarked on an intensive publicity campaign – 'all out on September the ninth'. The Labour Party and the TUC hastily banned the counter-demonstration to their supporters. This particular occasion illustrated the split in opinion in the labour movement, and indeed outside it, on the question of the tactics to be adopted by Mosley's opponents. The National Council of Labour, which was pledged 'to resist to the utmost any attempt to plant Fascism in this country', was against organizing opposition at Mosley's meetings, believing that such opposition not only led to violence, but gave Mosley the very publicity he wanted. The way to deal with fascism in Britain, it was held, was to keep away from Mosley's meetings, while ceaselessly educating people in the horrors and dangers of fascism and doing everything possible to strengthen the labour movement. But the Labour left, in particular the League of Youth, argued, as the Communist Party did, that Mosley would gain support unless opposition was mobilized against him whenever possible, that he had friends in high places and would come to power as Hitler had done if the movement buried its head in the sand. And it was not only the left in the labour and trade union movement who were arguing like this. Many students and professional people felt the same. The result was that in the ensuing years calls for action against Mosley met with a great response, whether those calls emanated from the Communist Party or from one or other of the *ad hoc* anti-fascist bodies which sprang up from time to time.

One of these occasions was 9 September 1934. Some two and a half thousand Blackshirts assembled and Mosley spoke to them surrounded by a cordon of six thousand police. His voice was inaudible above the booing from outside. Meanwhile a crowd estimated at 100,000 to 150,000 congregated round the anti-fascist platforms less than a quarter of a mile away. It was one of the largest Hyde Park demonstrations seen, and a foretaste of things to come.

Following Olympia and its aftermath the more respectable of

Mosley's supporters had begun to cool off, while some of the influential people who had given the movement backing also began to hesitate. The prevailing wind at the top had veered sharply against Mosley, not so much because of his aims and objects as because of what were thought of as his methods. The kind of ostentatious thuggery displayed at Olympia seemed to be provoking the very left-wing disorders which it was desirable to avoid. Left-wing subversion could often be dealt with by more subtle means than a head-on clash. And in so far as left-wing movements required a show of strength, the police had recently been reorganized on more effective lines. For those who still worried about Invergordon there was the Incitement to Disaffection Bill now going through the House. Meanwhile it was ludicrous to suggest, as Mosley's rich backers appeared to do, that Britain had slipped so far towards social revolution as to require a fascist movement to save it. So at the top Mosley began to be regarded as a bit of a nuisance, though not at that stage as anything worse. And the police, who were conditioned to the idea that threats to law and order came only from the left, went on treating Mosley with the same kind of indulgence accorded to university students during a rag. They reserved the firm hand and the show of strength for Mosley's opponents.

The increasing tendency towards the firm hand and the show of strength was, however, already causing apprehension among liberal-minded professional people, some of whom believed that the threat of fascism did not come mainly from Mosley at all, but rather from the erosion of traditional freedoms on which the authorities seemed to be engaged. The behaviour of the police towards the hunger marchers had made a deep impression. Under the shadow of these fears the National Council for Civil Liberties came into existence early in 1934. Its aim was 'to assist in the maintenance of the hard-won rights of citizens – especially freedom of speech, press and assembly – from all infringement by executive or judicial authority'. The president of the Council was E. M. Forster, and its list of fifty vice-presidents included leading people in the scientific, literary and academic world, such as H. G. Wells, J. B. Priestley, Professor Julian Huxley, Dr Ivor Jennings, as well as politicians like A. P. Herbert, Dingle Foot, and Clement Attlee. The Council's first challenge was the Incitement to Dissaffection Bill, under which a person could be jailed for two years for possessing any document which could be construed as subversive if disseminated among the armed forces. People who had expected the Bill to be directed against Mosley's private army were sharply disillusioned. It became clear that anyone possessing not just revolutionary literature, but even pacifist literature, could be prosecuted under it.

The Council for Civil Liberties called great conferences of explanation around the Bill – like the joint one with the London Trades Council attended by one thousand six hundred accredited delegates. And it made a nonsense of the Bill by using its terms to stage a mock trial of David Low, who was accused of seducing a soldier from his allegiance by means of a cartoon. The soldier was played by Kingsley Martin, editor of the *New Statesman,* and the learned and senile judge who presided was played by Aylmer Vallance, editor of the *News Chronicle.* The Council's campaign was partially successful, and the Bill was substantially modified before it became an Act.

The Blackshirts meanwhile, turned openly to anti-semitism. Mosley had already failed to get the kind of mass following among the lower middle class that had helped to bring Hitler to power. The lower middle class in Britain were indeed differently situated from their opposite numbers in Germany. There were proportionately fewer petty proprietors, whose ruin had provided such fruitful soil for fascist ideas. Here they consisted to a much greater extent of salaried and blackcoated workers, whose position was not only less insecure than that of manual workers, but, with the fall in prices, was to some extent improving. By 1934 there was hope among them – not despair. No reason to turn to Mosley.

Neither had Mosley succeeded in getting any following among the unemployed – perhaps because the largest concentrations were in the areas where the trade union tradition was strongest, rather than in the shifting populations of the big cities. And any unemployed man who really wanted to kick against the pricks tended to join the NUWM. In the end it was on the anti-Jewish question alone that Mosley did succeed in building up some sort of following.

Jews in Great Britain in 1933 probably numbered not more than three hundred and thirty thousand or 0·8 per cent of the total population. But in 1933 began the first trickle of refugees from Germany which was to continue right up to 1939. Some of the refugees were 'political' – social democrats, trade unionists, Communists, liberals, pacifists, escaping from Germany illegally. But nearly 90 per cent of them were not 'political' but Jewish, and in many cases the Germans were prepared to let them go after stripping them of all their possessions; what they needed was entry permits to other countries. The first refugees were the victims of the terror which began during the night of the Reichstag fire in 1933; in subsequent years each wave of persecution, each Jewish pogrom, each tightening of anti-Jewish laws in Germany increased the thousands of desperate victims seeking sanctuary.

The British government, however, adopted a much more restrictive attitude towards the refugees than did the French or some other governments. Broadly speaking, the refugees were not granted entry permits unless they could prove that they either had means of support or intended to re-emigrate elsewhere. They were not allowed work permits except for domestic service, which meant that unless they were among the few who had private assets in countries outside Germany, their support depended on financial guarantees and hospitality from private individuals or voluntary organizations. Self support by use of their own skills or knowledge was usually debarred. The support given to the voluntary refugee organizations, both Jewish and others, in their fund-raising activities was very considerable, for there was widespread horror among the British public at Hitler's treatment of his victims. But the process of getting refugees into this country appeared to be surrounded by legal obstacles and red tape.

The result was that, allowing for re-emigration, the total number of Jewish refugees from Germany or German-occupied territories by the time the war broke out was probably not more than fifty thousand – a relatively small number. Yet this number was used by certain organizations to create the impression that

Britain was being 'over-run' by Jews, and that something must be done to deal with the 'Jewish Problem' in Britain. Much anti-semitic propaganda was finding its way into the country direct from Nazi Germany, and there were various organizations involved in anti-semitic activities, ranging from the Imperial Fascist League peddling obscene stories about Jewish ritual murder, right up to the seemingly highly respectable Anglo-German Fellowship, which provided a sort of platform for the justification of Hitler's activities, including his treatment of the Jews.

Mosley concentrated on the East End of London, particularly Bethnal Green, Shoreditch and Stepney. In the East End lived about half the Jewish population in Britain at the time. They were not refugees from Hitler but most had been born and bred in the East End, where in some boroughs they formed 25 per cent of the population. Living side by side with them were large numbers of Roman Catholics, particularly Irish dockers. Jew and Gentile had lived fairly peaceably side by side in these areas for a generation or more, but they did not mix much or intermarry; quite apart from the religious differences, the way of life, the culture, the outlook, the occupations differed. Jewish workers were to a great extent concentrated in the clothing, furniture and fur trades; there were relatively few of them in docks, engineering or heavy industry generally. Where there are racial differences, a certain amount of racial antagonism is often latent; where there is also poverty and squalid misery, it is not difficult to stir up racial antagonism, bring it to the surface in the form of open racial strife. This the Blackshirts did.

All grievances were blamed on the Jews. The big Jewish chain-stores were taking away the livelihood of the small shopkeepers; unscrupulous Jewish businessmen were undercutting British enterprises by the use of sweated labour; Jews were causing unemployment by taking people's jobs; all political parties (except the BUF) were parties of Jewry; the press, the cinema and parliament were subject to the organized corruption of Jewish finance; the Jews were trying to embroil us in a war against Hitler's Germany. Blackshirt speakers talked about Jewish 'submen' and the 'sweepings

of foreign ghettoes'; words like 'corruption' were constantly associated with the word 'Jew'.

The Blackshirts paraded the streets of the East End rhythmically
shouting 'Yids! Yids! We gotta get rid of the Yids!' as they
marched. As they paraded with bands and flags through the back
streets they would be followed by little crowds of working people;
they claimed to be recruiting members fast. P. J. (Perish Judah)
appeared in monstrous white-washed letters in the streets and even
the more explicit 'Kill the Jews'. Continuous back-street meetings
were held – often in Jewish streets – in which insulting language
was used about Jews. Thus: 'The Jews among us are a cancer and
every foul disease. The situation calls for surgical operation, and
we Fascists intend making that operation. We will extirpate them
thoroughly from our public life.'[9]

While such speeches were being made, the police stood round
in considerable numbers. If a member of the public shouted back
he could be pounced on by the police and hustled away from the
meeting; if he resisted he might be arrested and charged with
'insulting words and behaviour'. This sort of pattern of events was
defended by some who said the police were trying to keep the
peace and avoid disturbances. But others were more and more
indignant that Jew-baiting should be allowed *without* disturbance.
When fights broke out they were often not so much between
audience and fascists as between the audience and the police who
were shielding the fascists. Among Jews and anti-fascists the conviction grew that the police were on the side of the fascists.

On 5 March 1936, Herbert Morrison, MP for South Hackney,
gave a lengthy account in the House of Commons of intimidation
and violence against Jews in the East End. He mentioned a Shoreditch Jewish shopkeeper who had been told he would be murdered
and his shop burned down; and another who had had his windows
deliberately smashed by fascists hurling bricks and stones; another
who had been forced to close early because of disturbances and
threats of violence against his customers; a man who had been
set upon when alone and so badly beaten up that he was forced to
have hospital treatment for a fortnight; a local blackshirt leader
who had spat in the face of a Jewess when she asked him to stop

writing 'kill the dirty Jews' on her wall. And he mentioned that a well known Jewish public figure had tried to get police protection without success.

Sir John Simon, the Home Secretary, replied that in this country 'we are not prepared to tolerate any kind of Jew-baiting', and went out of his way to deny allegations that the police discriminated in favour of the fascists. The East End MPs expressed their gratification at the Home Secretary's attitude. However, a little over two weeks later a curious episode took place in quite another part of London. On an evening when Sir Oswald Mosley was addressing a meeting in the Albert Hall, mounted police used quite abnormal violence in breaking up an open air anti-fascist protest meeting in Thurloe Square, Kensington, riding their horses into a tightly-packed little crowd, striking down with their batons on people who were taken by surprise and were offering no resistance, and causing serious injuries. The Home Secretary was asked for a public enquiry, but refused. The National Council for Civil Liberties then held its own public enquiry and reported that the mounted police had 'seemed more concerned with inflicting injuries than with dispersing the crowd'.

Meanwhile in the East End, the Home Secretary's words seemed to have changed nothing. The anti-Jewish campaign continued as before; the young men began to mutter; members of some Jewish organizations began to talk of organizing their own strong-arm gangs for protection. In the Stepney Communist Party, which was growing in membership, there were endless arguments, some members saying that 'bash the fascists whenever you see them' was the only tactic.[10] By 10 July 1936, F. C. Watkins, MP for Central Hackney, was telling the House that he had received many letters from Jewish people who had been followed into back streets and beaten up by fascists, and George Lansbury, MP for a Poplar constituency, said that in every East End district there was real terror among the Jewish population, while Percy Harris, Liberal MP for Bethnal Green said: 'there is a feeling going right through the East End that somehow or other the police are acting in collusion with the fascists', adding that he did not personally believe there was a word of truth in that suggestion.

In the late summer of 1936 Mosley announced a major East London event for Sunday 4 October – an anniversary rally and march to which blackshirts from all over the country would be drafted. It was to assemble on parade in military formation in Royal Mint Street with Mosley 'inspecting the troops'; it would then march up Leman Street, past Gardners Corner and along Commercial Road right through the heart of East London. The plan caused consternation; the Mayors of Bethnal Green, Stepney, Hackney, Poplar and Shoreditch spent over an hour on 1 October at the Home Office urging that the march be banned. They were unsuccessful. Equally unsuccessful was the Jewish People's Council against Fascism, which had secured a hundred thousand signatures from East End people asking for the march to be banned. The petition was presented to the Home Secretary on 2 October by a deputation which included James Hall, Labour MP for White-chapel, A. M. Wall, secretary of the London Trades Council, and Father Groser, an Anglo-Catholic priest, well-known and influential in the East End. The deputation failed in its object.

A day or two earlier the London Communist Party and the Independent Labour Party issued a call to London workers to rally in thousands at Gardners Corner and in Cable Street and block the march. The Jewish Ex-Servicemen's Association supported the call. Overnight the streets were covered with whitewashed slogans – 'All out on 4 October'; 'Bar the road to fascism'; 'They shall not pass'. The last slogan echoed that of the Spanish Republican Government where the civil war had just begun.

The call to block the march was received in many quarters with as much consternation as the announcement of the march itself; the organizations which had issued the call were small in membership, but experience had shown that such calls could evoke a great response. George Lansbury, who had earlier urged the Home Secretary to divert the march, issued a statement urging people to stay away; the *Daily Herald* and the *News Chronicle* on 1 October implored their readers to follow this advice, the latter saying 'The Communist has no more right to break up a Fascist meeting than the Fascist has to break up a Communist demonstration. If the opponents of Fascism wish to retain the public sympathy, which is their best asset, they will heed Mr Lansbury's wise and public-spirited advice.'

When 4 October came, all police leave was stopped, six thousand foot police and the whole of the mounted division were drafted into the area. But hours before the time when the fascists were to assemble, the streets were blocked with people. 'The greatest East End crowd in living memory – one estimate is three hundred thousand – awaited the Fascists,' reported the *News Chronicle* correspondent the next day. The foot and mounted police laboriously cleared Royal Mint Street with the aid of several baton charges to enable the fascists to assemble, and there they stood surrounded by police. The next task facing the police was to carve a way through to enable the fascists to march. Bit by bit, with repeated baton charges up Leman Street and elsewhere, and throwing cordons of foot police across all side streets, Leman Street and the Minories were at last cleared with much booing, dodging and running by the crowd, some heavy baton wielding, and actual physical pressure by foot police. But at the end of it all, round Gardners Corner and the adjoining thoroughfares, the main crowd was still solidly jamming the streets chanting 'they shall not pass' in a confused roar of sound. And behind them, in backstreets all the way to Limehouse, so it was said, others were preparing to play their part should the fascists get that far. Meanwhile, a tram which had been deliberately abandoned by its driver at the junction of Commercial Road and Leman Street had been joined by others to make an effective road block at a key point.

If the Gardners Corner-Commercial Road route were abandoned, there was still another main route east via Cable Street. It was thought that the police would try to avoid taking this route because it was known as a 'rough area'. Now it lived up to its reputation. A barricade formed with the contents of a nearby builders yard was thrown across the street. As the mounted police moved forward, marbles were thrown under horses' hooves, while the foot police were met with flying bricks and bits of broken paving stone. In the ensuing tussles and attempted arrests some police were 'captured' and locked into empty shops. Gradually the foot police forced their way up to the barricade, threw a cordon round it and laboriously dismantled it, but another barricade had been thrown up farther back and everything was prepared for a third behind that. And it became clear that it was not only the people down in the roadway who would have to be dealt with; the windows and roofs were alive with women hurling down bottles at the police. Soon the road was thick with the glass of old sauce and vinegar bottles, their smell sharp in the air.

When Mosley finally arrived, an hour late, to 'review the troops' he was told by Sir Philip Game, the Chief Commissioner of London police, that the projected march through East London had got to be abandoned. Finally the fascists were escorted westward through deserted city streets to disperse ignominiously on the embankment.

'The Leader of the British Union places on record the fact that this is the first occasion on which the British Government has openly surrendered to Red Terror,' said Sir Oswald in a press statement published the next day. The Mayor of Stepney also issued a statement:

> I have never seen the people of East London so thoroughly aroused and angry during the whole of my experience. I understand that many were hurt, workers and policemen, and this could all have been prevented had the Home Office and Commissioner of Police done before the march what they were compelled to do during the march itself.

The government's answer was the Public Order Act which prohibited the wearing of political uniforms in public; it also placed power in the hands of the police to ban any political processions and in this respect appeared to be aimed as much against Mosley's opponents as against Mosley. It was in fact invoked in North East and East London in the summer of 1937 to stop all processions, both fascist and anti-fascist.

It was not invoked when Mosley tried to stage another great march through Bermondsey on 3 October 1937, in spite of urgent requests from a Bermondsey deputation led by its mayor to the Home Secretary. Bermondsey had a big Irish Catholic population but very few Jews; it was therefore argued that his Jew-baiting policy would not lead to a breach of the peace there. But Bermondsey was a solid Labour borough with a great socialist tradition, and on the afternoon of 3 October 1937 there was a vast concourse of people in Long Lane preparing to stop the march. Thousands of police had again been drafted in and once again there were baton charges. Once again barricades were thrown up. Once again Mosley's march had to be diverted from its advertised route. Organized opposition to Mosley was not indeed confined to London, but showed itself wherever he tried to gain a foothold – in South Wales, in Lancashire, in the universities.

Although individual acts of intimidation and violence against Jews were still continuing in the East End, it was by this time clear that Mosley had lost whatever substantial following he had once had. This reinforced the arguments of those in the labour movement who had always thought that British tolerance and good sense made any danger of fascism in Britain remote, and who were continually suggesting that the calls to action against Mosley were a Communist-inspired tactic to make trouble for trouble's sake. To which the counter-argument from the left was of course that if Mosley had lost support it was *because* of the opposition shown from Olympia onwards.

But indeed the passions aroused at the time around the Mosley issue cannot be dissociated from the events taking place in the outside world. To many who participated in the huge anti-fascist demonstrations at the time, Mosley was the symbol of an international menace – a menace about which the National Council of Labour, though keenly aware of its existence, seemed unprepared to do much except urge the need to educate the British public to vote differently at the next general election. Yet all over Europe democratic strongholds appeared to be going down in front of Hitler, Mussolini, Franco, with, it was believed, the connivance of the British government. And there seemed to be a sinister parallel in the government's tolerance of Mosley and its behaviour towards the fascist dictators abroad. It was this that gave the later anti-fascist demonstrations their spirit of desperate urgency. 'Fascism means War' was more than the slogan chalked up to encourage people to turn up, it was a whole analysis of the world

L

threat in face of which a tactical argument was raging. Loud on the ground, the argument seemed to become inaudible in the higher reaches of society, where the readers of *The Times* were being assured that one more concession to Hitler could pave the way to peace in our time.

Attitudes to the
Outside World

In the end the inexorable advance of fascism was to dominate the view of the outside world from Britain, creating new divisions and alignments, changing the attitudes of social groups both to one another and to wider political and moral questions. So great were these changes that the years at the start of the decade were to seem in retrospect curiously remote.

In pre-Hitler years governing circles appeared more pre-occupied with the stresses within the Empire than with any threat from outside. The Empire which circled the world and on which the sun never set had been part of everyone's childhood teaching. There had been maps with a quarter of the earth's surface tinted pink; history books which told of Britain's mission to civilize backward peoples; story books which told of the white man's struggle with savage tribes. But the adult world was by now uneasily aware of the long shadows that seemed to herald the approach of sunset after all. The rising tide of Indian nationalism had involved successive governments in elaborate counter-moves – enquiries, reports, negotiations with Gandhi, revised constitutional measures – avowedly with the intention of leading India to responsible self-government. Those on the far political left denounced such moves as a façade behind which repression continued. Those on the far political right, of whom Winston Churchill was one, fought a tough rearguard action, trying to hold off the inevitable.

In this, Churchill and others like him had the sympathy of many people whose personal ties with the Empire inclined them to look with suspicion on moves towards colonial self-government. There were the retired Indian Army officers and ex-colonial civil servants who clustered in the Home Counties and south coast resorts, and their successors who returned home on extended leave. There were businessmen who had previously served a year or two with the colonial branch of their firm, and others who had temporarily sought careers in tea or rubber planting. And then there were the naval families whose whole lives revolved round the Empire. In the big naval towns people of all classes, including the working class, were very Empire-minded. They were Empire-minded too in many Lancashire towns, where prosperity in the cotton industry appeared to depend on Empire markets. Yet outside these centres with a direct connection, there were many working people for whom the Empire meant little. Though the newspapers were always reminding them of its importance, it seemed remote and profoundly uninteresting like many other things they had been taught at school.

Outside the Empire, Russia was the main source of uneasiness to the governing class at the beginning of the thirties. For although the young Soviet Republic was not reckoned to offer any military threat – indeed she was thought to be militarily weak – the ideas which her very existence fostered had spread to many parts of the world and seemed to offer a challenge to the established order in every country. This challenge was powerfully reinforced by the Soviet Union's apparent immunity from the 1931 slump which had affected the whole capitalist world. Most British newspapers were actively engaged in combating the spread of these ideas, denigrating everything done in Russia and suppressing anything which might tell in the new regime's favour, and most middle and working-class people regarded Russia with dislike and contempt. Dislike because the Soviet system was thought of as a bloodstained tyranny. Contempt because the Russians were thought to be backward and incompetent.

A minority of socialists and Communists thought the exact opposite of what the newspapers told them – indeed every newspaper story (and many of them were false*) hardened their opinion

---

* The basic theme of most newspaper comment was that the Five Year Plan was a failure and that the regime was on its last legs. But the basic theme was often embellished by grotesque propaganda stories – for example, the one current in the twenties that Russian women were nationalized, or the one started by the *Sunday Chronicle* on 23 October 1932, that as part of its fanatical anti-God campaign the

that everything said in the newspapers was lies. They argued that the Soviet people, having got rid of their capitalist and landlord oppressors, were freer than those of other nations, and that, in building socialism, the Soviet Union was building the world of the future. Within the organized labour movement, where socialist aims were part of a deep-rooted tradition, there were many who wanted passionately to see the Soviet Union succeed. The vision of a society run by working people for working people had generated a new kind of hope for some who all their lives had seen people kicked around, degraded by the means test, humiliated by the nagging fear of losing their job.

In those pre-Hitler years it could not be clear to anyone that fascism would be the main-spring of a future world war. War was thought of in terms of the First World War. That war was still vivid in the memory. Eight hundred thousand Englishmen had lost their lives in it. Physically a future war was envisaged as an extension of 1914–18, the same long drawn out static trench warfare, but with a new dimension of horror added to it – aerial bombardment, probably with poison gas. The idea of gas was much more frightful than the idea of high explosive. It conjured up visions of whole cities crawling with blinded and choking people.

And attitudes to war in the pre-Hitler years reflected the after-thoughts about the First World War. During the twenties there had been much questioning about the causes of that war, much cynical debunking of its alleged motives, much heart-searching. Few people still believed that it had been a war to end wars, or indeed a war to make the world safe for democracy.

'Your King and Country need you' had been the recruiting call in 1914–18. So when, on 9 February 1933, a resolution 'that this House will in no circumstances fight for its king and country' was carried by 275 votes to 153 at an Oxford Union debate, the words had a very special significance. To some, the words 'king and country' still symbolized noble effort and noble sacrifice. To others – particularly the questioning young – they represented the

---

Soviet Government was smuggling into this country matchboxes with the figure of Christ as a trade mark. The matchboxes were actually of Indian origin, where they were popular with devout Indian Christian converts.

hypocritical rallying cry to lure millions to the slaughter in the interests of commercial greed on both sides. The resolution became known as the Oxford 'pacifist' resolution, but the truth was that though all pacifists could support it, so could many non-pacifists who might be quite prepared to fight for freedom and democracy, but who thought that 1914–18 had not been about that at all.

In working-class organizations anti-war resolutions were common. Few of them received any attention in the newspapers. But this resolution from a handful of Oxford students caused a major sensation. The reason was clear. If the middle class, and above all the officer class, was going to question the basic values of society, then indeed there was a breach in the rock of stability. The Oxford resolution was a sign of this breach which was already letting loose a sizeable stream. The left-wing student movement in England was something new.

The Times tried to treat the Oxford resolution lightly. Under the caption 'Children's Hour' it devoted a leader to explaining that it was not a symptom of universal decadence. Others disagreed. The *Daily Express* denounced the 'woozy-minded Communists, the practical jokers, the sexual indeterminates of Oxford'.[1] The *Daily Mail* spoke of 'posturers and gesturers';[2] the *Daily Telegraph* of 'Besmirching Oxford's Fair Fame'.[3] Winston Churchill delivered a speech to the Anti-Socialist and Anti-Communist Union in the Queen's Hall. 'They had all seen with a sense of nausea,' he said, 'the abject, squalid, shameless avowal made in the Oxford Union.'[4]

At an Oxford Union meeting a week later, the president was asked about an alleged consignment of white feathers. 'Two consignments of white feathers have been received,' he replied. 'White feathers are therefore available for all members who voted for the motion last week, at the rate of two per member. It may be possible to increase the number in the next few days.' The House cheered.[5]

The final episode was a move on 2 March to expunge the resolution from the minutes. It was made by various life members who rather officiously came down to Oxford for the occasion. They included Lord Stanley, Randolph Churchill and Quintin Hogg.

The motion to expunge the resolution, which attracted the highest attendance for many years, was defeated by 750 votes to 188.

The Oxford debate, which occurred just before Hitler came to power in Germany, was in part a reflection of the kind of thought prevailing in the labour movement, where it was widely believed that the First World War had been caused by imperialist rivalries, and that all governments shared responsibility for it. The arms race which had preceded it, stimulated by pressure from the private arms firms, had been, it was thought, a subsidiary cause. Later in that same year of 1933, the Annual Conference of the Labour Party at Hastings unanimously passed a resolution which spoke of the 'deepening of imperialist and capitalist rivalries as a direct cause of war'. It stated that the working class of any country had no quarrel with the working class of any other country, pledged itself to take no part in war and to resist it, and to examine the possibility of a general strike in the event of war, and urged approaches to secure international action by workers in other countries on the same lines. Sir Charles Trevelyan, who moved the resolution, reminded delegates that it was the organized workers who had stopped open war with Russia after 1918.

The belief that peace depended on the action of the workers against their own governments was fortified by the apparent impotence of the League of Nations when Japan invaded Manchuria in 1931. The League of Nations had been created after the First World War with the avowed object of preventing future wars by a system of collective security, including the collective use of economic and military sanctions to deter an aggressor if possible, and stop him if he refused to be deterred. But faced with its first test, the League had done nothing but talk, mainly, it was alleged, under the influence of the British government.

To many, faced with this situation, the pacifist position – personal renunciation of war and weapons – seemed the right answer. When the Reverend Dick Sheppard wrote to the press on 16 October 1934, asking those of his sex who wanted to repudiate violence to send him a post-card expressing willingness to vote in support of a resolution 'We renounce war and never again, directly or indirectly, will we support or sanction another', he received a hundred thousand replies. Some months later at a packed meeting at the Albert Hall, with well known writers like Siegfried Sassoon and Edmund Blunden on the platform, the organization which was later to be known as the Peace Pledge Union came into existence. To Dick Sheppard and many of his followers, war was a denial of Christianity. But his movement temporarily embraced many who were not Christians, and many who were not even pacifists in the sense that they believed in non-violence. Its early sponsors ranged from churchmen like Donald Soper, writers like Aldous Huxley, artists like Eric Gill to George Lansbury, until 1935 leader of the Labour Party, and Ellen Wilkinson, of the Labour left wing.

The pacifist influence was strong in certain sections of the labour movement – particularly in the Women's Co-operative Guild, the great mass organization for working-class housewives, which inaugurated the selling of white peace poppies on Armistice Day.

But in the labour movement as a whole, the pacifist attitude was never the dominant one. And events after Hitler came to power in 1933 were to cause a shift in perspective. By the end of that year the German government had announced its decision to rearm and to follow Japan out of the League of Nations. From then on the attitudes taken up in the Hastings resolution no longer seemed so appropriate. You could not organize joint action against war with the German working-class movement when that same movement had been smashed to smithereens. After Russia joined the League in 1934 the latter could no longer be regarded as an exclusively capitalist institution. There were innumerable cross currents, as usual, but more and more opinion in the labour movement began to shift towards trying to make a reality of the collective security system laid down under the League covenant.

It was in this situation that the League of Nations Union conceived the idea of taking a poll of public opinion on the subject of the League and collective security. The League of Nations Union, a body founded to promote the objects of the League, had Viscount Cecil at its head, and had many times received semi-official support and encouragement. It now invited other national bodies to serve on a National Declaration Committee which would sponsor the projected ballot on collective security and international disarmament. Thirty-eight bodies agreed, including the Labour Party and the Trades Union Congress, the Co-operative Movement, the Liberal Party, churches, peace societies, women's organizations and so on.

But the Conservative Party refused to cooperate at national level, leaving its local organizations to decide their attitude for themselves. This in itself was revealing. For Britain was a member of the League of Nations and paid lip service to its intentions. But the truth was that Conservative opinion, both at top and bottom, had long since become extremely divided about the League, and distrustful of the implications of membership. The powerful Beaverbrook press, for example, wanted isolation, make Britain strong, unilateral rearmament. The service chiefs disliked the League because it inhibited freedom to rearm. To such schools of thought a ballot about the League seemed an affront. In the event, only a minority group of Conservative MPs expressed support for the ballot, believing that the hostility of their colleagues, open or secret, was a mistake.

The ballot was intended to pose to the people five questions, one of which was divided into two parts. They were 1. Should Britain remain a member of the League? 2. Are you in favour of all-round reduction of armaments by international agreement? 3. Are you in favour of all-round abolition of national military and naval aircraft by international agreement? 4. Should the manufacture and sale of armaments for private profit be prohibited by international agreement? 5. Do you consider that if a nation insists on attacking another, the other nations should compel it to stop by (a) economic and non-military measures (b) if necessary military measures?

Thus this ballot, which became known as the peace ballot, was not a pacifist ballot. It did not suggest unilateral disarmament but disarmament by international agreement. And it clearly and deliberately raised the possibility of collective military measures against an aggressor.

The project involved distributing a form to every possible household, and collecting it again with the answers and signatures of those who answered. The eventual form used had room for six people to give their respective answers and signatures to each of the six questions, and, moreover, space for additional comment from those signing. Some of the sponsors had cold feet initially – not surprisingly. They argued that a limited poll only should be aimed at. But this was before the days when a limited public opinion poll could be regarded as scientific or valid. The majority of the sponsors were determined on as large a poll as possible, and a call went out for local Declaration Committees to be set up in every parliamentary constituency to conduct the ballot. They *were* set up – over a thousand of them – sometimes on the initiative of the local League of Nations Union branch, sometimes on the initiative of one or more of the other organizations concerned, co-ops, trade unions, peace societies, churches and so on. In the end no less than half a million volunteers came forward to help conduct the ballot.

Voting started in some areas in the late summer of 1934. Perhaps only those who have taken part in any sort of poll or canvass can appreciate what was involved. A form, or more than one form, had to be left at every house, and then called for when it was completed. At many houses it meant calling several times and finding everyone out, then finding everyone in, but the form lost and another needed. It meant calling at houses where the house-holder shouted at you and looked as though he might throw things at you, and at houses where the people were totally indifferent and apathetic. It meant having discussions with people who had strong opinions, and giving explanations to those who were puzzled. In rural areas it meant long journeys on foot to collect forms from isolated farms and cottages. The local Declaration Committees included people from all social classes. In Huddersfield, for example, the committee consisted of a Church of England canon, a teacher, a trade union official, a manufacturer, a railwayman, a bank clerk, some weavers, several social workers and an education expert.[6] In some areas it seemed to be the Co-op guildswomen and members of Labour Women's Sections who were wearing out their shoe leather.

Financially the whole operation was run on a shoe string; the headquarters expenses amounted to no more than £12,000 for everything, including printing, and any expenses in the localities had to be raised locally.

The *Manchester Guardian,* the *Daily Herald* and the *News Chronicle* were all backing the ballot, but most of the Conservative press – *The Times, Daily Telegraph* and *Daily Mail* – was doing its best to ignore it, while Beaverbrook's *Daily Express* advised the public to throw the ballot papers in the dustbin. 'Have nothing to to do with the Ballot of Blood,' it said. 'When the papers reach you, tear them up.'[7] And later it reported that anger at the Ballot of Blood was mounting – thousands were tearing up ballot papers.[8]

Some leading members of the government did not conceal their hostility. Sir John Simon, the Foreign Secretary, said that question four about the private manufacture of arms 'is not a question on which, without reasonable information of the arguments on either side, the verdict of the uninstructed should be invited'.[9] This statement seems to have done Sir John some harm and the ballot some good. Question four was a very topical one. A Senate enquiry into the international arms traffic was uncovering sensational details in the United States, and was indeed to be followed by a Royal Commission on the question in Britain in 1935. Meanwhile the left was busy selling literature with titles like *Patriotism, Ltd* and *Merchants of Death.*

The National Declaration Committee received its first completed result at the end of November 1934 from the little village of Scaldwell in Northamptonshire. For the next six weeks results were trickling in, mainly from small places. They all showed an identical voting pattern – a huge affirmative majority for the first five questions, a smaller majority, but still substantial, for question five (b). The sponsors kept their fingers crossed. They wondered what would happen when the returns from the big cities came in. The answer came with Bristol on 6 January 1935 – a huge affirmative reply, and 51½ per cent of the people had voted. After this, the pattern of voting was no longer in doubt, it was the same whereever it came from – what was going to matter was the size of the poll. By the end of January the first million had been passed; in February Conservative Bournemouth returned a 53 per cent poll: Rossendale in the north replied with a 73 per cent poll; Lincoln came up with a 60 per cent poll. In March, Manchester and Sheffield recorded huge votes; April added two and a half million to the total; in May it was revealed that the Welsh constituencies of Cardigan, Montgomery and Merioneth had recorded polls of over 80 per cent – more people had voted than in a General Election.

When the final results were published on 27 June 1935, they exceeded the wildest expectations of all involved. Eleven and a half million people had voted. And the answer 'yes' was in overwhelming majority to all five questions.* It was the largest amateur poll ever conducted in any country, and the most gigantic demonstration of public opinion which could possibly have been hoped for.

It had become clear, while the ballot was on, that people were taking it very seriously; that in many households a lot of thought and discussion had gone into completing it. The pattern of voting revealed that this was so: there was no automatic 'yes' to each question. Indeed while eleven million voted 'yes' to the first question, not more than six and three-quarter million voted 'yes' to question five (b) which raised the matter of military sanctions against an aggressor. This question was indeed the one which provoked most heart-searching – whether after economic sanctions had failed to stop aggression, military measures should be invoked. The 'no's' to this question included many who took either a

* The numbers voting on each question are given below. 'Doubtfuls' were those who answered in such a way that the meaning was not clear. 'Abstentions' were those who failed to answer that particular question though they answered others. Christian pacifists were permitted a special classification for question five.

Ques- tion	Yes	No	Doubt- ful	Absten- tion	Christian Pacifist	Totals
I	11,090,387	355,883	10,470	102,425	—	11,559,165
2	10,470,489	862,775	12,062	213,839	—	11,559,165
3	9,533,558	1,689,786	16,970	318,845	—	11,559,165
4	10,417,329	775,415	15,076	351,345	—	11,559,165
5 (a)	10,027,608	635,074	27,255	855,107	14,121	11,559,165
5 (b)	6,784,368	2,351,981	40,893	2,364,441	17,482	11,559,165

pacifist position, or a left-wing position where it was thought dangerous to give any capitalist government the go-ahead to use force. But the large number of abstentions shows that many were uncertain of this question, no doubt feeling that military sanctions meant war, whereas the whole purpose of the League was to stop war. Even so those answering 'yes' to question five (b) were in a big majority.

The purpose of the Peace Ballot was not to pose the superfluous query as to whether people preferred peace to war, but to find out, and indeed to suggest to them, the principles upon which peace could be pursued and maintained. But it soon ceased to be just a ballot and became a crusade, and for the half million volunteers who conducted it, at any rate, a crusade for the most important thing in the world – to stop another war. Within four years they were all to be engulfed in another war – perhaps the saddest outcome in history for any great movement. For no one can say that they didn't try.

And indeed no one can say that they were wrong. Collective action to deter the fascist dictators in the thirties might not have prevented the Second World War, but since no such action was taken, no one is in any position to be dogmatic about it. The 'uninstructed', as Sir John Simon had called them, had expressed the view that if one nation attacked another, the other nations should compel it to stop, by economic sanctions, and if necessary military measures. Their rulers were to chart another course altogether, that of appeasing the fascist powers, which was to take them all the way to Munich.

Indeed the government months before had started on its road of appeasement with the Anglo-German naval agreement, signed in May 1935, which gave Hitler the right to build submarines. Soon after, in the autumn of 1935, Mussolini embarked on the conquest of Abyssinia, and the British government, much shaken by the Peace Ballot and with a general election pending, appeared initially to be taking a tough line, calling for sanctions against Italy by the nations in the League. But by the end of the year the government was sponsoring the notorious Hoare-Laval pact which offered Italy everything she wanted in Abyssinia. And though the storm which followed caused the withdrawal of this particular deal, the oil sanctions which could have been decisive were never applied, much less naval sanctions, and Italy got away with it. It was the second major step towards conniving at fascist aggression. More connivance was to follow.

It is sometimes alleged that the climate of opinion which produced the Oxford resolution was a major factor enabling the British government – in particular the Chamberlain government after 1937 – to pursue the policy of appeasing the fascist powers. Public opinion, it is suggested, in favour of 'peace at any price', supported Chamberlain against the others – 'the others' being the minority represented by Churchill – who said Britain should resist and rearm. Such assumptions project the attitudes of the pre-Hitler era at the beginning of the thirties into the post-Hitler era. They fail to take account of what developed from 1935 onwards. The Peace Ballot did not show a demand for peace at any price, but for a collective stand against aggression. And to an increasing extent thereafter, the real division of outlook in the country was to be not 'peace at any price' versus the others, but 'anti-fascism' versus the rest.

This realignment was not peculiar to Britain. In France formidable para-military fascist organizations had been met with a rapidly growing alliance of the Socialists, Communists and Radicals which ultimately developed into a Popular Front. After a critical look at the deep divisions between social democrat and communist workers in Germany which had prevented successful resistance to Hitler, the Seventh World Congress of the Communist International had in the summer of 1935 called for a united anti-fascist struggle in every country. Though firmly outlawed by the Labour Party, the British Communist Party was finding people in a mood to listen to its calls for anti-fascist unity. For the organized working-class movement was by this time consciously and militantly dedicated to the idea of resisting fascism. Hitler meant the smashing of all working-class organizations which had been so painstakingly built up over decades – the trade unions, the Co-ops – all the means by which working people could protect themselves against being 'pushed around'. Understanding

on this question of fascism seemed to have filtered down to the
least politically aware working-class family. And in addition to
this, many professional people and others of the middle class with
liberal opinions who valued free speech and human rights were in
no doubt about their attitude and were unusually aroused.

But in the sophisticated circles at the top the climate of opinion
was quite different. Here was going on a complicated diplomatic
game to keep out of war – perhaps by winning over Mussolini,
perhaps by coming to terms with Hitler, whose bellicosity
appeared to be directed against Russia and 'Bolshevism' rather
than against Britain.[10] And so a rapid stream of opinion spread
out among influential circles in favour of conciliating the fascist
powers. If Hitler wanted to carry out a crusade against Bolshevism, it was argued *sub rosa,* let him – Britain could stay out.
Important people were entertained at the Olympic games in Berlin, and came back much impressed. The labour camps for the
unemployed there offered a solution which ought to be considered
here. Of course, Hitler's solution to the Jewish problem was not
appropriate to Britain – but then, after all, the Germans *had* a
Jewish problem. The Hitler youth were imbued with impressive
strength of purpose, in comparison with the demoralized attitudes
of youth at home. Ribbentrop, Hitler's ambassador in Britain, was
a good fellow. Open admirers of Nazi Germany included Lord
Londonderry[11] (coalowner and former Air Minister, and a leading
figure in the Anglo-German Fellowship) and the Conservative
MP Sir Henry Channon and his wife Lady Honor Channon of
the Guinness family; of the Channons, Harold Nicolson recorded
in his diary: 'they think Ribbentrop a fine man, and that we should
let gallant little Germany glut her fill of the reds in the East and
keep decadent France quiet while she does so . . .'[12]

Lord Astor, owner of the *Observer,* was one of those working
for agreement with Germany. 'There is complete ignorance in the
public mind as to the reasons why some people desire to negotiate
a settlement with Germany,' he wrote while on a visit to America.
'This is largely due to the intensive and widespread anti-German
propaganda being conducted by Jews and Communists. Newspapers are influenced by those firms which advertise so largely in

the press and are frequently under Jewish control.'[13] The Astors held regular weekend houseparties at Cliveden, their country house, where people in key positions, like Geoffrey Dawson, editor of *The Times,* exchanged views with diplomats and Cabinet ministers, including the Prime Minister, Neville Chamberlain. In time appeasement began to be identified with the so-called 'Cliveden set'.[14]

An alarmed and dissident group of Conservatives, headed by Churchill saw the threat to British security involved in appeasement but got nowhere. The left, meanwhile, were convinced that the whole object of appeasement was to encourage Germany against the Soviet Union – this seemed the only rational explanation for what was going on. It is in this context that the issue of British rearmament must be seen, an issue on which the labour movement was much divided – inevitably so, since there could not be a simple 'for' or 'against' under the circumstances. There were those who thought that the threat from Germany made rearmament imperative. Meanwhile those who took a pacifist position and thought all armaments wrong, found themselves joining forces with militant anti-fascists who thought that you could not acquiesce in handing over arms to Hitler's friends in the British government.

The division of opinion into anti-fascists versus the rest reached its most acute form over the issue of the Spanish Civil War which broke out in July 1936. The war began as an armed rebellion of Spanish officers, headed by General Franco, against the Spanish Republican government. General Franco was quickly supported not only by most of the army, but by the Falange fascists, various monarchist groups, almost the whole of the Church hierarchy, the largest landowners of the south, and ultimately certain sections of the middle class. The Republican government, against whom the rebellion was directed, consisted at the time of the rising exclusively of Liberal Republicans; it had come to power the previous February as a result of the victory at the polls of the 'Popular Front' combining liberals, socialists and communists.

Within weeks of the outbreak of the civil war, it became clear that Germany and Italy were heavily involved on Franco's side, supplying not only weapons and advisers, but regular troops on a considerable scale. The Spanish government, trying to buy arms from abroad with which to put down the rebellion, found itself blocked by the British and French governments, who had decided on a policy of 'non-intervention'. This policy, the argument for which was that all European powers should avoid getting embroiled in something that was a purely Spanish affair, was to be pursued throughout the two and a half years of the civil war. It denied the Spanish government the right to buy arms, and would, in view of the active intervention of the fascist powers, have led rapidly to the Republic's downfall, had it not been that the Soviet Union began to sell arms to the Republican government, and ultimately to send in equipment on a substantial scale.

British opinion was divided on the question of the Spanish Civil War, though by no means equally divided. Some sections strongly supported General Franco right from the beginning. He was thought to be a patriot, saving his country from the Reds; he represented law and order, whereas the government side represented anarchy; he upheld Christianity against those who would destroy it. This was the standpoint of newspapers such as the *Daily Mail*, the *Daily Sketch* and the *Observer*. In the latter paper J. L. Garvin, who wrongly expected Madrid to fall to Franco in a matter of weeks, carried on a vigorous and sustained pro-Franco campaign. 'The fall of Madrid will mean the shattering and humiliating defeat of Moscow as the open partner of Communist revolution in other countries,' he wrote as early as 25 October 1936.

As the Spanish government under the impact of the rising was reconstituted to include some Socialists and Communists, as the Spanish Communist Party, initially rather small, grew in strength during the progress of the war, and as the Russians began to supply arms to the Republican government, so voices such as those of Garvin could claim that their classification of the Republicans as 'Reds' was entirely valid. Meanwhile not only church-goers in England were outraged by the stories of the burning of churches and the persecution of nuns on the Republican side. Some Conservatives, of whom Churchill was one, had great misgivings at the possible threat to British interests if the fascists were established in Spain. However, there were powerful elements in the Conservative Party who regarded the cause of Franco as their own.

The strongly pro-Franco view was, however, never adopted by more than a small minority of people in this country, judging by the public opinion polls, which showed that support for Franco ranged at different times from 7 to 14 per cent, whereas support for the Republican government ranged at different times from 57 per cent to 72 per cent. When *Left Review* took a poll of writers in 1937 only five of them supported Franco, sixteen declared themselves neutral, but a hundred supported the Republic.

The majority of British people wanted the Republican government to win. Not all of them, however, were against the 'non-intervention' policy, which the government was initially successful in presenting as a neutral policy, aimed purely at avoiding an all-European conflagration. Thus at the Labour Party Conference of 1936 'non-intervention' was supported, mainly on two grounds: it was thought that it might force Germany and Italy to stay out, and it was seen as a means of keeping Britain out. As it became clear that 'non-intervention' was doing nothing to stop Italy and Germany, but was merely depriving the Republicans of the means of survival, opinion underwent a rapid change. Four weeks after the Labour Party Conference the Labour leaders declared that the Spanish government should have the right to buy arms, and in 1937 both the Labour Party and the TUC unanimously denounced the non-intervention policy.

All the same, the Labour leaders were to be accused by many in the movement of dragging their feet over Spain. For indeed nothing could exceed the passionate involvement of many of those who sided with the Spanish Republic. For them the conflict seemed to sum up all the great issues of the day, the defence of a freely elected government against overthrow by an armed reactionary clique, the cause of civil liberty and human rights, the universal cause of poor people against their rich oppressors. 'It is better to stand and die than to live on your knees,' La Pasionaria had said, evoking a response not just in Spain but half the world over. And to halt the advance of the fascist powers had begun to seem a life and death matter to the rest of the world, and not just to Spain. When the little undefended town of Guernica was destroyed by German bombers, it seemed like a foretaste of things to come. If Germany and Italy get away with it here, it was argued, it will be our turn next. And yet the British government, by non-intervention, appeared to be *helping* them to get away with it.

It was not only the dedicated left who thought like this. It was not only, even, the organized working class who thought like this. The attitude spread right through to liberal-minded middle class and professional people and beyond.

Simultaneously there was a perceptible shift in the attitude to the Soviet Union. Up till the Spanish War almost nobody had approved of Russia except the extreme left, who were thought by the rest of the world to be rather starry-eyed about the whole thing. But now that Russia was the only country actively supporting the Spanish government, and Litvinov was leading the fight at the League of Nations both for Spain and collective security against fascism, the attitude to the Soviet Union underwent a cautious change.

It was in this climate of opinion that the dominant Labour leadership appeared to many to be failing to match up to the situation. Particularly among the frustrated left wing there was widespread impatience with a 'constitutional' posture which seemed to lay more stress on getting people to vote Labour at the next election than on forcing changes in present government policy, while the TUC leaders were resisting calls for challenging the government by industrial action and appeared anxious to channel activity into relief work for the victims of the war.

Yet the very size of relief activities testified to the strength of feeling. At national level there was a National Joint Committee for Spanish Relief, chaired by the Duchess of Atholl, a Conservative MP who, incidentally, quarrelled with her local Conservative Association about 'non-intervention'. Also on the Joint Committee was Eleanor Rathbone, Independent MP for the Combined Universities, Wilfred Roberts, a Liberal MP, D. R. Grenfell, a Labour MP and miners' agent, and the Earl of Listowel, a Labour peer. The Joint Committee acted as coordinator for the activities of many organizations such as the Society of Friends, the Save the Children Fund, the Salvation Army; it also had links with the trade unions. Although there was no doubt which way its sympathies lay, it avoided asking its constituent members for a formal declaration of support for the Republican cause, instead getting agreement to send aid 'where the need is greatest'.

In individual localities there were few such inhibitions, and indeed the backbone of the movement was the local Aid Spain Committee. Almost every town had its local committee, collecting tins of milk, bars of soap, and money for medical aid, and holding meetings to explain the cause of Republican Spain. These committees varied in their composition. In working-class districts they were often rather like enlarged trades councils, with delegates from trade union branches, together with representatives of the Co-op Guilds, the local Labour parties and other organizations wanting to help. In many of them church organizations were involved. In other areas they were a lot less formal – perhaps just a group of people wanting to do something. In the more middle class areas members of the local Left Book Club might form the nucleus.

Some Aid Spain Committees set themselves the goal of collecting a ton of food – equal to five thousand tins of milk or other food. It meant leafleting a street one night, knocking on the doors the next. The response was often astonishing; even in the poorest working-class streets people seemed to come readily to the door with their gifts. Twenty-nine foodships were sent to Republican Spain as gifts, including a number stocked up by local people and firms in the big ports such as Liverpool, Hull, Glasgow and Tyneside. These foodships were separate from the commercial vessels which were still trading with Republican Spain, despite Franco's blockade, one of whose captains, 'Potato Jones', gained an almost legendary fame for risking the blockade unprotected by the British navy.

And there were local collections for medical supplies. The first British ambulance unit with British nurses and doctors left for Spain in August 1936. Many more were to follow, and several cities sent their own ambulances bought with money raised locally.

When four thousand Basque children were admitted to Britain as refugees a week or so after Coronation Day, it was on the strict understanding that they must not be a charge on public funds. But voluntary funds flooded in. Housed in a transit camp at Southampton thrown up at short notice by volunteers mobilized by the Southampton Trades Council who borrowed tents from the army, many of these children went later to private families and stayed with them until they grew up.

The mining areas were among the most active in support of Republican Spain. The Miners' Federation of Great Britain, having already made substantial contributions from its funds, decided in May 1938 to raise £83,000 by means of a levy of 2s 6d per member. A levy was the customary way of supporting fellow miners in an industrial dispute, but the usual sort of levy would be perhaps 3d a head. A levy as large as 2s 6d was unprecedented. Will Lawther of the Durham miners, whose young brother had been killed in Spain, told the 1938 TUC that of the £68,000 which had so far come in, £16,000 had come from two Distressed Areas. In all it was estimated that some £2 million worth of cash and goods was contributed from this country to help Republican Spain[15] – in those days a very big amount.

Despite the determination of the dominant TUC leadership to avoid 'unconstitutional' action[16] feeling ran so high as time went on that there were token strikes in some of the large engineering factories, such as De Havilland and Dorman Long, where the engineers downed tools and marched down Whitehall demanding arms for Spain.

But the most significant 'unconstitutional' action was the formation of the British Battalion of the International Brigade. The International Brigades were formed of volunteers from many nations, and played a major part in the fighting on the Republican side. Two thousand British were among them, at first as individuals attached to various units, but soon to form their own British Battalion. Five hundred were killed, and twelve hundred wounded. After January 1937 it became illegal to volunteer to fight in Spain, or to recruit volunteers, or to arrange their passage to Spain. The operation was carried through in this country by the Communist

Party, which discreetly escorted groups of volunteers on weekend tickets to Paris (this did not then require a passport), and handed them over to the French Communist Party which conducted them on foot over the Pyrenees. About half the British volunteers were Communists. Of the rest, some were in the Labour Party or Independent Labour Party, and some were of no political party.

Though there were writers and scientists and other intellectuals among the British volunteers, including some young men of great promise who lost their lives, 80 per cent of them were working class. They came from all over the country, many from Scotland, many from Wales, many from the Distressed Areas. Some had been unemployed; some threw up jobs to join. There were miners, engineers, building workers, and indeed all trades were re-presented, the first two to volunteer being clothing workers. So that many of the local Aid Spain Committees had their own local lad at the front, and felt thereby a close personal involvement. His letters home to his family would be read out at meetings; his dependants, if he had any, visited and helped, though money for dependants was mainly raised under the auspices of the national Dependants' Aid Committee. Pride in the British volunteers was great throughout the labour movement and C. R. Attlee, the leader of the Parliamentary Labour Party, visited them at the front, and lent his name to what became known as the Attlee Company of the British Battalion.

There were great meetings with great oratory and great names. Like the one which packed the Albert Hall in June 1937 to raise funds for the Basque refugee children, when the Duchess of Atholl took the chair, Heinrich Mann and Professor Paul Langevin came to speak, and a Guernica sketch given by Picasso was auctioned. Or the one in January 1939 when nine thousand people assembled in the Empress Hall, Earls Court, to welcome the returned members of the International Brigade, to hear Harry Pollitt speak and Paul Robeson sing about Joe Hill, and to answer an appeal from Isabel Brown with a collection of £3,800. Or the last desperate 'Save Spain' meeting in the Queens Hall on 25 January 1939, with David Low the cartoonist, Stafford Cripps, Lady Violet Bonham

Carter, Aneurin Bevan and others, when J. B. Priestley said that he felt that he was moving in the middle act of a great tragedy. By this time the demand for the Labour leaders to unite all anti-Chamberlain forces, from dissident Conservatives on the right to Communists on the left, in a Popular Front had mounted to a crescendo. The Labour leaders resisted this pressure and expelled its chief advocates, including Cripps and Bevan, from the Labour Party.

But the last act had really begun a few months earlier with the Munich crisis. Throughout the spring and summer of 1938 Hitler, who had already annexed Austria, had been putting pressure on Czechoslovakia, using the German minority in the Czech Sudetenland as a pretext. During August and early September the threats were mounting. The Czechs, however, were powerfully armed, with elaborate fortifications, comparable to the French Maginot line, situated precisely in the Sudeten border districts. Moreover, Czechoslovakia had a mutual assistance pact with both France and Russia. By mid-September the French cabinet was nervously debating whether to fulfil France's obligations to Czechoslovakia if the latter was attacked by Germany.

It was at this point on 15 September that Prime Minister Chamberlain flew to see Hitler at Berchtesgaden amid the congratulations of most of the British press, which emphasized that he was sixty-nine and had never flown before. When he returned Chamberlain had discussions with the French, ostentatiously excluding the Russians who had continued to declare that they would fulfil their obligations to the Czechs if the French did so too. A few days later it emerged bit by bit that there was an Anglo-French Plan to transfer great areas of Czechoslovakia to Germany, and that, moreover, irresistible pressure had been put upon the Czechs to accept this proposal.

How was all this presented to the British public? The two and a half million readers of Beaverbrook's *Daily Express* were fed with praise of Chamberlain, interspersed with suggestion that the issues at stake in Europe were not Britain's concern anyway. Rothermere's *Daily Mail* with one and a half million readers plugged a 'trust Chamberlain' motif, while printing personal and friendly interviews with Hitler and adopting a bullying tone with the Czechs.[17]

The Labour press was, however, taking a different line. As early as 7 September, the General Council of the TUC had issued a joint statement with the executives of the Labour Party and the Parliamentary Labour Party which declared:

> Every consideration of democracy forbids the dismemberment of the Czechoslovakian State ... The time has come for a positive and unmistakable lead for collective defence against aggression and to safeguard peace. The British government must leave no doubt in the mind of the German government that it will unite with the French and Soviet governments to resist any attack upon Czechoslovakia.

Labour and trade union leaders continued to make speeches along these lines in the ensuing days, and the Anglo-French Plan was condemned on 21 September as a 'shameful surrender to the threats of Herr Hitler ... with every surrender to violence, peace recedes'. On that day it was decided to launch a 'Stand by the Czechs' campaign, and indeed three thousand meetings all over the country were quickly organized.

The *Daily Herald*, Labour's official newspaper, which had two million readers, printed all these statements. But it has to be recorded that many of them were tucked away inside, while the paper's front page and editorials appeared to be following Labour's policy with somewhat faltering steps.* The Cadbury-owned *News Chronicle* appeared to be doing its best to stand by the Czechs, though the only newspaper with no hesitations was the small-circulation *Daily Worker,* which continued to denounce what it called the Hitler-Chamberlain alliance from beginning to end. But the Left Book Club mobilized its members to distribute two and a half million leaflets on the Czech crisis.

In such ways the message got through. The group known as 'Mass Observation' attempted to explore public feeling at the time; its conclusion was that after the terms of the Anglo-French

---

* For example on 15 September, 'Good Luck Chamberlain' and on 19 September on the Anglo-French Plan: 'In a critical international situation hasty comment without all the facts can make a critical situation more critical.'

Plan became known there was a great movement of mass opinion moving faster than the newspapers. The observers carried out three hundred and fifty interviews on 21 and 22 September asking the simple question 'What do you think about Czechoslovakia?' Replies were classified into four groups: 1 *Indignant* (Chamberlain policy wrong, we should stand up to Hitler). 2 *No War* (It may be unfair to the Czechs, but we want peace above everything). 3 *Pro-Chamberlain* (he is a good man, he has saved peace). 4 *Don't know*. Of the men questioned on these two days, no less than 67 per cent were in the *indignant* category, 2 per cent only were in the *no war* category, 14 per cent only in the pro-Chamberlain class, 17 per cent were *don't knows*. An example of the *indignant* class was a London bus conductor:

What the hell's he got the right to go over there and do a dirty trick like that? It'll have the whole world against us now. Who'll trust us? It's like throwing your own kid to the wolves. We helped make it a country and then Chamberlain comes along and wants to buy that swine off. There'll be a war sooner or later, then there'll be nobody to help us.

The women were much more divided. Not more than 22 per cent were in the *indignant* class. Only 16 per cent were in the *no war* class and 27 per cent were *pro-Chamberlain*. But as many as 35 per cent were *don't knows*, for it was the habit among married women to refer all political questions to their husbands. Even so, taking men and women together, the *indignants* outnumbered the combined *no wars* and *pro-Chamberlains* by four to three.

'Stand by the Czechs' demonstrations were meanwhile gathering momentum. That in Trafalgar Square on 18 September was very large indeed; on the evening of Sunday 25 September, 'Whitehall was packed from wall to wall with people', according to the *News Chronicle,* which came out with large photographs of the demonstration carrying posters which said 'Stop Hitler'.[18] But news of these demonstrations was virtually suppressed by the Conservative press.

Chamberlain, however, had flown once more to see Hitler on 22 September, this time at Godesberg, triumphantly presenting his Anglo-French Plan for the dismemberment of Czechoslovakia, only to find that Hitler considered the plan too slow, and was now demanding the *immediate* occupation by German troops of the Czech territories concerned, with all Czech installations, including fortifications, to be handed over intact. The Czechs rejected this ultimatum and had indeed began to mobilize. Chamberlain returned with the new Godesberg demands, and on 26 September the Government announced that if Czechoslovakia was attacked Great Britain would stand by France and Russia.

Suddenly there appeared to be a war situation, though why Hitler should choose to go to war when he had been offered 90 per cent of what he wanted without war could be clear to no one – nor indeed why Chamberlain should be preparing to fight for a country which he had previously wanted to dismember.* For those who tried to follow the news, its very illogicality was to add to the nightmarish quality of the next three or four days.

But certain things seemed all too real. Loud-speaker vans were touring the streets telling people where to go for gas masks; trenches were being dug in the parks; the air was thick with announcements – that the navy was being mobilized, that fifty million ration cards were ready, that there were plans to evacuate school children. And Air Raid Precautions volunteers – mostly unpaid, spare-time – found themselves called upon to work non-stop handing out gas masks to the millions now queueing up. The ARP workers did their best to keep up everyone's spirits, exchanging facetious jokes with the shuffling queues. But it wasn't really funny. Gas had been too many people's private nightmare ever since the First World War. And everyone knew that you couldn't fit a gas mask on a baby.

After it was all over there was an extraordinary outburst from the Administrative Chief of the Home Office ARP Department:

---

* The *Daily Herald* had by this time apparently forgotten that it had denounced the dismemberment of Czechoslovakia. On 27 September it explained that the only issue was whether the Czech territories should be subjected to 'an ordered transfer within a reasonable period' or whether Hitler should take them by force – exactly Chamberlain's argument.

This has got to be said and might as well be said at once. People who are known as the governing classes of this country have, broadly speaking, done very little to help local authorities. It has been a very serious thing that ARP has had to be organized largely by officials and the local authorities, and that most of the personnel are the industrial workpeople of this country.[19]

But on 28 September, Chamberlain announced that he had been invited to meet Hitler once again, this time at Munich. The Munich agreement signed two days later gave Hitler the Czech territories he wanted without firing a shot, together with all the elaborate fortifications and defence installations.

There were emotional scenes in Downing Street and much adulation in the press ('Be glad in your hearts. Give thanks to God. The wings of peace settle about us and the people of Europe').[20] But down below, natural relief at having emerged from what seemed like a bad dream soon gave way to shame and disgust when the terms of the Munich agreement became fully known.

It has since been argued that if Britain had fought then instead of later, she would have done so on far more advantageous terms, with not only France as ally, but the Soviet Union and Czechoslovakia itself. However that may be, it was not the argument used by anti-fascist opinion at the time, even though many were quite prepared to fight, and indeed volunteers had been going to the Czech embassy to offer their services. The argument, however, had always been that a collective stand by the peace-loving powers – headed by Britain, France and Russia in particular – would deter Hitler from going to war at all. This was the collective security thesis propounded ever since the peace ballot, but never implemented.

September 1938 may have been the last occasion when such a stand was possible, though left opinion never admitted this, but continued to call upon Britain to join France and Russia in a mutual assistance pact against fascist aggression. By February 1939 the Spanish Republic had fallen, by March 1939 Hitler had occupied the rest of Czechoslovakia, by August 1939 the Soviet Union, cold-shouldered and rejected by the Western democracies for so long, finally signed a non-aggression pact with Hitler.

When, on 1 September, Hitler attacked Poland, it signified, as Chamberlain said, that everything he had worked for, hoped for and believed in had 'crashed in ruins'.

And on 3 September 1939, just as millions of Sunday dinners were going into millions of ovens, the British people heard that they were at war at last. All in all, they had hardly deserved their rulers.

Conclusion

> The clever hopes expire
> Of a low dishonest decade

wrote W. H. Auden in September 1939. For the ruling politicians the epitaph is not unjust. And yet there was more to the thirties than the downward slither into war and the failure of the left to arrest it. The movements of resistance and protest against poverty and fascism did not simply die away with the outbreak of war. The changes begun in those bitter years, though only to be seen clearly much later, were real and irreversible.

For one thing, a new attitude to poverty was established. For the first time the pre-ordained inevitability of poverty and insecurity began to be widely challenged. When the Beveridge Report with its interlocked recipes for 'freedom from want' appeared in 1942, it was in response to the pressure of opinion built up in the thirties, above all through the movement against the means test on the unemployed.

It is easily forgotten how much of the social legislation which we now take for granted as part of the fabric of British life was as recently as the thirties either non-existent or embryonic. There were no family allowances, no universally available free medical treatment, no free secondary education except for a handful of children, no free milk in schools except for a tiny minority. There were still relatively few council houses. Old age pensions were a pittance, which many people were not entitled to anyway. It was the demonstrations, the exposures of malnutrition, the hunger marches, which helped to create and focus a demand for state guarantees against poverty which no subsequent government could ignore. Rightly or wrongly, great numbers of people came to believe that the kind of pattern later known as the Welfare State would bring freedom from the insecurity and deprivation from which they had suffered. In future, governments would be held responsible for any major rise in unemployment – a fact which has limited the freedom of successive administrations to carry through deflationary policies on the scale of 1931.

True, all these stirrings and pressures met with a resistance which in some fields was almost fanatical – a resistance which cannot be explained solely in terms of financial expediency dictated by the slump. It seemed as though the social advances of the twenties, meagre though they were by later standards, had inspired a sort of fear in the governing class, just as the 1926 General Strike had engendered fear. The response was a swing back to philosophies of an earlier epoch, and a desperate stand to preserve intact the old class relationships. In face of the challenge of socialist thought, some groups in the upper reaches of society toyed with fascism; and many felt a greater sympathy with their opposite numbers in fascist Germany and Italy than they had ever felt with their own poor at home. But it was not their influence that proved the most lasting.

For the conscious growth of anti-fascist and democratic feeling especially linked with the Spanish Civil War was another important legacy of this period. The British working class and radical movement had traditionally been militant on economic and trade union matters rather than political ones. Now far-reaching political questions – such as racialism, militarism, national independence and fascism – became mass issues on which millions of people were involved in some kind of protest action, and the subject of intense discussion within the labour movement.

It is easy to say now, with hindsight, that there was never any serious chance that Britain would go Fascist or ally itself with the fascist powers in war. At the time both possibilities seemed open. Right-wing Conservative erosion of traditional rights, though less dramatic, evidently had more weight behind it than black-shirted mob violence, and with continuing trade recession could have become much more formidable. Even during the war public knowledge of what Fascism and Nazism meant to ordinary people was derived less from government propaganda than from that of the liberal and labour movements. Not until the liberation of Belsen and Auschwitz in 1945 did the official news machine begin to catch up.

Meanwhile deference and respect for one's superiors perceptibly declined. The unspoken belief that the rich and expensively educated had a natural right to rule and manage was deeply shaken by their manifest inability to deal either with unemployment or with Hitler. The abdication fuss did not indeed alienate sympathy from the monarchy – loyal citizens contriving to be almost equally sorry for Edward VIII and his successor George VI – but the image of royalty as a semi-divine institution could never be restored.

Cynicism among the common people paradoxically gave rise in war conditions to a new self-confidence. 'Let us have a go, we can't make a worse mess of it than they have' – such was the philosophy of innumerable workers who set up joint production and efficiency committees in the war factories (a move without precedent in the First World War).

As for the rank and file in the armed forces, they were notably more independent and critical of their officers, much less disposed to accept leadership and war aims from their class superiors than the Tommies of the First World War. There seems little doubt that the whole movement of organized protest and anti-fascism helped to colour the sceptical patriotism of other ranks and their refusal to vote Churchill in as peacetime leader in 1945. Nor should we forget the millions of civilians sheltering from Hitler's bombs under the stairs or down the London tubes, who silently resolved 'Never again, if we come through this – never again a Britain as it was in the thirties'.

Short Guide to Further Reading

General

C. L. Mowat, *Britain Between the Wars*, 1955.
R. Graves and A. Hodge, *The Long Weekend: A Social History of Great Britain 1918–39*, 1940.
J. B. Priestley, *English Journey*, 1934.
A. M. Carr Saunders and D. Caradog Jones, *A Survey of the Social Structure of England and Wales*, 1937.

Economic

S. Pollard, *The Development of the British Economy 1914–1950*, 1962.
British Association, *Britain in Depression*, 1935; *Britain in Recovery*, 1938.
G. C. Allen, *British Industries and their Organization* (second edn.), 1951.
M. Dobb, *Studies in the Development of Capitalism*, 1946.
E. Hobsbawm, *Industry and Empire*, 1968.

Unemployment and the Distressed Areas

W. Hannington, *Ten Lean Years*, 1940.
Ellen Wilkinson, *The Town that was Murdered*, 1939.
Fenner Brockway, *Hungry England*, 1932.
R. C. Davison, *British Unemployment Policy since 1930*, 1938.

Trade Union and Industrial

G. D. H. Cole, *British Trade Unionism Today*, 1939; *Short History of the British Working Class Movement*, 1948.
H. Pelling, *A History of British Trade Unionism*, 1963.

J. Hilton (ed.), *Are Trade Unions Obstructive?*, 1935.
A. Hutt, *Postwar History of the British Working Class*, 1937.
W. Citrine, *Men and Work*, 1964.
A. Bullock, *Life and Times of Ernest Bevin*, 1960.
A. Horner, *Incorrigible Rebel*, 1960.
R. P. Arnot, *The Miners in Crisis and War*, 1961.
J. Jeffreys, *The Story of the Engineers*, 1946.
H. Clegg, *General Union*, 1954.
J. Gollan, *Youth in British Industry*, 1937.

Living Standards

G. D. H. and Margaret Cole, *Condition of Britain*, 1937.
A. Bowley, *Wages and Income since 1860*, 1937.
J. Hilton, *Rich Man, Poor Man*, 1944.
J. Burnett, *Plenty and Want*, 1966.
B. Seebohm Rowntree, *Human Needs of Labour*, 1936; *Poverty and Progress*, 1941.
J. Boyd Orr, *Food Health, and Income*, 1936; *As I Recall*, 1966.
G. C. M'Gonigle and J. Kirby, *Poverty and Public Health*, 1936.
R. Titmuss, *Poverty and Population*, 1938.
J. Kuczynski, *Short History of Labour Conditions in Great Britain*, 1946.
A. Hutt, *Condition of the Working Class in Britain*, 1933.

Housing and Town Development

Marion Bowley, *Housing and the State*, 1945.
E. D. Simon, *Rebuilding Britain*, 1946.
R. Durant, *Watling*, 1939.
Bournville Village Trust, *When We Build Again*, 1941.
P. Willmott, *The Evolution of a Community. A Study of Dagenham*, 1963.

Fascism

R. Benenson, *Political Violence and Public Order*, 1969.
Colin Cross, *The Fascists in Britain*, 1961.

Culture and Recreation

R. Williams, *Communications*, 1962.
J. Reith, *Into the Wind*, 1949.

M

J. Symons, *The Thirties*, 1960.
J. Lindsay, *After the Thirties*, 1956.
P. Rotha, *The Film Till Now*, 1949.
A. Briggs, *The History of Broadcasting in the United Kingdom*, Vol II, 1965.

Memoirs and Biography

H. Macmillan, *Winds of Change 1914–1939*, 1966.
H. Nicolson, *Diaries and Letters 1930–39*, 1966.
T. Jones, *A Diary with Letters 1931–1950*, 1954.
C. Cockburn, *I Claud . . .*, 1967.

References and Notes

Chapter 1: Economic and Political Setting

1 Harold Macmillan, *Winds of Change* (1966), p. 283.
2 Lord Swinton, *Sixty Years of Power.*
3 See Citrine's autobiography, *Men and Work*, for details of such contacts between himself and Baldwin.

Chapter 2: 1931 The Political Watershed

1 *Report of the Committee on Trade and Industry*, set up by the Labour government in 1929.
2 *Committee on National Expenditure Report*, Cmd. 3920.
3 *Daily Mail*, 25 August 1931.
4 See the account by Len Wincott, who was serving on HMS *Norfolk*, reprinted in *Mutiny* by T. H. Wintringham (1937).
5 See *Labour Research*, October 1931.
6 *Daily Herald*, 17 September 1931.
7 See *The Mutiny at Invergordon*, by Kenneth Edwards, a retired Lieutenant-Commander (1937).
8 Including Len Wincott (ibid) and Fred Copeman, whose account of the mutiny appears in his memoirs *Reason in Revolt* (1948).
9 J. R. Clynes, *Hansard*, 11 September 1931.
10 *Liberal Magazine*, November 1931.

Chapter 3: The Unemployed and the Means Test

1 Unemployment Insurance (Anomalies) Regulations, actually made under an Act which had been passed by the previous Labour government.

2   Unemployment Insurance (National Economy), No. 2 Order.
3   According to evidence to the Royal Commission on Unemployment Insurance 1932, in January 1931 twelve County Boroughs gave an allowance of under 20s for a man and wife apparently without any additional rent allowance. They were: Croydon (15s), Chester (16s), West Bromwich (16s 6d), Darlington, Dudley (17s), Portsmouth (17s 6d), Grimsby, Rochdale, Wallasey, West Hartlepool, Wigan (18s), Southampton (18s 6d). Another ten County Boroughs gave only 20s. Several of the County Councils had equally small fixed sums for man and wife, but many of the latter had no fixed scale at all.
4   *Daily Herald*, 14 September 1932.
5   *Daily Herald*, 27 September 1932.
6   *Manchester Guardian*, 12 November 1932.
7   Listed in *Labour Research* diaries covering the period or in *Daily Herald*, 11 October 1932.
8   *Daily Herald*, 1 November 1932.
9   *Hansard*, 19 October 1932.
10 Broadcast from Lossiemouth, 19 December 1932, reported in the *Liberal Magazine*, January 1933.
11 See *Manchester Guardian* and other newspapers, 24 February 1934. The signatories were: Lascelles Abercrombie, Ambrose Appelbee, C. R. Attlee, G. H. Bing, Vera Brittain, Dudley Collard, A. P. Herbert, Harold Laski, Kingsley Martin, Evelyn Sharp Nevinson, Henry W. Nevinson, D. N. Pritt, Edith Summerskill, H. G. Wells, R. Kidd (Secretary).
12 *Hansard*, 28 January 1935.
13 *Report of the Unemployment Assistance Board*, 1935, Cmd. 5177, p. 15.
14 ibid., p. 206.
15 ibid., p. 198.
16 ibid., p. 249.
17 ibid., p. 192.
18 ibid., p. 78.
19 ibid., p. 15.
20 ibid., p. 110.
21 *Report of the Unemployment Assistance Board*, 1938, Cmd. 6021, p. 2.
22 ibid., p. 5.
23 ibid., p. 47.
24 ibid., p. 38

25 ibid,. p. 50.
26 *The Times*, 22 February 1938.

Chapter 4: *Industrial Graveyards*

1 For the whole history of cartellization, see D. L. Burn, *Economic History of Steelmaking*, and H. Owen, *Steel: The Facts*, 1946.
2 For the Jarrow scheme, see E. Wilkinson, *The Town That Was Murdered*, 1939.
3 *Report of the Royal Commission on Merthyr Tydfil*, 1935, p. 19.
4 ibid, p. 15.
5 PEP *Report on the Location of Industry in Great Britain*, 1939, p. 251.
6 Pilgrim Trust, *Men Without Work*, 1938.
7 Allen Hutt, *Condition of the Working Class in 1934*. This book documents conditions in Lancashire as well as in the Distressed Areas proper.
8 J. B. Priestley, *English Journey*, 1934.
9 *Report of Commissioner for Special Areas of Scotland*, 1937–38, p. 55.
10 *Report of Commissioner for Special Areas of England and Wales*, 1937–8, p. 43.
11 J. B. Priestley, *English Journey*, 1934.
12 A. L. Horner, *Incorrigible Rebel*, 1960, p. 97.
13 See also Wal Hannington, *The Problem of the Distressed Areas*, for social conditions.
14 *Reports of Investigations into the Industrial Conditions in Certain Depressed Areas*, Cmd. 4728, 1934, p. 83.
15 *First Report of Commissioner for the Special Areas of England and Wales*, July 1935, p. 16.
16 *Hansard*, 7 December 1934.
17 *Hansard*, 20 November 1934.
18 *Hansard*, 3 December 1934.
19 *Report of Commissioner for Special Areas of England and Wales*, 1936.
20 *Report on West Cumberland*, by Rt Hon J. C. C. Davidson, MP, Chancellor for Duchy of Lancaster, in Cmd. 4728, 1934.
21 *Report of Commissioner for the Special Areas of England and Wales*, 1935, p. 65.
22 ibid., p. 74.
23 PEP *Report on Location of Industry in Great Britain*.
24 Cmd. 4957, 1934, *Report on Durham and Tyneside*, p. 94.

25   Report of Commissioner for the Special Areas of England and Wales, 1935, p. 86.
26   Report of Commissioner for the Special Areas of England and Wales, 1936, p. 6.

Chapter 5: The Growing Communities

1   Bournville Village Trust, *When We Build Again*, 1941.
2   P. Willmott, *The Evolution of a Community: A Study of Dagenham*.
3   *Royal Commission on the Distribution of the Industrial Population*, 1940.

Chapter 6: Inside the Workshops

1   West Midlands Group on Post-War Reconstruction, *Conurbation*, 1948.
2   Factory Inspector's Report, 1935, p. 65.
3   K. Liepmann, *The Journey to Work*.
4   Factory Inspector's Report, 1935, p. 42.
5   ibid.

Chapter 7: Industrial Workers: Backs to the Wall

1   Milne Bailey, *Trade Union Documents*, p. 427.
2   Alan Bullock, *The Life and Times of Ernest Bevin*, p. 396.
3   See *Class Against Class*. General Election Policy of CPGB 1929. Also *The New Line*. Report of 10th Congress, CPGB. 1929.
4   See William Gallacher, *Last Memoirs*, p. 221, for a frank critical treatment of this issue.
5   W. Citrine, *Men and Work*, p. 316.
6   Reported *Manchester Guardian*, 22 March 1932.
7   *Labour Research*, October 1932, Special Supplement on the Cotton Industry.
8   Daniels and Campion, *The Cotton Textile Industry*, in British Association, *Britain in Depression*, 1934.
9   *Cotton Factory Times*, 4 October 1935.
10   Wage figures derived from Ministry of Labour figures, and from index by Ramsbottom published in the *Journal of the Royal Statis-*

tical Society. For details of calculation see J. Kuczynski, *Short History of Labour Conditions in Great Britain*, 1946.

Chapter 8: Industrial Workers: Recovery and the Fight for Trade Union Organization

1 *Trade Union Difficulties in New Areas*, in G. D. H. Cole, ed. *British Trade Unionism Today*, 1939, p. 242.
2 A. L. Horner, *Incorrigible Rebel*, p. 139.
3 Quoted in R. Page Arnot, *The Miners*, Vol. II, p. 211.
4 ibid.
5 H. Pelling, *History of British Trade Unionism*, Penguin Books.
6 H. A. Marquand, *Organised Labour in Four Continents*, p. 183.
7 J. Jefferys, *Story of the Engineers*.
8 H. Clegg, *General Union in a Changing Society*.
9 ibid.
10 E. J. Hobsbawm, *Labouring Men*: Essay on *Trends in the British Labour Movement*.
11 H. A. Marquand, *Organised Labour in Four Continents*, p. 817.
12 H. Pelling, *History of British Trade Unionism*, p. 105. (Penguin ed.)
13 A. Bullock, *Life and Times of Ernest Bevin*, p. 520.
14 Bullock, ibid.
15 Bullock, ibid., p. 610.
16 See V. L. Allen, *Trade Unions and Government*.
17 W. Citrine, *Men and Work*, p. 360.
18 G. D. H. Cole, *British Trade Unionism Today*, 1939.
19 Concluding words of G. D. H. Cole, ibid, p. 540.

Chapter 9: Wages Real and Unreal

1 This calculation is made for 1930–62 from *Key Statistics of the British Economy 1900–62*, London and Cambridge Economic Service, which is based as far as possible on the Ministry of Labour cost of living index (less inaccurate for the two ends of the decade than for the middle) and for 1962–70 on the official Retail Price Index as given in the *Statistical Abstract*.
2 C. G. Routh, *Occupation and Pay in Great Britain, 1906–60*.
3 Ministry of Labour official index, and Professor A. Bowley's index compiled for the London and Cambridge Economic Service.

4   Even though a cautious and scrupulous worker like Professor A. Bowley (*Wages, Prices and Incomes since 1860*, p. 30) was so conscious of its deficiences that he called the $\dfrac{\text{Wage-Rates}}{\text{cost of living}}$ column of his table 'quotient' rather than 'real wages'.

5   See chapter 8 on industrial workers and the trade unions.

6   Figures from H. W. Richardson, *Economic Recovery in Britain 1932–39*, p. 73.

7   B. S. Rowntree, *The Human Needs of Labour*, 1936. See chapter 14 on Eating and Not Eating.

8   Colin Clark, estimate given in G. D. H. and M. Cole, *Condition of Britian*, 1937, p. 258.

9   J. Kuczynski in *Hunger and Work*, 1938.

Chapter 10: Class Structure and Class Outlook

1   Based on A. L. Chapman and R. Knight, *Wages and Salaries in the United Kingdom, 1920–38*.

2   Leak and Maizels, *The Structure of British Industry*, published by the Journal of the Royal Statistical Society, 1945.

3   J. Hilton, *Rich Man, Poor Man*, delivered as BBC talks in 1938, published in 1944.

4   J. E. Meade, *Efficiency, Equality and Ownership of Property*, 1964, p. 27.

5   Harold Macmillan, *Winds of Change 1914–1939*, 1966, p. 195.

6   Thomas Jones, *A Diary with Letters 1931–1950*, 1954, p. 286. Jones was a former Cabinet Secretary, and Chairman of the Pilgrim Trust.

7   Harold Macmillan, ibid. p. 197.

8   Harold Nicolson, *Diaries and Letters 1930–39*, 1966.

9   Francis Williams, *A Pattern of Rulers*.

Chapter 11: Babies and the Birth-rate

1   E. Lewis-Faning, *Report on an Enquiry into Family Limitation and its influence on Human Fertility during the past fifty years*. Volume I of the Papers of the Royal Commission on Population, 1949.

2   ibid. The Enquiry showed that over 60 per cent of couples married in 1930–4 had by 1946 practised some kind of birth control. But while 40 per cent of those in Social Class I (professional and

non-manual) had used birth control appliances, (i.e. sheath, cap, tablets), only 25 per cent of those in Social Class 3 (unskilled) had done so, while 38 per cent of this latter group used 'non-appliance' methods only, which in practice nearly always meant *coitus interruptus.*

3 *Hansard,* 15 April 1935.
4 *Hansard,* 10 February 1937.

Chapter 12: Educational Pyramid

1 *Report of Consultative Committee on Secondary Education* (Spens Report) 1938, p. 221.
2 Hadow Reports on the state of primary schools (1931) and infant schools (1933).
3 Committee on National Expenditure Report, Cmd. 3920, paras. 501, 502.
4 *Hansard,* 13 February 1936.
5 *Hansard,* 26 May 1936.

Chapter 13: Homes, Landlords and Building Societies

1 *Hansard,* 15 December 1932.
2 *Daily Telegraph,* Building Society Supplement, 29 May 1933.
3 *The Times,* 30 January 1940.
4 *Daily Telegraph,* 18 May 1933.
5 *Hansard,* 12 December 1932.
6 C. G. Ammon MP gave chapter and verse for what was going on in Camberwell in this respect in the House of Commons, 2 March 1938.
7 *News Chronicle,* 29 June 1939.

Chapter 14: Eating and Not Eating

1 For further details see John Burnett, *Plenty and Want,* 1966.
2 See, for example, the diets published by Seebohm Rowntree in *Poverty and Progress,* 1941; the *Report of the Committee on Tuberculosis Services in Wales,* 1938; and the Ministry of Labour survey of weekly budgets for agricultural workers in 1937–8.
3 *The Medical Officer,* 6 May 1933.

4   G. C. M'Gonigle and J. Kirby, *Poverty and Public Health*, 1936.
5   Most conclusively, the investigation of Seebohm Rowntree, published in *Poverty and Progress*, 1941 (see p. 212).
6   Not the revised and more expensive standard worked out by Rowntree for his York survey in 1936.
7   P. Sargant Florence and others, *Nutrition and Size of Family*. Report for Birmingham Social Service Committee, 1939.
8   Orr, *Food, Health and Income*, p. 17.
9   For the optimum standard, Orr used the standards compiled by Stiebeling of the Government Bureau of Home Economics, US.
10   Orr, *As I Recall*.
11   Rowntree, *The Human Needs of Labour*, 1937, p. 124.
12   This was a consolidating Act, provision for free school meals for necessitous children having originally been made in Acts of 1906 and 1914.
13   Thus in Manchester in 1938–9, 10·6 per cent were fed, in Leeds 4·6 per cent, in Birmingham 4 per cent and in Sheffield 2·2 per cent.
14   For much information in this section we are indebted to an unpublished paper by F. Le Gros Clark, *A Social History of the School Meals Service* (1964). An abbreviated version was published by the National Council of Social Service.
15   e.g. the schemes in the Rhondda and Jarrow financed by the National Birthday Trust (see Report of the Commissioner for the Special Areas (1937–8)).
16   Based on J. R. Stone and D. A. Rowe, *Consumers' Expenditure in the United Kingdom 1920–38*, Cambridge Department of Applied Economics.

Chapter 15: The Sick and the Old

1   The contrasts between different areas were exhaustively analysed in 1938 by Richard Titmuss in his first book *Poverty and Population*.
2   *Report on Maternal Mortality in Wales*, 1937, (Cmd. 5423).
3   Widows', Orphans' and Old Age Contributory Pensions Act of 1925 provided a pension for men aged sixty-five from 1928 onwards.
4   See, for example, *The New Survey of London Life and Labour*, Vol. III, *The Eastern Area*, chapter 10.

5 Seebohm Rowntree, *Poverty and Progress: Second Social Survey of York*, 1941.
6 *Hansard*, 1 December 1937.
7 Evidence submitted to Interdepartmental Committee on Social Insurance, April 1942, Cmd. 6405, p. 239.
8 *Hansard*, 23 November 1938.
9 *Hansard*, 1 December 1937.
10 *Hansard*, 21 February 1934.
11 *The Times*, 19 August 1940.

Chapter 16: New Patterns of Living

1 *Hansard*, 10 December 1937.
2 *The Motor*, 20 October 1931.
3 *The Motor*, 10 April 1934.
4 *Autocar*, 20 April 1934.
5 *Hansard*, 10 April 1934.
6 *Hansard*, 4 March 1936.
7 *Hansard*, 28 April 1936.

Chapter 17: Leisure and the Rise of the Mass Media

1 J. R. Stone and D. Rowe, *Consumers' Expenditure in the United Kingdom 1920–38*, C. L. Mowat, *Britain Between the Wars*.
2 See chapter 16, section on motoring and cycling.
3 The Youth Hostels Association, for example, founded in 1930, had 297 hostels and 93,000 members by 1939.
4 Mary Grieve, *Millions Made My Story*.
5 See J. Reith, *Into the Wind*.
6 For further information, see B. Paulu, *British Broadcasting*.

Chapter 18: The Radical Trend in Culture

1 Estimates by Professor J. Huxley in *Scientific Research and Social Needs*, and by J. D. Bernal in *Social Function of Science*.
2 Quotations in this paragraph are from the symposium *Unit One: The Modern Movement in Art and Sculpture*, (ed. H. Read) 1934. See also *Circle*, (ed. J. L. Martin, Ben Nicholson and Naum Gabo,) 1937.

3   A. Blunt in C. Day Lewis (ed.), *The Mind in Chains*, 1937, which also contains essays by H. Read, A. Calder-Marshall, J. D. Bernal and others.

4   RIBA *Journal*, June 1967, article on *Architects' Copartnership*, by three partners.

5   See Osbert Lancaster, *Progress at Pelvis Bay*, *Homes Sweet Homes*.

6   E. M. Forster, *Two Cheers for Democracy*.

7   For a detailed study of right wing social ideas and attitudes in the writings of Eliot, Yeats, Pound and Wyndham Lewis, see J. Harrison, *The Reactionaries*.

8   Paul Rotha, *The Film Till Now*, p. 551.

9   See C. Day Lewis, *The Buried Day*, and E. Upward, *In the Thirties*.

10 *Partisan Review*, Summer 1967.

11 See, for example, Storm Jameson in *Fact* (quoted in J. Lindsay, *After the Thirties*).

12 *Keep Culture Out of Cambridge*, in P. Sloan, (ed.), *John Cornford, a Memoir*, 1937.

13 W. H. Auden, *Spain*. Published as pamphlet, 1937.

14 Too numerous to quote here, including C. Day Lewis, *Buried Day;* Philip Toynbee, *Friends Apart*; P. Stansky and W. Abrahams, *Journey to the Frontier*, a biography of Julian Bell and John Cornford; Carmel Guest, (ed.), *David Guest, a Memoir*; Esmond Romilly, *Boadilla*; John Sommerfield, *Volunteer in Spain*; and others.

15 Harry Kemp in *Cambridge Left*, 1934.

16 Rex Warner, 1933, reprinted in R. Skelton (ed.), *Poetry of the Thirties*.

17 The recent reprinting of the volumes of *Left Review*, unavailable for many years, enables the interested reader to check this judgement.

18 Auden to Robin Skelton, quoted in Skelton's introduction to his *Poetry of the Thirties*. See also Julian Symons, *The Thirties*, and Jack Lindsay, *After the Thirties*, for two well-illustrated accounts of left wing literary life. Lindsay's is pro-Communist, Symons' not.

19 Claud Cockburn, in *The Review*, No. 11–12, has noted how important homosexuality was as an influence on the attitudes of some important writers.

20 Louis MacNeice, *The Sunlight on the Garden*.

21 See J. W. Beach, *The Making of the Auden Canon*, 1957.

Chapter 19: Fascists and anti-fascists

1 Oswald Mosley, *The Greater Britain*, 1934 edition, p. 185.
2 *Sunday Dispatch*, 29 April 1934.
3 *Tatler*, 30 May 1934.
4 *The Greater Britain,* (ibid.), p. 35.
5 Quoted by Gerald Barry in a broadcast, 8 June 1934; reprinted in *Fascists at Olympia*, 1934, a record of eye-witnesses.
6 *Yorkshire Post*, 9 June 1934.
7 *Hansard*, 14 June 1934.
8 *Daily Telegraph*, 9 June 1934.
9 Speech made by a fascist in Victoria Park, quoted by E. Thurtle, Labour MP for Shoreditch, in the House of Commons, 5 March 1936.
10 See *Our Flag Stays Red*, by Phil Piratin who was Communist MP for Mile End, Stepney, 1945–50.

Chapter 20: Attitudes to the Outside World

1 *Daily Express*, 13 February 1933.
2 *Daily Mail*, 11 February 1933.
3 *Daily Telegraph*, 14 February 1933.
4 *The Times*, 18 February 1933.
5 *The Times*, 17 February 1933.
6 Recorded in *The Peace Ballot: The Official History* by Dame Adelaide Livingstone, 1935.
7 *Daily Express*, 12 November 1934.
8 ibid., 14 November 1934.
9 *Hansard*, 8 November 1934.
10 Thomas Jones, a former Cabinet Secretary who was close to Stanley Baldwin, wrote in a letter to a friend in May 1936: 'Hitler feels quite unequal to standing up alone to Russia . . . He is therefore asking for an alliance with us to form a bulwark against the spread of Communism. Our PM is not indisposed to attempt this as a final effort before he resigns after the Coronation next year, to make way for Neville Chamberlain'. (Thomas Jones, *A Diary with Letters 1931–1950* (1954), p. 209.)
11 See Londonderry's *Ourselves and Germany,* 1938.

12   Harold Nicolson, *Diaries and Letters 1930–39* (1966), entry for 20 September 1936.

13   Thomas Jones, ibid., p. 390.

14   See Claud Cockburn, *I Claud* . . . (Penguin 1967) for the origin of the phrase 'the Cliveden Set'. See also Thomas Jones, ibid., p. xxxviii.

15   This figure of £2 million was given to the authors by Mrs Isabel Brown, the star money raiser during the Spanish Civil War. She was one of the initiators of the Spanish Medical Aid Committee and was its representative on the National Joint Committee. Her husband, Ernest Brown, was in charge of the National Joint Committee's organizing committee.

16   See, for example, the statement by W. Citrine, general secretary of the TUC, to the 1938 TUC.

17   See, for example, the issues of the *Daily Mail* for 19, 20 and 21 September 1938.

18   *News Chronicle*, 26 September 1938.

19   *The Times*, 27 October 1938.

20   *Daily Express*, 30 September 1938.

Appendix

Tables on which the figures in this book are based

Figure 1 (page 42)

NUMBERS UNEMPLOYED: GREAT BRITAIN

Month		Total on Register	Of which:		
			total on insurance benefit	total on means test★	others disallowed uninsured, etc.
1931	August	2,733,782	2,537,344	—	201,038
	December	2,509,921	1,362,384	762,273	385,264
1932	June	2,747,343	1,334,862	945,069	467,412
	December	2,723,287	1,213,813	1,039,374	470,100
1933	June	2,438,108	1,009,479	995,588	433,041
	December	2,224,079	865,372	935,791	422,916
1934	June	2,092,586	880,198	817,031	395,357
	December	2,085,815	963,038	727,975	394,802
1935	June	2,000,110	920,179	708,617	371,314
	December	1,868,565	831,334	687,859	349,372
1936	June	1,702,676	756,827	567,058	378,391
	December†	1,628,719	744,437	578,987	305,295
1937	June	1,356,598	582,619	574,157	199,882
	December	1,665,407	896,019	555,927	213,461
1938	June	1,802,912	1,073,755	530,763	198,394
	December	1,831,372	1,076,387	553,596	201,387
1939	June	1,349,579	695,689	488,146	165,744

★ On Transitional Payments until the end of 1934: on the Unemployment Assistance Board after.

† Revised system of counting – not comparable with previous years.

Note: This table excludes Northern Ireland, and it excludes the peak month which was January 1933. It will be observed that from 1932 until the end of 1937 the numbers on the means test combined with those disallowed under the anomalies act or uninsured exceeded those drawing unemployment benefit. Many of those disallowed would disappear from the register altogether in subsequent months, so that the figures were certainly underestimated from December 1931 onwards but to what extent cannot be calculated. (Source: Ministry of Labour Gazettes for the months concerned.)

Figure 2 (page 48)

MOVEMENT OF POPULATION WITHIN GREAT BRITAIN 1931–8 (IN THOUSANDS)

	1931	1938	Increases or decreases
Great Britain	44,795	46,208	1,413
England and Wales	39,952	41,215	1,263
Greater London	8,952	8,700	496
Rest of South East	5,274	5,790	516
Northumberland, Durham	2,243	2,204	—39
West Midlands (Mid. I)	4,534	4,751	217
South Wales	1,898	1,783	—115
Rest of Wales	696	683	—13
Scotland	4,843	4,993	150

(Source: National Register, Statistics of Population, and Registrar General's Estimate. Quoted in C. L. Mowat, *Britain Between the Wars*.)

Figure 3 (page 49)

DISTRIBUTION OF PEOPLE INSURED UNDER THE UNEMPLOYMENT INSURANCE ACTS

	Insured in thousands				Per cent of total insured	
	1923	1929	1932	1937	1923	1937
London and Home Counties	2,421	2,802	3,027	3,453	22·4	26·0
Lancashire	1,697	1,780	1,840	1,826	15·7	13·8
W. Riding, Notts. and Derby	1,403	1,501	1,559	1,614	13·0	12·2
Staffs., Warwick., Worcs., Leics. and Northants.	1,212	1,332	1,402	1,554	11·2	11·7
Northumberland and Durham	619	613	652	648	5·7	4·9
Mid-Scotland	792	794	832	868	7·3	6·6
Glamorgan and Monmouth	457	435	457	437	4·2	3·3
Rest of Great Britain	2,225	2,443	2,631	2,844	20·5	21·5
Total	10,826	11,700	12,400	13,244	100	100

(Source: Royal Commission on Distribution of the Industrial Population, 1940.)

Figure 4 (page 67) (*Ministry of Labour Report, 1938.*)

Certain industries showing marked decreases in workers in employment (in thousands)

	June 1923	June 1929	June 1938
Coalmining	1,176	870	701
Cotton	439	478	251
Woollen and Worsted	240	204	163
Iron and Steel	185	164	152
Percentage of above to total all industries	21·1	16·0	10·7

Certain industries showing marked increases in workers in employment (in thousands)

	June 1923	June 1929	June 1938
Distributive trades	1,143	1,557	1,875
Miscellaneous services*	476	617	844
Building	586	742	906
Construction and repair of motor vehicles, cycles and aircraft	170	228	355
Electrical trades†	129	185	312
Public works contracting	95	129	218
Miscellaneous metal trades	143	176	237
General engineering, engineers, iron and steel founding	500	529	586
Road transport (other than train and bus)	116	160	176
Printing, publishing and bookbinding	206	257	265
Total	3,669	4,722	5,979
Percentage of above to all industries	37·9	44·1	50·4

* Entertainments, sport etc., hotels, laundries, dyeing and dry cleaning, professional services.

† Electrical engineering, electrical mining and contracting, cables, apparatus, lamps etc.

N

Figure 5 (page 130)

TRADE UNION MEMBERSHIP IN THE THIRTIES (IN THOUSANDS)

	All Trade Unions	*Affiliated to TUC★*
1920	8,334	6,418
1926	5,218	4,164
1930	4,839	3,719
1931	4,624	3,613
1932	4,444	3,368
1933	4,392	3,295
1934	4,590	3,389
1935	4,867	3,615
1936	5,295	4,009
1937	5,842	4,461
1938	6,053	4,669
1939	6,244	4,867
1945	7,803	6,671

★ Numbers represented at the Congress of the following year.

Figure 6 (page 131)

CHANGES IN MEMBERSHIP OF LARGE UNIONS

Numbers Represented at Trades Union Congress in following year
(in thousands)

	1930	1933	1938
MFGB	600	500	584
NUR	320	272	366
ASLE&F	48	45	53
RCA	54	58	64
TGWU	384	370	634
AEU	154	135	333
Boilermakers	62	50	55
ETU	27	28	64
AUBTW	57	55	65
ASW	116	101	137
Painters	37	30	45
NAFTA	19	14	21
Plumbers	22	20	27
TA	33	34	37
NUPBW	45	45	71
Natsopa	21	21	27
Amalgamated Weavers (cotton)	159	113	88
Tailors and Garment Workers	40	50	90
Boot and Shoe Operatives	80	77	86
NUDAW	119	130	182
Shop Assistants	40	43	78
Agricultural Workers	30	30	45
NUPE	13	12	50
NUGMW	257	229	417

Figure 7 (page 140)

MINISTRY OF LABOUR COST OF LIVING INDEX (AS PUBLISHED IN THE 1930s)
COMPARED WITH THE LATER CAMBRIDGE INDEX (1938 — 100)

	Ministry of Labour index	Cambridge index
1929	105·1	105·8
1930	101·3	102·8
1931	94·6	98·5
1932	92·3	95·9
1933	98·7	93·8
1934	90·4	93·7
1935	91·7	94·5
1936	94·2	95·2
1937	98·7	98·2
1938	100·0	100·0

(Source: *Wages and Salaries in the United Kingdom, 1920–38*, Chapman and Knight; *Consumer's Expenditure in the United Kingdom*, Stone and Meade, vol. 2.)

Figure 8 (page 141)

WAGE RATES, PRICES AND REAL WAGE RATES (1930 = 100)

	Money wage rates* men, manufacturing	Cost of living index†	Cambridge consumer price index‡	Real wage rates cost of living index	Real wage rates Cambridge index
1929	100	103·7	102·9	96·4	97·2
1930	100	100·0	100·0	100·0	100·0
1931	97	93·4	95·8	103·7	101·2
1932	97	91·2	93·5	106·3	103·8
1933	94	88·6	91·2	106·1	103·1
1934	94	89·2	91·1	105·4	103·2
1935	97	90·5	91·9	107·1	105·5
1936	97	93·0	92·6	104·3	105·7
1937	103	97·4	95·5	105·7	105·8
1938	106	98·7	97·3	108·7	108·9

* Bowley's index, from London and Cambridge Economic Service, Key Statistics of the British Economy 1900–1962, recomputed on base 1930.
† Ministry of Labour official index.
‡ Consumer price index published by J. R. Stone in *Measurement of Consumer Expenditure and Behaviour in the United Kingdom, 1920–38*, recomputed on base 1930.

Figure 9 (page 142)

AVERAGE ANNUAL REAL EARNINGS (1930 = 100)

Earnings per employee per man-year, all industries

	Average annual money earnings	Average annual real earnings (on cost of living index)	Average annual real earnings (Cambridge index)
1929	100·2	96·5	97·6
1930	100·0	100·0	100·0
1931	98·6	105·6	102·9
1932	97·0	106·5	103·5
1933	96·4	108·8	105·6
1934	97·4	109·2	106·9
1935	98·8	109·2	107·5
1936	100·7	108·3	108·7
1937	102·6	105·2	107·4
1938	105·7	107·1	108·6

(Cols. 1 and 2 are from Chapman and Knight, *Wages and Salaries in the United Kingdom,* published before J. R. Stone's new Cambridge consumer price index was completed. Col. 3 is computed by applying Stone's index to the earnings figures in Col. 1.)

Figure 10 (page 160)

OCCUPATIONAL CLASS AND INDUSTRIAL STATUS AT CENSUS DATES OF GAIN-FULLY OCCUPIED POPULATION IN GREAT BRITAIN (IN THOUSANDS)

	1921	*1931*	*1951*
1 Professional:			
higher	195 (1·01%)	240 (1·14%)	434 (1·93%)
lower	680 (3·52%)	728 (3·46%)	1,050 (4·70%)
2 Employers and proprietors	1,318 (6·82%)	1,409 (6·70%)	1,118 (4·57%)
Managers and administrators	704 (3·64%)	770 (3·66%)	1,246 (5·53%)
3 Clerical workers	1,300 (6·72%)	1,465 (6·97%)	2,404 (10·68%)
4 Foremen, inspectors, supervisors	279 (1·44%)	323 (1·54%)	590 (2·62%)
Manual Workers			
5 Skilled	5,573 (28·83%)	5,619 (26·72%)	5,616 (24·95%)
6 Semi-skilled	6,544 (33·85%)	7,360 (35·00%)	7,338 (32·60%)
7 Unskilled	2,740 (14·17%)	3,115 (14·81%)	2,709 (12·03%)
All	19,333	21,029	22,514

(Source: tables based on census figures in *Occupation and Pay in Great Britain, 1906–1960,* G. Routh.)

Figure 11 (page 166)

BIRTH AND THE BIRTH RATE

	England and Wales		Scotland		United Kingdom	
	Number	rate per 1,000 popula- tion	Number	rate per 1,000 popula- tion	Number	rate per 1,000 popula- tion
1900–2		28·7		29·5		28·6
1910–2		24·5		25·8		24·6
1920–2		22·8		25·6		23·1
1931	632,081	15·8	92,220	19·0	749,974	16·3
1932	613,772	15·3	91,000	18·6	730,079	15·8
1933	580,413	14·4	86,546	17·6	691,560	14·9
1934	597,642	14·8	88,836	18·0	711,843	15·3
1935	598,756	14·7	87,928	17·8	711,420	15·2
1936	605,292	14·8	88,928	17·9	720,129	15·3
1937	610,557	14·9	87,810	17·6	723,779	15·3
1938	621,204	15·1	88,627	17·7	735,573	15·5
1965		18·1		19·3		18·3

Figure 12 (page 243)

ROAD VEHICLES – GREAT BRITAIN

	Motor Vehicles no. of licences current	private cars	motor cycles	commercial	buses
August 31					
1931	2,189,650	1,076,128	603,728	348,969	86,208
1932	2,213,012	1,118,521	577,827	357,058	84,667
1933	2,271,699	1,195,882	540,594	372,273	85,352
1934	2,391,059	1,298,440	524,012	401,479	85,388
1935	2,543,577	1,455,721	499,712	414,760	85,223
1936	2,706,555	1,604,948	479,943	438,565	84,523
1937	2,881,034	1,762,098	462,439	460,343	84,393
1938	3,039,683	1,916,226	436,231	471,156	87,536

(Source: Statistical Abstract, No. 83.)

Figure 13 (page 244)

ROAD BUILDING

Expenditure out of loans for capital works

	England and Wales £000	Scotland £000
1930–1	18,850	1,028
1931–2	18,961	1,178
1932–3	10,234	738
1933–4	8,696	544
1934–5	7,231	501
1935–6	8,254	449
1936–7	9,743	643
1937–8	12,163	798
1938–9	13,467	770

Figure 14 (page 245)

ROAD ACCIDENTS – GREAT BRITAIN

	killed	injured	total
1931	6,691	202,119	208,810
1932	6,667	206,450	213,117
1933	7,202	216,328	223,530
1934	7,343	231,603	238,946
1935	6,502	221,726	228,228
1936	6,561	227,813	234,374
1937	6,633	226,402	233,035
1938	6,649	226,711	233,359

Index